D. H. LAWRENCE
AESTHETICS AND IDEOLOGY

D. H. LAWRENCE

Aesthetics and Ideology

ANNE FERNIHOUGH

CLARENDON PRESS · OXFORD
1993

Oxford University Press, Walton Street, Oxford OX2 6DP
Oxford   New York   Toronto
Delhi   Bombay   Calcutta   Madras   Karachi
Kuala Lumpur   Singapore   Hong Kong   Tokyo
Nairobi   Dar es Salaam   Cape Town
Melbourne   Auckland   Madrid
and associated companies in
Berlin   Ibadan

Oxford is a trade mark of Oxford University Press

Published in the United States
by Oxford University Press Inc., New York

British Library Cataloguing in Publication Data
Data available

Library of Congress Cataloging in Publication Data
Fernihough, Anne.
D. H. Lawrence : aesthetics and ideology / Anne Fernihough.
Includes bibliographical references and index.
1. Lawrence, D. H. (David Herbert), 1885–1930—Aesthetics.   2. Art
and literature—England—History—20th century.   3. Criticism—
England—History—20th century.   4. Aesthetics, Modern—20th
century.   5. Social problems in literature.   I. Title.
PR6023.A93Z62834   1992   823'.912—dc20   92-46669
ISBN 0-19-811235-1

Typeset by Graphicraft Typesetters Ltd., Hong Kong
Printed in Great Britain
on acid-free paper by
Bookcraft Ltd.
Midsomer Norton, Bath

For my mother,
and in memory of my father

ACKNOWLEDGEMENTS

I should like to thank, for their help and encouragement in different ways, Tony Atkins, Carl Baron, John Beer, Michael Bell, Christopher Butler, Peter Collier, Juliet Dusinberre, Terry Eagleton, Andrew Entwistle, Andrew Lockett, Adrian Poole, James Simpson, Karina Williamson-McIntosh, and especially Rupert Wood.

CONTENTS

INTRODUCTION

Why should he insist on the bodylessness of beauty, when we cannot know of any save embodied beauty?

(Lawrence on Shelley)

The term 'aesthetics', in its Greek derivation, denotes the study of sense experience rather than the study of art. It is not surprising, therefore, that when aesthetics was founded as a discrete discipline by Baumgarten in 1735, it focused attention on experiences, perceptions, and judgements of the beautiful, all of which referred primarily to the responding subject, not to the art-work itself.[1] Kant, in categorizing aesthetic judgements as 'judgements of taste', located the aesthetic squarely within the experiencing subject rather than the artefact. In the *Critique of Judgement* (1790), he argued that judgements of taste are concerned not with the object as such, but with the pleasure or pain experienced by the subject. To say that something is beautiful is not, for Kant, to ascribe any property to it: 'Nothing in the object is signified; on the contrary, in this feeling the subject is aware of itself as it is affected by the representation.'[2] Here we find Kant's most explicit articulation of the subject-centred basis of his aesthetic.

Lawrence almost always uses the term 'aesthetic' pejoratively, with an acute awareness of the subjectivist standpoint of traditional art theory: 'The ego', he comments on Clive Bell's theory of significant form, 'shuts itself up and paints the inside of the walls sky-blue, and thinks it is in heaven.'[3] For Lawrence, things themselves (by which he means something like 'the body' or 'the material world', and emphatically not the Kantian *Ding-an-sich*), have been the blind spot of mainstream aesthetic philosophy. In a characteristically mythopoeic gesture, he connects this denigration of the material, substantive world with humanity's neglect or suppression of its own creaturely nature. In analysing our experiences of the beautiful and in making aesthetic judgements, we are, argues Lawrence, simply reinscribing the severance, in

---

[1] The term 'aesthetics' was first used in its current sense by Alexander Gottlieb Baumgarten in his *Meditationes philosophicae de nonnullis ad poema pertinentibus* (Halle, 1735). This work is available with a parallel English translation: *Reflections on Poetry*, trans. K. Aschenbrenner and W. B. Holther (Berkeley, Calif., 1954).

[2] Kant, *Critique of Judgement*, sect. 1. 204, trans. H. W. Cassirer, in *A Commentary on Kant's Critique of Judgement* (New York and London, 1938), 179.

[3] 'Introduction to These Paintings', in *Phoenix: The Posthumous Papers of D. H. Lawrence*, ed. Edward McDonald (London, 1936), 551–84 (p. 567). This essay was first published as the introduction to *The Paintings of D. H. Lawrence* (London, 1929).

Western cultures, of mind and body, and the subsequent privileging of the mind. His version of the myth of a 'fall' into self-consciousness and idealism (a myth he inherited in the first instance from Nietzsche) is well known; it replaces the more orthodox biblical account of a fall into carnal knowledge. One of its consequences, for Lawrence, is that humanity is now 'doomed to view [the world] objectively', and he sees this objectivity to be synonymous with a dangerous *subjectivity*, for reasons which will become apparent in later chapters.[4] He carries the theme of a postlapsarian culture right through to his last novel, *Lady Chatterley's Lover* (1928), where Connie Chatterley is warned that 'Once you start the mental life you pluck the apple. You've severed . . . the organic connection. And if you've got nothing in your life but the mental life, then you yourself are a plucked apple . . . [and] it's a natural necessity for a plucked apple to go bad.'[5] In seeking to trace this fall, Lawrence, again following Nietzsche, finds a landmark in the philosophy of Plato: the Platonic Ideal (which implies a degradation of the phenomenal world) is 'the worm, the foul serpent of our epoch, in whose coils we are strangled'.[6] He detects one of the most recent manifestations of this Platonism in the art theories of his Bloomsbury contemporaries, Clive Bell and Roger Fry.

Lawrence's condemnation of a certain idealist tendency in art theory should not be allowed to obscure the fact that, throughout his career, he was evolving an elaborate aesthetics of his own (though 'aesthetics', as I have already indicated, is not the term he would have chosen). *Women in Love* (1920) is very much a novel about art and aesthetics, set in an atmosphere of cultural ferment: Halliday's flat is decorated with 'one or two new pictures . . . in the Futurist manner'; Gudrun has introduced some reproductions of Picasso into the Brangwen household; Loerke is busy expounding doctrines of aesthetic autonomy.[7] There is, of course, a strong sense in

---

[4] 'Apocalypse, Fragment 2', in *Apocalypse and the Writings on Revelation*, ed. Mara Kalnins (Cambridge, 1980), 177–94 (p. 182). This fragment was previously unpublished.

[5] *Lady Chatterley's Lover* (London, 1972), 48.

[6] '[Germans and English]', in *Phoenix II: Uncollected, Unpublished and Other Prose Works by D. H. Lawrence*, ed. Warren Roberts and Harry T. Moore (London, 1968), 244–9 (p. 247). This essay first appeared in *Das Inselschiff* (1927), 285–293, as 'Ein Brief von D. H. Lawrence an das Inselschiff'. See also 'A Propos of *Lady Chatterley's Lover*', in *Phoenix II*, 485–515 (pp. 510–11), and 'Him With His Tail in His Mouth', in *Reflections on the Death of a Porcupine and Other Essays*, ed. Michael Herbert (Cambridge, 1988), 307–17. Compare Nietzsche, 'The Birth of Tragedy', in *The Birth of Tragedy and The Genealogy of Morals* (New York, 1956), 1–146, and 'Twilight of the Idols', in *Twilight of the Idols and The Anti-Christ* (Harmondsworth, 1968), 19–112 (pp. 106–7). 'A Propos of *Lady Chatterley's Lover*' was first published in its final form in London, 1930, as a book; 'Him With His Tail in His Mouth' was first published in the original *Reflections on the Death of a Porcupine* (Philadelphia, 1925).

[7] *Women in Love*, ed. David Farmer, Lindeth Vasey, and John Worthen (Cambridge, 1987), 74, 250, 430. Middleton Murry was responsible for the first reproduction of a Picasso in England, in the first issue of *Rhythm* (Summer 1911), and it is quite likely that Lawrence saw it.

which the artists and aestheticians of this novel represent, for Lawrence, the nadir of the mythical fall into self-consciousness, as Catherine Carswell, who read the manuscript of *Women in Love*, was quick to recognize.[8] Paradoxically, however, it is through art that Lawrence seeks redemption from this 'fallen' condition. When, later in his career, he complains that the Bloomsbury art-critics are guilty of what he calls *abstracting* Cézanne's 'good apple', he refers on one level to the apple of the tree of knowledge, the consumption of which, in his own mythology, precipitated the fall into self-consciousness, a fall which Bloomsbury art theory is seen to reinscribe. But on another level, he refers to Cézanne's painted apples, his famous still-lifes in oil. The most important aspect of Cézanne's still-lifes, for Lawrence, is their acknowledgement that 'matter *actually* exists'; they stubbornly elude the dematerializing effects of an aesthetics of transcendence.[9]

We are faced with the paradox that Cézanne's art, for Lawrence, *de-aestheticizes* matter. In a curious way, Lawrence's writings on art make palpable again the original impulse behind the founding of aesthetics, which was to make a space within philosophy for the body itself. In *The Ideology of the Aesthetic*, Terry Eagleton, having traced the development of the aesthetic as far as Schopenhauer, reflects that 'A discourse which began as an idiom of the body has now become a flight from corporeal existence'.[10] Lawrence, in his long 'Introduction to These Paintings' (1929), records this same flight into insubstantiality: the Impressionists 'made the grand escape from the body. They metamorphosed it into a pure assembly of shifting lights and shadows'; they 'made the . . . grand escape into freedom, into infinity, into light and delight. They escaped from the tyranny of solidity and the menace of mass-form.'[11] The aesthetic would seem to be two-edged, capable both of celebrating the senses and implicitly suppressing them. If the Impressionists have escaped the body, Cézanne's art constitutes, for Lawrence, both a means of reinstating the body into the aesthetic response, and an assertion of the materiality which exceeds our finite, subjective perceptions.

Yet Lawrence's emphasis on matter, on what he calls the 'substance and *thereness*' of Cézanne's art, does not, strictly, make him a materialist. Indeed, it would be extremely difficult to 'place' a writer like Lawrence, whose tendency was to take up and drop certain positions as it suited his rhetorical purposes. Though he never ceases to denounce idealism and 'the ideal', Lawrence constantly risks reifying the body into what is merely another transcendental category. Terry Eagleton stresses the need to prevent the

---

[8] Catherine Carswell, *The Savage Pilgrimage* (London, 1932), 38. See below, p. 26.

[9] 'Introduction to These Paintings', 570, 568.

[10] Terry Eagleton, *The Ideology of the Aesthetic* (Oxford, 1990), 171.

[11] 'Introduction to These Paintings', 564, 563.

body becoming 'another privileged anteriority', and indeed the body becomes precisely this in much of Lawrence's work.[12] In a novel like *The Plumed Serpent* (1926), for example, 'blood-consciousness' is its own authorization, authorizing, in this case, authoritarianism itself. Far too often, Lawrence privileges some esoteric region *within* the body which might just as well be a metaphysical domain.

Yet if Lawrence's politics is sometimes brutally authoritarian, his aesthetics can often be seen by contrast as pluralistic and even *anti*-authoritarian. It is not always fair to see Lawrence's insistence on the body as simple inverted idealism, and especially not where his writings on art and literature are concerned. Kierkegaard reminds us that 'the particular cannot be thought', and this is a problem which Lawrence repeatedly addresses in his art-criticism, premissing his aesthetic on precisely those recalcitrant fragments which defy incorporation into a unified theory.[13] In this sense, his 'aesthetic' is a kind of 'anti-aesthetic', cutting through theory. At times, though, it risks becoming in its turn another 'aesthetic', a risk which is intrinsic to any meditation upon 'art' as a category. The philosopher Martin Heidegger shows how to apply language to art is to force art into the (European) realm of aesthetics and its implicit idealism, because 'language itself rests on the very same metaphysical distinction between the sensuous and the supra-sensuous, in that the structure of the language is supported by the basic elements of sound and script on the one hand, and signification and sense on the other'.[14] Like all writers who try to use language against itself, Lawrence often finds himself trapped by his rhetoric of the body. Tony Pinkney has recently confronted a related problem in terms of the revenge of classicist transcendentalism, which is 'premised upon the abolition of the disorder of Nature', upon Lawrence's anti-classicist project; for classicism 'has an uncanny ability to inhabit, virus-like, literary forms which seem initially to contradict it, and slowly, remorselessly, to remake them into its own original shape'.[15]

It will by now be apparent that Lawrence's art-criticism, far from being confined to the realm of art, concerns itself with the stance of the work of art towards reality itself. And this stance, far from being the transcendent one which the term 'aesthetic' has come to imply, quintessentially represented in

---

[12] *The Ideology of the Aesthetic*, 197.

[13] Søren Kierkegaard, *Concluding Unscientific Postscript*, trans. D. F. Swenson, introd. Walter Lowrie (Princeton, NJ, 1941), 290.

[14] 'A Dialogue on Language', in *On the Way to Language*, trans. Peter D. Hertz (New York, 1971), 1–54 (p. 15).

[15] Tony Pinkney, *D. H. Lawrence* (Hemel Hempstead, 1990), 72, 163.

Clive Bell's 'significant form' which elevates itself above the ('feminine'?) viscosity and contingency of day-to day living, gives priority to that viscosity, to the material and the bodily. This study does not address at any length the question of sexual politics in Lawrence's treatment of art, on the grounds that to have done so would have taken an entire book in itself and would not have left me the time or space to deal with the other ideological questions which have preoccupied me. Lawrence is, of course, by no means alone in employing genderized vocabulary in matters of aesthetics; in this he has a long line of predecessors. Indeed, at its very inception the aesthetic was seen to be a specifically 'feminine' category, mediating, as 'woman' had tradition-ally done, between the rational and the bestial. Through some curious twist of philosophical history, however, the aesthetic mysteriously changes gender in many of the modernist manifestos, becoming in Bell's theory of significant form the prerogative of those who have risen above the mire and the fret of day-to-day living, 'the life of the plains', and 'climbed the cold, white peaks of art'.[16] We are left with the paradox that Lawrence, in so many ways a stridently masculinist thinker, attempts to restore those aspects of the aes-thetic (viscosity, bodiliness) traditionally regarded as 'feminine'.

The extraordinary history of Lawrence's literary reputation (adulation turned to bitter vilification in a startlingly short space of time) hinges on two main factors. The first of these was of course the somewhat belated recognition of misogynistic elements in Lawrence's work, with the publication of Kate Millett's *Sexual Politics* (1970). The second has been the flourishing and demise of a post-Romantic critical idiom deeply informed by notions of the organic. Lawrence's popularity in the 1960s and early 1970s was inseparable from the fact that Leavis's influence still prevailed in many academic quar-ters. Lawrence and his critics seemed to enter into a closed circle: post-Romantic criticism found in Lawrence an echo of its own basic tenets, so that writer and critic were mutually confirming. Just as the organic was appropriated by critics like Leavis to uphold Lawrence's reputation, so with the impact of a revived structuralism and its aftermath, the same notion of the organic was used to dismiss Lawrence out of hand.

Two controversial figures have added a renewed impetus to this discred-iting of the organic. Paul de Man hit the headlines in December 1987 with the discovery of his contributions to the Belgian collaborationist newspaper *Le Soir* during the 1940s. Many critics were then tempted to interpret his

---

[16] *Art* (London, 1914), 35, 33. Genderizing the issue more explicitly, Bell declares that 'the perfect lover, he who can feel the profound significance of form, is raised above the accidents of time and place' (p. 36).

career, from American New Critic to arch-deconstructionist, in terms of a guilt-ridden unravelling of an organicist aesthetic ideology now, perhaps *too* conveniently and patly, associated with Nazism.[17] The other controversial figure is Martin Heidegger; a renewed emphasis on *his* collaboration was sparked off by the publication of a book by Victor Farias, *Heidegger et le nazisme* (1987). Derrida, Habermas, and Gadamer have been among the prominent philosophers who have addressed themselves to the question whether Heidegger's philosophy itself is contaminated by his collaboration.[18] As a result, much energy has been spent alerting critics to the dangers inherent in that branch of post-Romantic aesthetic ideology that draws analogies between literary language or art on the one hand, and natural growth on the other.[19]

It is important to bear in mind here that attacks on organicist theories of art and literature frequently stem from the fact that this organicism is seen to betray a certain *idealism*, either overt or covert. Organicism is almost invariably seen, in other words, to connect to the aesthetics of transcendence that Cézanne's art, in Lawrence's view, subverts. This connection between organicism and idealism comes out very clearly in Barbara Johnson's essay, 'The Surprise of Otherness', a particularly eloquent and incisive example of the recent critical writing on de Man's wartime journalism. In this essay, Johnson applauds de Man's insistence that 'the too-easy leap from linguistic to aesthetic, ethical, or political structures has been made before, with cata- strophic results'. She goes on to draw a direct causal link between idealism and the holocaust:

If idealism can turn out to be terroristic, if the defence of Western civilization can become the annihilation of otherness, and if the desire for a beautiful and orderly society should require the tidying action of cattle cars and gas chambers, it is not enough to decide that we now recognize evil in order to locate ourselves comfortably in the good. In Nazi Germany, the seduction of an image of the good was precisely the road to evil.[20]

---

[17] See Werner Hamacher, Neil Hertz, and Thomas Keenan (eds.), *Responses on Paul de Man's Wartime Journalism* (Lincoln, Nebr., 1989). An example would be A. Stoekl in 'De Man and Guilt', 375–85 (p. 376): 'Even near the end of his life, de Man was positing a textual "machine" whose method of accounting for the production and excusing of guilt will sud- denly be seen as a necessary (and also highly suspect) strategy when one recognizes the gravity of the implications of the writings that were kept secret for so long.'

[18] See esp. Arnold I. Davidson (ed.), 'Symposium on Heidegger and Nazism', *Critical Inquiry*, xv/2 (Winter 1989), 407–88.

[19] See e.g. Christopher Norris, *Paul de Man: Deconstruction and the Critique of Aesthetic Ideology* (New York and London, 1988), pp. xi–xii; Eagleton, *Literary Theory* (Oxford, 1983), 21–2.

[20] Barbara Johnson, 'The Surprise of Otherness: A Note on the Wartime Writings of Paul de Man', in Peter Collier and Helga Geyer-Ryan (eds.), *Literary Theory Today* (Oxford, 1990), 13–22 (p. 21).

The reference to Nazism immediately brings to mind Bertrand Russell's notorious remark that Lawrence's views 'led straight to Auschwitz'.[21] Many of the accusations levelled against his organicist theories have been very similar to those levelled against de Man and Heidegger. Moreover there are, as I will try to show, very intricate and deep-rooted links between Lawrence's work and Heideggerian philosophy. But one of the most obvious links between Lawrence and Heidegger is their shared hostility towards what they see to be the inherently idealist bent of Western culture. For both of them, aesthetics brings into sharp focus a disabling opposition at the heart of Western metaphysics, namely the distinction between the sensuous and suprasensuous worlds, and, indeed, for both of them the expression 'Western metaphysics' is a virtual tautology. One cannot help noticing, moreover, that Barbara Johnson's sentiments on idealism and the holocaust, written with all the benefit of hindsight, were expressed by Lawrence some sixty years previously at a time when he could not have known that his premonition would come true quite so quickly:

Back, before the idealist religions and philosophies arose and started man on the great excursion of tragedy. The last three thousand years of mankind have been an excursion into ideals, bodilessness, and tragedy and now the excursion is over. And it is like the end of a tragedy in the theatre. The stage is strewn with dead bodies, worse still, with meaningless bodies, and the curtain comes down.[22]

The point I wish to make here is that Lawrence, accused by Russell of carving the way to Auschwitz, never ceased to warn against the dangers of an unbridled idealism. Auschwitz, the apotheosis of an idealism in which the body had become utterly dispensable, would, I believe, have utterly horrified Lawrence. His output as a writer places the neat link between organicism and idealism under violent strain.

Barbara Johnson's point that 'In Nazi Germany, the seduction of an image of the good was precisely the road to evil' is an extremely important one. Language is slippery, so slippery that good and evil can slide into one another. As a defence against such linguistic instability, Johnson advocates de Manian vigilance: our function as literary critics, she argues, is to 'become aware of the repressions, the elisions, the contradictions and the linguistic slippages that have functioned unnoticed' and to see texts and values in 'a more complex, more *constructed*, less idealized light'. In view of this, it seems time to confront the constructedness of the organic metaphor itself. We should do so not only to guard against right-wing mysticism, but also, perhaps, to understand more clearly the organic metaphors underlying

[21] Bertrand Russell, 'Portraits from Memory, III: D. H. Lawrence', *Harper's Magazine*, ccvi/1233 (Feb. 1953), 93–5 (p. 95).   [22] 'A Propos of *Lady Chatterley's Lover*', 511.

more positive ideologies of (to choose the most obvious example) green and ecological thinking. In a sense, of course, the organic metaphor, like the metaphor of the 'natural', was one of the first and most obvious targets of deconstruction. But in another, perhaps deeper sense, the 'organic', like 'logocentrism', has remained largely undeconstructed, and treated as the stable entity against which the deconstructive enterprise can define itself.

Johnson argues that deconstruction came into being 'not out of "hostility" to the moral values of Western civilization . . . but out of a desire to understand how those values are potentially already different from *themselves*'.[23] If we have genuinely learnt this lesson we can, surely, apply it to the term 'organic' itself, recognizing the good in the evil as well as the evil in the good, however unsettling it may be to do so. For the 'organic', like the 'natural' (and like, for that matter, the 'constructed'), derives its political impetus from the particular linguistic and historical configurations in which it finds itself. One has only to think of the way in which organicist metaphor surfaces in the critical writing of a feminist modernist like Woolf to recognize the very different political resonances it can carry in different situations. Moreover, though my own sympathies lie far more with Barbara Johnson's 'constructedness' than with ideas of the organic or natural, I also recognize that rigid adherence to the notion of the 'constructedness' of all cultural categories can be as ideologically loaded as speaking of the 'natural' or the 'organic'. Hence the resurfacing of a qualified essentialism among some contemporary feminist theorists, who argue that to discard essentialist or biological categories at this point in the history of the emancipation of women is premature, in view of the fact that society still behaves as though 'women' existed.[24] Fredric Jameson alerts us to the need for historical contextualization of the 'natural':

It is certainly the case that a belief in the natural is ideological and that much of bourgeois art has worked to perpetuate such a belief, not only in its content but through the experience of its forms as well. Yet in different historical circumstances the idea of nature was once a subversive concept with a genuinely revolutionary function, and only the analysis of the concrete historical and cultural conjuncture can tell us whether, in the post-natural world of late capitalism, the categories of nature may not have acquired such a critical charge again.[25]

---

[23] 'The Surprise of Otherness', 21.

[24] See e.g. Denise Riley, '*Am I That Name?': Feminism and the Category of 'Women' in History* (Minneapolis, 1988), 112: 'it is compatible to suggest that "women" don't exist—while maintaining a politics of "as if they existed"—since the world behaves as if they unambiguously did'.

[25] Fredric Jameson, 'Afterword' to *Aesthetics and Politics: Debates Between Bloch, Lukács, Brecht, Benjamin, Adorno* (London, 1977), 196–213 (p. 207).

I do not for a moment wish to suggest that all Lawrence's uses of the organic metaphor are, in my view, politically desirable. Most of them are emphatically not, and in the first chapter of this study I confront one of the ugliest manifestations of the organic in the form of the anti-Jewish rhetoric surrounding the figure of Loerke in *Women in Love*. I recognize, of course, that the fictional context of such rhetoric rules out any simple identification with Lawrence's own views. If I seem, at times, to switch too easily from non-fiction to fiction and back again, it is because such rhetorical patterns, in novels or otherwise, say much about the cultural and intellectual context in which Lawrence was working, and carry political implications which stretch far beyond the bounds of authorial intention.

I should also stress that I do not wish to be read as advocating the continued use of the term 'organic' in literary critical discourse. As a term it is perilously slippery and prone to all manner of political appropriation. But at the same time, the dangers of an amnesia which simply dismisses out of hand those writers who have had recourse to some notion of the 'organic' in the past, regardless of the differing ways in which they have used it, cannot be overlooked. One of my enabling premises in the first part of this study is that the concept of the organic is too often hypostatized; there has been a tendency for certain uses of the term to eclipse others. The organic has many faces, some more benign than others, but for the purposes of my argument here it is two-faced, like Janus.[26] If one face points towards something politically ominous, the other points towards something more positive, which acts as a vital antidote to the more dangerous concept of the organic. I go on to suggest that Lawrence's organicist aesthetic is not always dangerously mystifying or idealizing, but can lead to a retrieval of the material world, to an acknowledgement, precisely that 'matter *actually* exists'.

The opening chapter of this book confronts Bertrand Russell's charge that Lawrence's views 'led straight to Auschwitz', looking in detail at Lawrence's connections with the *völkisch* ideologies prevalent in Germany in the 1910s and 1920s, from which, among other cultural and political phenomena, both Heideggerian philosophy and Nazism emerged. The historians Werner Sombart and Oswald Spengler were among the most prominent figures in this cultural climate. Lawrence first left England for Germany in 1912, and came into direct contact, through Frieda von Richthofen and her circle, with this cultural ethos (Sombart was a close friend of Frieda's sister, Else Jaffe). Moreover, since by then Lawrence was already well versed in Nietzsche, he

[26] See 'Introduction to *The Dragon of the Apocalypse* by Frederick Carter', in *Apocalypse and the Writings on Revelation*, 43–56 (p. 48). This essay was first published in *The London Mercury* (July 1930).

would have been familiar with many of the tenets of these *völkisch* ideologies in which Nietzsche was a key figure. Lawrence has often been distinguished from other male modernists (Conrad, Joyce, Eliot) on the grounds that he is a quintessentially *English* writer; Lawrence's claim 'I am English, and my Englishness is my very vision', was of course the epigraph to Leavis's *D. H. Lawrence: Novelist* (1955). One of the purposes of my study is to argue that, on the contrary, Lawrence cannot be fully understood apart from the specifically *German* philosophical tradition in which he was already immersed before meeting Frieda; contact with the von Richthofen circle served to familiarize Lawrence with some of its most recent developments. I attempt to link a certain *völkisch* organicism in Lawrence's thought (an organicism which roots cultures in their native soil, linking together culture and national destiny) with anti-Semitism. Without wishing to suggest that Lawrence's views 'led straight to Auschwitz', as Russell would have it, I try to show how Lawrence uses a nexus of imagery (centring on disintegration, decomposition, etc.) which would later be appropriated in the services of Nazism. That it would be so appropriated Lawrence could not have foreseen; that it *was* so appropriated we should not forget.

The second chapter then goes on to trace, in Lawrence's writings on art and literature, a second concept of the organic, differing radically from the idealist, *völkisch* brand, and leading to a retrieval, rather than abolition, of the material world. Lawrence's literary and art criticism is implicitly based on the belief that language and the external/material world are disjunct, and that the one should not be allowed to appropriate the other. For Lawrence defines art in opposition to a realist or mimetic model of language, according to which language attempts to suppress its own rhetorical status, aspiring to transparency and thereby appropriating the world as its own. This mimetic model of language depends, as Barthes was later to observe, on 'the supposed exteriority of the signified to the signifier'.[27] Premissed as it is on a form/content split, it is seen by Lawrence to be the prerequisite of scientific discourse, and by extension, scientific method and its practical manifestation, technology.

In asserting its own materiality, art, in Lawrence's view, whether it be visual or literary, creates a disjunction between itself and the outside world which fractures and complicates the meanings at work within it. In other words, the refusal to claim transparency, or one-to-one correspondence between elements of art-work and world, opens up the way to semantic complexity, making art the site of plural and conflicting meanings. Because

---

[27] Roland Barthes, 'The Last Word on Robbe-Grillet', in *Critical Essays*, trans. Richard Howard (Evanston, Ill., 1972), 197–204 (p. 198).

this critical stance does not give rise to the unifying, totalizing meaning often associated with the organic, I call it the 'fractured organic'. I then go on to argue that Lawrence's 'modernist' aesthetics can be seen as an attempt to articulate what is essentially the distinction between a pre-Saussurean (mimetic or logocentric) and a post-Saussurean ('differential') model of language. And whilst the term 'logocentric' has only infiltrated our critical vocabulary in the last twenty years or so, it is a peculiarly apt term to use in connection with Lawrence's critique of mimetic language, since he frequently uses the term 'Logos' himself in connection with the tendency for words to reify and gain a fixed hold on our view of the world.[28] I see modernist aesthetics, then, to be repeating moves which were being made quite independently in Continental linguistic philosophy at around the same time. Ironically and importantly, language first had to be recognized as a self-contained structure (and, in this sense, as 'organic'), before the notion of a purely differential meaning, and its post-structuralist legacy, could come into being.

Although this book as a whole is concerned primarily with Lawrence as art-critic, with his views *on* art and literature rather than with his artistic practice, I go on to suggest that there are ways in which Lawrence as writer foregrounds polyvalence in his work and undermines the idea of an essential link between signifier and signified. Paradoxically enough, in view of Lawrence's current reputation, his attack on logocentrism and on a model of language which assumes a bounded, coherent self in mastery of an objective, outer world, links him to contemporary French feminist theory. As Julia Kristeva has expressed it, 'in a culture where the speaking subjects are conceived of as masters of their speech, they have what is called a "phallic" position. The fragmentation of language in a text calls into question the very posture of this mastery.'[29] It is precisely this posture of mastery that Lawrence attacks in his own critical writing, arguing famously that we should trust the tale, not the artist, and that a work of art 'must contain the essential criticism on the morality to which it adheres'.[30]

For Lawrence, the erosion of the signifier/signified link is connected to the play of the unconscious in language. Like the French feminists who draw so heavily on Lacan's work, and like his own contemporary Freud, he is

---

[28] See 'Democracy', in *Reflections on the Death of a Porcupine*, 63–83, esp. pp. 69, 75. This essay first appeared in 1919 in *The Word*, a periodical published in The Hague.

[29] 'Oscillation Between Power and Denial', trans. Marilyn A. August, in *New French Feminisms*, ed. Elaine Marks and Isabelle de Courtivron (Amherst, Mass., 1980), 165–7 (p. 165).

[30] *Studies in Classic American Literature* (1923; London, 1964), 2; 'Study of Thomas Hardy', in *Study of Thomas Hardy and Other Essays*, ed. Bruce Steele (Cambridge, 1985), 1–128 (p. 89). 'Study of Thomas Hardy' was first published in its complete form in *Phoenix*.

engaged in a monumental attack on the Cartesian *cogito [ergo] sum*, on the idea of the unified subject as the given, exposing this belief in one's unity and self-knowledge as an illusion of mastery. In spite of this, though, Lawrence feels absolutely no sympathy for Freud's project. In Chapter 3 I look closely at this hostility towards Freud; it is rooted in what Lawrence sees to be a fundamental contradiction at the heart of Freud's enterprise, namely that Freud is at once attempting to subvert the Cartesian rationalist tradition and working from within its confines. Because of this, his epistemological project fails to reach the body (the unconscious) that it has made its prime object of study; it also represents, for Lawrence, an attempt at psychic imperialism.

The second part of the book explores Lawrence's connections with Bloomsbury art theory and criticism, opposing the received view that Lawrence and Bloomsbury were poles apart. I argue that Lawrence's hostility towards Bloomsbury aesthetics is based on a recognition of the idealism in Bell's theory of significant form, but also, when looked at from a different angle, on a crucial misreading of Bloomsbury formalism, a failure to recognize its intuitive basis. I try to stress the importance for both Lawrence and the Bloomsbury art-critics of the body in aesthetics, where the body is taken to mean a physiological/emotional response to art (as opposed to an exclusively linguistic or conceptual one); both base their theories on an organicist belief in the *integration* of the cognitive and the sensuous in the aesthetic response. I then go on to challenge the notion of a Lawrence–Bloomsbury opposition from the point of view of linguistics, attempting to show how the Bloomsbury emphasis on aesthetic autonomy is best understood not as an attempt to sever art from life completely, but as a reaction against what it sets up as a naïvely mimetic model of language and art. This brings Bloomsbury closer to Lawrence than literary history has generally allowed, since, like Bell and Fry, Lawrence uses the shibboleth of a naïvely mimetic language (which could never exist in practice) in order the more effectively to articulate his own views on the language of art. Like Bell and Fry, Lawrence objects to pseudo-photographic painting because it attempts, in his view, to naturalize the accidents of meaning, and like Bell and Fry he privileges Cézanne as the most important modern painter.

The last four chapters draw out the connections between Lawrence's views on art and his critique of the impact of capitalistic industrialism and technology on the environment. The link between logocentrism and violence or coercion is something which Lawrence's criticism, more than that of any other post-Romantic thinker, seeks to forge. I try to show how some of Lawrence's ideas on this subject originate in his readings of Victorian commentators on art and the environment, such as Carlyle and Ruskin, but are developed in ways which have more in common with Martin Heidegger

than with Lawrence's Victorian predecessors; I then go on to trace the
extensive connections between the aesthetics of Lawrence and Heidegger.
This is not a question of direct influence, for which there is no evidence; it
is rather the case, as I have already indicated, that Lawrence and Heidegger
shared many (largely *völkisch*) influences. Although one scarcely thinks of
them as contemporaries (Heidegger outlived Lawrence by forty-six years),
they were in fact born within four years of each other, Lawrence in 1885 and
Heidegger in 1889. Most prominent among the *völkisch* influences on them
was, of course, Nietzsche, the philosopher from whom they both learned so
much but also *against* whom they both reacted. A great deal has already been
written on Lawrence and Nietzsche. Instead of devoting too much space to
that already well-documented intellectual encounter, I have chosen instead
to focus on Lawrence and Heidegger, about whom practically nothing has
been said, even though they take up, use, and repudiate Nietzsche in closely
corresponding ways.[31] They both bring Nietzsche forward into the age
of technology, adapting his thought to a more fully fledged critique of industrial capitalism, whilst seeing him, curiously, as a kind of philosophical
technologist himself.

The last chapter turns again to the vexed question of the relationship
between art and politics, stressing the importance, for Lawrence, of an 'anti-
imperialistic' aesthetics, and opposing the view that his theory of art should
be read in terms of political extremism (more specifically, of fascism). The
anti-imperialism implicit in Lawrence's critique of 'white consciousness'
is central to his aesthetics.[32] For Lawrence, the 'white consciousness' that
characterizes Western culture is the direct result of the demotion of the
body. 'White' here has resonances both of a bloodless, dispassionate,
dematerializing use of the intellect, and of the imperialism that has characterized the overweening white man: unburdened of its corporeality, the
intellect, for Lawrence, becomes expansive and appropriative.

In his art-criticism, Lawrence makes little or no distinction between literature and the visual arts: essays ostensibly about literature, such as 'Study of
Thomas Hardy', make frequent references to painting, and it is quite typical
of Lawrence that an essay entitled 'Morality and the Novel' should open
with a meditation on Van Gogh.[33] For that reason, I too have ventured to
discuss painting as well as literature. Without wishing to deny important

---

[31] The section on Heidegger in Michael Bell's book on Leavis can, in view of Lawrence's
influence on Leavis, be seen to articulate links between Lawrence and Heidegger. See *F. R.
Leavis* (London, 1988), esp. pp. 36–54.

[32] In *Studies in Classic American Literature*, Lawrence diagnoses 'the collapse of the white
psyche' (p. 59), by which he implies an overemphasis on the intellect at the expense of the
body.

[33] 'Morality and the Novel', in *Study of Thomas Hardy and Other Essays*, 169–76. This essay
was first published in the *Calendar of Modern Letters*, 2 (Dec. 1925), 269–74.

differences between the two media, I have focused, through what could be described as a semiotic approach, on what they have in common. My prime concern though, is with Lawrence as *critic* or *theorist* of art, and with models of *reading* or *interpreting* works of art and literature, not with Lawrence's novelistic, poetic, or painterly practice. Whether Lawrence's critical views are borne out by his writerly or painterly practice is an interesting question, though not one which this book sets out to address at any length. Moreover, Lawrence in some of his most challenging art-criticism seems quite deliberately to offer a model for *reading* art and literature rather than producing it. It is the *critic's* task, he famously urges, to 'save the tale from the artist who created it'.[34] This injunction is an intriguing one, coming as it does from a writer whose strident didacticism is notorious. It is tempting to see Lawrence's anti-subjectivist, anti-humanist stance (his claim that the author is never fully in control of his work) as a safety net for the extremist nature of some of his own fiction; saving the tale from the artist suggests that it is left to the *reader* to rectify the excesses of the author. Yet the invitation to read against the grain seems, ultimately, both productive and liberating. Its implicit pluralism is the necessary antidote to the rigid dualities and hierarchies, the totalizing systems, that Lawrence erects in other areas of his thinking.

Lawrence's comments on art, as these introductory remarks have suggested, go far beyond what are normally considered the bounds of art. He extends his aesthetic theories to embrace the world itself, arguing that humanity's desire for interpretative mastery of the world leaves the *body* of the world very much out of account, with devastating results:

Strange as it may seem, for thousands of years, in short, ever since the mythological 'Fall', man has been preoccupied with the constant preoccupation of the denial of the existence of matter, and the proof that matter is only a form of spirit. And then, the moment it is done, and we realize finally that matter is only a form of energy, whatever that may be, in the same instant matter rises up and hits us over the head and makes us realize that it exists absolutely, since it is compact energy itself.[35]

Lawrence continually warns, then, against the dangers of abstracting from the body, believing that all forms of transcendence entail a forgetting of the material universe. The catastrophes that Lawrence witnessed in his own lifetime (not least the First World War), were seen to be the culmination of 'centuries and centuries of weaning away from the body of life'.[36] Heidegger, who shares with Lawrence a (largely German) organicist heritage, has, like Lawrence, been accused of aesthetic mystification. Yet he deplores a situation

---

[34] *Studies in Classic American Literature*, 2.
[35] 'Introduction to These Paintings', 568.   [36] 'Study of Thomas Hardy', 115.

in which 'the earth and its atmosphere become raw material', and in which 'man becomes human material, which is disposed of with a view to proposed goals'. He shows how dispensable the body has become in our technological tradition, citing Rilke's comment that technology is an 'act without an image'; through art, Lawrence, like Rilke and Heidegger, finds a way of restoring these effaced images.[37]

[37] 'What Are Poets For?', in *Poetry, Language, Thought*, trans. Albert Hofstadter (New York, 1971), 89–142 (pp. 111, 127).

THE TOTALIZING ORGANIC:
LAWRENCE AND FASCISM

1. Deconstructing the Organic

Cézanne's apple provides an apt image with which to begin a discussion of Lawrence's views on art, not only because of its biblical connotations, but because it suggests the organicity that has in recent years become one of the most controverted topics within aesthetics. In the Introduction I commented on the fact that a great deal of critical energy has been spent stressing the perils of organicist analogies, largely as a result of the de Man and Heidegger affairs. I also indicated there that many of the charges that have been levelled against Lawrence are very similar to those more recently levelled against de Man and Heidegger, and that I believe there to be very deep-rooted and intricate links between Heideggerian aesthetics and what Lawrence has to say on the subject of art, which I explore in later chapters. Bertrand Russell's allegation, that Lawrence's views 'led straight to Auschwitz', has too often been dismissed or evaded; it has also far too often been swallowed unquestioningly among a new generation of students no longer prepared to dirty their hands with Lawrence. Recent overviews of Lawrence's work tend to match totalitarianism with totalitarianism. Lawrence was fascistic, the general line of argument runs, *therefore* we should not read him. If we pursue this line of thought, purging from our reading lists all works considered ideologically unsound, we are bound, sooner or later, to witness the return of the repressed. Only by working through, time and again, those thought-processes that *can* (and, historically, did) lead to fascism, will we remember that they can and did do so. It still seems imperative to face up to the question of the organic in Lawrence's thought.

Christopher Norris, in his study of Paul de Man, saw the notion of the organic to be the main strand in a 'potent, post-Romantic aesthetic ideology', where 'potent' had resonances of 'dangerously powerful'; he argued convincingly throughout his study that the principle of organicity can lead to a dangerous mystification.[1] I should perhaps make it clear at the outset that I agree wholeheartedly with Norris's claim, and that, as I stressed in the

---

[1] Norris, *Paul de Man*, pp. xviii, 149, 165.

Introduction, I do not wish to be read as advocating the continued use of the term 'organic' in literary critical discourse. I made the point there that the 'organic', as a term, is far too vague and slippery to be useful, and is open to all kinds of political appropriation. None the less, what I would like to stress is the fact that some of the ways in which the term 'organic' *has* been used in the past by critics and philosophers have been more positive than the current attitude towards the term would suggest, and that a writer's use of the term 'organic' should not be treated as an automatic cue for dismissing that writer out of hand. Without wishing to refute Norris's claim, then, it seems necessary to look a little more closely at this concept of the organic; few other concepts in contemporary critical theory are so complacently dismissed as outworn, reactionary, and irresponsibly obfuscating. The organic occupies a position within post-structuralist criticism comparable to that of essentialism within much recent gender theory; rarely scrutinized or interrogated, it is presented as the naïve Other of deconstructive rigour and vigilance, as the monolith whose shadow delineates (and validates) the enlightened play of *différance*.

What is so consistently forgotten in current criticism is that the application of the adjective 'organic' to texts has often been quite consciously metaphorical or analogical. The organic metaphor is of course a paradoxical and potentially dangerous metaphor, in that it appeals to an idea that is precisely the opposite of metaphor, the idea of the 'natural', of the way things are. Yet a text is palpably *not* the same sort of thing as a plant or a piece of coral. It seems to me that this patently obvious fact is simultaneously acknowledged and suppressed in critical discussions of the organic. Much deconstructive criticism, committed to exposing the metaphorical nature of ostensibly non-metaphorical usage, frequently exposes the constructedness of the organic only to replace one logocentrism with another, namely the belief that the organic *always* and *necessarily* claims an essential link between language and world. In other words, having exposed the fact that the organic makes a false claim on the world, critics are often content to leave off their analysis at that point and treat the organic as a fixed, stable phenomenon, *always* insidiously naturalizing and *always* ideologically unsound. Frequently, then, deconstructive criticism treats 'organicism' in the same way as it treats 'logocentrism', not as another metaphor to be unpicked, but as a stable point of reference against which the deconstructive enterprise can define itself. For it is necessary to have something against which deconstruction *can* define itself. We find ourselves in the familiar *mise en abîme* of post-structuralist thought, in that 'organic' and 'logocentric' are themselves merely signifiers, subject to the same deferral of meaning as all others.

The metaphorical or analogical nature of claims that texts or artefacts are organic is amply borne out by the fact that this organicity is used to imply so many different, and conflicting, things. For many critics, the organic implies a determinism that prevents change, the unfurling of a destiny that cannot be halted, just as the fully grown plant is already present in the seed. This is something John Beer brings out very clearly, commenting on European theories of the organic:

Those theories had concentrated mainly on vegetable growth, focusing therefore upon the unity in diversity to be seen in the growth of a vegetable, realizing the 'idea' that had always been implicit in its seed. They were inevitably conservative in nature, since they encouraged the conception of an evolution which took place according to inward laws. To interfere with such natural workings out, whether in the vegetable creation or in society at large, could be seen, therefore, as destructive. All that might be countenanced was something in the nature of a pruning, which must take strict account of the organism in question and its natural form of development.[2]

Beer distinguishes between these 'traditional' European theories and their nineteenth-century English developments, which 'had to do with qualities such as "energy", "vitality" or "animation" '. Lawrence's affinities are, argues Beer, with the latter version of the organic: Lawrence 'devoted himself to those elements in romanticism which encouraged a view of art in terms of process rather than through survey of the finished products' and he 'developed a framework for looking at the world which would automatically stress the role of energies rather than of forms'.[3]

The European version of the organic which Beer describes does not allow for genuinely *radical* change ('radical' = 'from the root'). From this deterministic position it is a small step to a situation where the organic is used to attempt to root a culture in its native soil, to bind together language, culture, and national destiny (here race becomes the organism incapable of tolerating foreign bodies). Yet very often Lawrence uses organic imagery to suggest the opposite of this dependence on the past: 'The idea . . . must rise ever fresh, *ever displaced*, like the leaves of a tree, from out of the quickness of the sap.'[4] And for other critics, notably the American New Critics, the organic has, in practice, very little to do with the soil from which a poem has sprung; New Criticism severs the poem from its material, historical, or cultural origins and focuses attention on to the *body* of the text itself. Here the organic implies that the text, like the living organism, cannot be broken down into its

---

[2] John Beer, 'D. H. Lawrence and English Romanticism', *Aligarh Journal of English Studies*, x/2 (1985), 109–121 (pp. 110–11).   [3] Ibid. 111, 110.
[4] 'Fantasia of the Unconscious', in *Fantasia of the Unconscious and Psychoanalysis and the Unconscious* (London, 1961), 79–80, my emphasis.

component parts and put back together again; the life of the text is somehow inseparable from the fact that it is an 'organic whole'.

Germane to my argument here is Norris's treatment of the organic in his book on de Man. In spite of the book's many strengths, it seems to me that Norris conflates two usages of the term 'organic' which ought, strictly speaking, to be distinguished. In the introduction, he directs his criticism towards the organicity of New Criticism, by which he refers to a theory based on the integration of the sensuous and the cognitive in language itself (the form–content fusion) and the inextricability of the component parts of a poem; in the postscript, by contrast, he is concerned with the organic relation between language, culture, and national destiny ('organic' here implying 'springing from the [native] soil'). Notions of an indigenous, 'nationalist' literature and of history as a predestined evolution relate very obviously to this last sense of the organic, but they have very little to do with the actual practice of New Criticism; in fact, New Criticism as a whole tends to dissociate poetry from the material circumstances of its origination. The point of the New Critical version of the organic is not primarily that poems cannot be translated into another language without losing their (cultural) integrity; it is rather that they cannot even be translated into the other terms of *their own* language without losing their integrity. For several critics, the later de Man's denial of the historical basis of language is an attempt to expiate guilt associated with his contributions to a German-controlled newspaper.[5] But whatever guilt may have attached to de Man's 1940s journalism, it makes no sense to speak of the later de Man recoiling from a New Critical organicism which had in any case excluded the author and history from its domain. 'Organicity' for the New Critics does not relate poetry to the conditions of its origination (or, in other words, to the soil from which it has sprung); rather, the organic in this instance refers the reader back to the *body* of the poem itself.

For the New Critics, then, the poem is a self-contained entity, an 'organic whole'. Frequently, references to the organic stress this idea of an achieved whole, the notion of perfection or completion, and of something static or cyclic rather than something mobile or progressive. Yet when ideas of the organic were first invoked in Romantic aesthetics, they were invoked precisely to suggest an alternative to such perfection, completion, stasis, or cyclicality, since all of these were qualities associated with *classical* as opposed to *Romantic* art. The term often seems, nowadays, to have lost its original impetus and to have been subsumed by the classical model. Perhaps for some critics this is precisely the point, that Romantic notions of the organic were simply a reworking of classicism. But that the organic *need* not imply semantic unity

---

[5] See Introduction, n. 17.

or totality, and did not imply it for many of the earliest theorists of the organic, is hinted at by the German Romantic Jean Paul Richter's statement: 'Only dissimilarity raised to polemic fermentation can grow and sprout. No single element can produce flowers.'[6]

The organic as the germ of radicalism and change is strangely absent from current critical discourse; this would seem to be a puzzling case of amnesia in view of the fact that numerous Marxist aestheticians (Adorno, Bloch, Marcuse), not to mention Marx himself, all have cause, in their different ways, to defend some notion of the organic. The idea of 'organic wholeness' is, of course, frequently equated by Marxist critics with political totality, but it is also within certain Marxist discourses that we can find other, more positive readings of the organic. Through his emphasis on the organic, Lawrence is working around a nexus of ideas which point, politically, towards both left and right.

On the one hand, then, the organic can imply stasis or cyclicality, and on the other dynamism and change; it can imply a cultural rootedness, or, when looked at differently, a self-contained separateness. In the next chapter, I will go on to argue that it can imply both a transparency to natural forces and material opacity, both semantic totality and a rich polysemy. It is hardly surprising, then, that a writer who, like Lawrence, has such frequent recourse to the organic, should be not only a profoundly self-contradictory writer, but also one whom critics fail, very often, to approach in a sufficiently dialectical manner. Once the metaphoric or analogical status of the organic is brought completely into the open, the important question becomes not whether an argument is organicist or not, but *how* the organic is being used in a particular context. First, it seems necessary to confront one of the most negative aspects of Lawrence's organicism.

2. *Organicism,* Völkisch *Ideology, and* Women in Love

One disturbing model of the organic which is present in much of Lawrence's work, sometimes implicitly, sometimes explicitly, is that which attempts to root cultures in their native soil, binding together culture and national destiny. One of its more explicit formulations occurs in Lawrence's essay on Poe, where he states: 'For men who are born at the end of a great era or epoch nothing remains but the seething reduction back to the elements; just as for a tree in autumn nothing remains but the strangling off of the leaves and the

---

[6] Jean Paul Richter, cited in Kathleen M. Wheeler (ed.), *German Aesthetics and Literary Criticism: The Romantic Ironists and Goethe* (Cambridge, 1984), 15.

strange decomposition and arrest of the sap.'[7] Where this kind of organicism surfaces in Lawrence, Bertrand Russell's charge has obvious relevance. This kind of organicism was central to the *völkisch* ideologies prevalent in Germany in the 1910s and 1920s, from which, as I indicated in the Introduction, both Heideggerian philosophy and Nazism emerged. Lawrence first left England for Germany in 1912, and came into direct contact, through Frieda von Richthofen and her circle, with these ideologies.[8] The fact that Lawrence had already read Nietzsche meant that he would have been well prepared, philosophically, for such an encounter.

These *völkisch* ideologies were of course inseparable from the fact that Germany had been undergoing a period of rapid industrialization. It is well known that Germany's industrialization was an accelerated, intensified version of its British counterpart; the most intense period of industrial development in Germany was around 1870, fifteen years before Lawrence's birth, and the social and cultural upheaval it engendered was far more dramatic than its earlier British version. The historian Fritz Ringer tells us that 'German academics reacted to the dislocation with such desperate intensity that the specter of a "soulless" modern age came to haunt everything they said and wrote'.[9]

Pierre Bourdieu, in *L'Ontologie politique de Martin Heidegger*, and particularly in the opening chapter, 'La Philosophie pure et le Zeitgeist', amasses an abundance of detail in an effort to reconstruct the cultural matrix from which Heidegger's philosophy evolved, which was centred upon the apparently contradictory concept of a 'conservative revolution'. Since this was the same cultural climate with which Lawrence came into contact in 1912, Bourdieu's study is highly illuminating to students of Lawrence. In particular, Bourdieu focuses on the binary oppositions around which this cultural matrix was constructed (culture/civilization, *Gemeinschaft/Gesellschaft*, integration/disintegration, and so on).[10] Oswald Spengler emerges as one of the most prominent figures in this cultural climate (Bourdieu argues that Heidegger

---

[7] *The Symbolic Meaning: The Uncollected Versions of Studies in Classic American Literature,* ed. Armin Arnold (Fontwell, Arundel, 1962), 117.

[8] See Martin Green, *The Von Richthofen Sisters: The Triumphant and the Tragic Modes of Love* (London, 1974).

[9] Fritz Ringer, *The Decline of the German Mandarins: The German Academic Community 1890–1933* (Cambridge, Mass., 1969), 3.

[10] Bourdieu, *L'Ontologie politique de Martin Heidegger* (Paris, 1988), esp. pp. 31–2. The *Gemeinschaft/Gesellschaft* ('Community/Society') distinction was popularized by Ferdinand Tönnies, who used it as a title for one of his books, *Gemeinschaft und Gesellschaft* (1887). The distinction was used again by Julius Langbehn and by Oswald Spengler. Tönnies used organic analogies to describe communal ties, and mechanical analogies to describe societal ones; he was influenced by Marx, seeing capitalism to be the chief cause of the movement from community to society.

took up and euphemized a number of Spenglerian themes, p. 38). The first volume of Spengler's *Decline of the West* (*Der Untergang des Abendlandes*) appeared in 1918. The fact that it coincided with the final phases of the First World War accounted to a large extent for the startling impact it had on many of the leading philosophers of the day. Though many people disagreed violently with much of Spengler's thesis, no one could escape a sense of the timeliness of its gloomy prophesies. Lawrence himself was bound to feel the reverberations of this massively influential work, and indeed it is mentioned by its German title, almost in the same breath as Rilke,[11] at the opening of *The First Lady Chatterley*, in direct connection with Clifford Chatterley, 'a smashed man', whose physical paralysis, brought on by fighting in the war, is symbolic of a much deeper paralysis in society at large.[12]

Much of Spengler's work, as Bourdieu explains, was a vulgarized version of the philosophy of Sombart and Spann, and was popularized in its turn by the Youth Movement (*Jugendbewegung*), which was at its height in the period following the First World War (p. 16). There is another interesting link with Lawrence here when we consider that Werner Sombart, whose philosophy was such an important influence on both Spengler and the Youth Movement, was a friend of Frieda's sister, Else Jaffe.[13] In Sombart's work, Lawrence could have found all the arguments he was himself to use time and time again, against mechanical law, quantification, urbanization, and so on. Even if he never read Sombart's work at first hand, it seems more than likely that Frieda and her family would have discussed it with him.

It is worth summarizing Bourdieu's account of these *völkisch* ideologies, since they have a direct bearing upon interpretations of Lawrence's organicism. One of the key concepts was rootedness, in a native soil and among a native people, and the overriding feeling was one of alienation or rootlessness: humanity's kinship with the soil had been forgotten. This alienation was seen to have been caused by the tyranny of rationalism and the intellect in modern society, and a concomitant outwardness, an expansive materialism;

[11] For the importance of Rilke as a possible historical link between Lawrentian and Heideggerian thought, see below, pp. 123–4.

[12] *The First Lady Chatterley* (London, 1972), 2. Lawrence probably read John Gould Fletcher's review of *Civilisation or Civilisations: An Essay in the Spenglerian Philosophy of History*, by E. H. Goddard and P. A. Gibbons, which appeared in the *Monthly Criterion*, vi/3 (Sept. 1927). Lawrence contributed a series of essays entitled 'Flowery Tuscany' to the next three issues of the *Monthly Criterion* (vi/4, 5, and 6 (Oct., Nov., Dec. 1927)).

[13] See Green, *The Von Richthofen Sisters*, 27. See also *Lady Chatterley's Lover*, 11, where Connie is sent to Dresden shortly before the War, and participates in student activities which sound very like those of the Youth Movement. In the late 1920s, Lawrence was writing to Rolf Gardiner, who had been deeply influenced by *The Decline of the West* and later became involved in extreme right-wing politics. See Edward Nehls (ed.), *D. H. Lawrence: A Composite Biography*, 3 vols. (Wisconsin, 1959), iii. 71–84, 178–83.

'interiority', it was felt, must be brought back. The term 'disintegration' (*Zersetzung*) was used to evoke the weakening, in an industrial society, of the 'natural' bonds between people, and the erosion, through intellectual critique, of the traditional foundations of social cohesion.[14] Descriptions of city-dwellers as 'soulless automatons', as mere 'statistics' or 'ciphers' in regard to their position in what was now perceived to be the social 'machine' (suggesting a severance of organic links), pervaded the *völkisch* writing of the period. Man's will to dominate nature through technology only led (as in Heidegger's *The Question Concerning Technology*) to man being dominated by technology. This ideology emerged in the context of a cluster of profoundly unsettling world events: the First World War, the November 1918 revolution, the Kapp Putsch, the Versailles treaty, the French occupation of the Ruhr, hyper-inflation (1919–24), a period of brief prosperity and technological development, followed by another slump (1929). Bourdieu points to the irony that this *völkisch* discourse was a 'doctrine of the learned for the learned' (a similar irony has often been detected in Lawrence's anti-intellectualist stance). It was born and flourished first on the fringes of universities and among the intelligentsia, then it worked its way into university courses themselves, though in more refined and complex forms of which Heidegger's work was one example. Bourdieu relates its rapid success to various crises occurring within the universities, especially the threat posed to the Faculty of Letters by the increased status of the natural and human sciences (pp. 15–26).

It can be seen from this brief synopsis of Bourdieu's account that many of the grievances of the *Jugendbewegung* had much in common with those of the nineteenth-century British social commentators who had had to absorb the massive impact of the industrial revolution, and whom Lawrence had read as a young man (some of these are examined in Chapter 7). In particular, Carlyle started out from many of the philosophical and political premisses later espoused by Spengler and others: he repudiated an overintellectualized, materialistic culture, characterized by spiritual vacuity and homogeneity (this is perhaps not surprising in that Carlyle himself was writing in a German Romantic tradition and was strongly influenced by Kant). It is not difficult to see how, from such a position, he could go on to develop a brutally authoritarian politics, for, as Bourdieu points out in connection with the Youth Movement, as soon as the 'dehumanization' of industrialized society is linked, as it is in Carlyle, to the idea of democratic levelling (the idea of reducing human beings to statistics or ciphers), recourse is easily

---

[14] Bourdieu refers here to Ringer, *The Decline of the German Mandarins*. See esp. pp. 221–2.

made to 'natural categories' and to a 'natural hierarchy' grounded in biology, to the differences universally inscribed in 'nature' (p. 25). The *Jugendbewegung* paralleled similar moves in England made by Carlyle and later Lawrence, by positing a 'natural' (i.e. intellectual and spiritual) aristocracy, in place of an aristocracy based on (arbitrary) social rank. Bourdieu shows how the ecological theme of a 'return to nature' had become connected, without any obvious logical link, to a preoccupation with 'natural rights' (p. 25).[15] He cites as one of the more politically offensive products of this cultural ethos, Ernst Jünger's *Der Waldgang* (1951), in which the Worker, who represents the technological principle, an automaton or cipher, is opposed to the Rebel, poet, and natural leader, whose element is the forest (implying a region off the beaten track, and outside the normal boundaries of thinking, and suggesting Heidegger's *Holzwege*). The Rebel promises a return to origins and native soil, to the sacred and the secret; he has the natural strength of one who takes risks and who prefers death to the degradation and 'social security' of collective city life (pp. 28–9).

To return to Spengler, probably the best known of the *völkisch* ideologues: with Spengler we encounter full in the face the kind of organicist historiography criticized by Norris in the postscript to his book on de Man.[16] *The Decline of the West* replaces the causality of traditional historiography with Destiny, and the idea of a linear progression with that of 'a number of mighty Cultures, each springing with primitive strength from the soil of a mother-region to which it remains firmly bound throughout its whole life-cycle'.[17] For Spengler, cultures are best understood *morphologically*; they are analogous to living organisms, springing from the soil like plants and with the same unaccountability, flowering and then petrifying into rigid forms (this rigid stage Spengler, like Lawrence, calls 'civilization'), and eventually disappearing from the face of the earth, giving way to new seedling cultures:

---

[15] It is interesting that this, like so many aspects of *völkisch* ideology, issues later on not only in fascism but in radical green thinking. The eco-feminist Andrée Collard laments the loss of a culture in which the 'class-system' arises from 'a recognition of "specialness" and differences that have intrinsic survival value' (*Rape of the Wild* (London, 1988), 29). See below, pp. 171–2.   [16] *Paul de Man*, 177.

[17] Oswald Spengler, *The Decline of the West*, trans. Charles Francis Atkinson, 2 vols. (London, 1926), i. 21. The book was first published in two volumes as *Der Untergang des Abendlandes* (Vienna, 1918–22). As in Lawrence, those people at a late stage in the development of a so-called 'civilization' are seen to be the 'barbarians' of the narrative, and, like Lawrence, Spengler sees this barbarism in terms of an overdevelopment of the intellect: the soul–intellect antithesis, claims Spengler, 'is the differentia between Culture and Civilization' (*Decline of the West*, 32). He focuses on the term 'abstract', and its sense of 'withdrawn' ('abstract') from the sensual. The systematic spirit is abstract for Spengler, and belongs to a culture's ripest state; like the autumn leaf severed from the tree, a culture in this state must die (p. 102).

Civilizations are the most external and artificial states of which a species of devel-oped humanity is capable. They are a conclusion, the thing-become succeeding the thing-becoming, death following life, rigidity following expansion, intellectual age and the stone-built, petrifying world-city following mother-earth and the spiritual childhood of Doric and Gothic. They are an end, irrevocable, yet by inward neces-sity reached again and again. (p. 31)

Spengler's stress on rootedness and Destiny directly informs Heidegger's work, as does his analysis of an uprooted, metropolitan humanity succeeding an organically rooted one: 'In place of a type-true people, born of and grown on the soil, there is a new sort of nomad, cohering unstably in fluid masses, the parasitical city-dweller, traditionless, utterly matter-of-fact, religionless, clever, unfruitful . . .' (p. 32).

The cyclical nature of Spengler's conception of history sounds very like the Aztec myth of 'Worlds successively created and destroyed' which Law-rence posits in place of Darwinian theory.[18] Though Lawrence's only men-tion of Spengler occurs in *The First Lady Chatterley*, there is a strong possibility that he had heard of Spengler's theories or others very like them while writing *Women in Love*, to which the depiction of an overripe, putrefying 'civilization' is central. Though direct influence of *The Decline of the West* upon *Women in Love* seems unlikely (the 'Spenglerian' imagery was an es-tablished part of *Women in Love* before the publication in Germany of *The Decline of the West* in 1918), theories approximating very closely to Spengler's were in wide circulation. In the words of Fritz Ringer, 'In an emotional environment of this type, Oswald Spengler's *Decline of the West* was nothing more than a particularly thorough exploitation of a common theme.'[19] Moreover, as was mentioned above, many of Spengler's theories were derived from Sombart, Else Jaffe's close associate. Of course, British historians had not been without their own cyclical theories, and in particular the influential archaeologist Flinders Petrie had written *The Revolutions of Civilisation* (1911). In this book he relies heavily, as Spengler does, on organicist metaphor, taking his initiative from the Etruscans who believed 'that each successive race had its period of a Great Year in which it sprouted, flourished, decayed, and died'.[20] Like Spengler, Petrie equates the rise of democracy with the decay of civilization.

But, in view of the evidence we have of Lawrence's reading, it seems more likely that it was through another channel that Lawrence first encountered this notion of cultural flourishing and decadence. The single most important

[18] 'Mornings in Mexico', in *Mornings in Mexico and Etruscan Places* (London, 1956), 4.
[19] *The Decline of the German Mandarins*, 223.
[20] W. M. Flinders Petrie, *The Revolutions of Civilisation* (London and New York, 1911), 10.

philosopher for the *völkisch* ideologues was Nietzsche, whom, as we have already seen, Lawrence had already read before departing for Germany. Nietzsche had claimed in *The Case of Wagner* (1888) that 'decadence' had been the central theme of his philosophical career. And in *Ecce Homo* (1908) he boasted, 'I have a subtler sense for signs of ascent and decline than any man has ever had.'[21] If not directly from Nietzsche, Lawrence may have picked up ideas on decadence from A. R. Orage, the Nietzschean disciple, editor of and contributor to *The New Age*, the periodical which Lawrence is known to have read during the period 1908–9. Orage's rhetoric of a sick culture and a sick society was in all probability influenced by Nietzsche's *Twilight of the Idols* and *The Case of Wagner*. David Thatcher, in his study of Nietzsche's influence in England, tells us that Orage, together with Havelock Ellis, T. E. Hulme, and T. S. Eliot, was 'indebted to Nietzsche for a workable definition of "decadence", not in terms of pathology, as in Nordau, but in terms of an "anarchy of atoms" '.[22]

It seems probable, then, that Nietzsche, a direct influence on Lawrence, as well as on Spengler and the other *völkisch* ideologues whose ideas were in the air in the Germany of 1912, largely accounts for the remarkable similarities between *The Decline of the West* and *Women in Love*. It has already been suggested that many of the characters in *Women in Love* represent a 'fallen' humanity; their lives are characterized by rootlessness and sterility (a point examined in connection with Heidegger in Chapter 8). Lawrence's comments on this to Catherine Carswell sound Spenglerian both in their use of the analogy with natural growth and in their 'end-of-an-epoch' vocabulary. Carswell reports:

I asked him why must he write of people who were so far removed from the general run, people so sophisticated and 'artistic' and spoiled, that it could hardly matter what they did or said? To which he replied that it was only through such people that one could discover whither the general run of mankind, the great unconscious mass, was tending. There, at the uttermost tips of the flower of an epoch's achievement, one could already see the beginning of the flower of putrefaction which must take place before the seed of the new was ready to fall clear.[23]

A Spenglerian cultural 'autumn' is also implied in the alternative titles which Lawrence considered for the novel: *Love Among the Ruins, The Latter*

[21] *Ecce Homo: How one becomes what one is*, trans. R. J. Hollingdale (Harmondsworth, 1979), 38.

[22] David S. Thatcher, *Nietzsche in England 1890–1914* (Toronto, 1970), 274.

[23] *The Savage Pilgrimage*, 38. This 'end-of-an-epoch' vocabulary also suggests Baudelaire's *Les Fleurs du mal* (1857), which Lawrence had read in 1910. See *The Letters of D. H. Lawrence*, 7 vols. (Cambridge, 1979–   ), i, ed. James T. Boulton (1979), 179 (18 Sept. 1910). The Cambridge edition of the letters will be referred to throughout the book as *Letters*.

Days, and *Dies Irae.* Further, Hermione and her artistic friends are described as *Kulturträger* ('bearers of culture'), a term which has very specific historical reference to the class of German intellectuals (Fritz Ringer calls them the 'mandarins') who felt most threatened by industrial capitalism.[24] The antithesis *Women in Love* sets up between Hermione and the Breadalby set on the one hand, and Crich and the industrialists on the other, parallels the *Kultur–Zivilisation* antithesis evolved by the mandarins in an attempt to define their own position in relation to industrialization. They defined their own idea of what learning should be through the terms *Bildung* ('cultivation') and *Kultur.* They opposed to this *Zivilisation,* which had to do with practical knowledge, vocational training, and ultimately the 'outward' signs of progress in economics, technology, and social organization. Ringer explains how, eventually, *Zivilisation* came to signify 'outer' and *Kultur* 'inner': ' "Civilization" evoked the tangible amenities of earthly existence; "culture" suggested spiritual concerns.'[25] What is immediately apparent about the narrator's own position in *Women in Love,* though, is that it negates *both* Crich's materialism *and* Hermione's idealism, seeing them, in fact, as two sides of the same coin. There has to be some alternative, the novel seems to imply, to Crich's manipulation of the material world, but an alternative which does not deny the material realm altogether. It is above all in Lawrence's writings on art that such an alternative is posited.

Women in Love, then, cannot be exempted, at a thematic level, from a full-blooded, *völkisch* organicism, nor indeed from the racist positions to which this kind of organicism can lead. It is no accident, for example, that Loerke, the Dresden sculptor who puts forward a theory of an absolute aesthetic autonomy, a transcendental art–life dichotomy, is Jewish.[26] Lawrence's descriptions of Loerke constitute a catalogue of the anti-Jewish commonplaces that pervaded the work of Sombart and others at this period. According to Sombart in his monolithic *The Jews and Modern Capitalism (Die Juden und das Wirtschaftsleben,* 1911), the Jewish religion is 'a creation of the intellect, a thing of thought and purpose projected into the world of organisms, mechanically and artfully wrought'; Sombart is struck by 'the Jew's love for the inconcrete, his tendency away from the sensuous, his constant abiding in a world of abstractions'; he argues that 'Jews have the gift of adaptability in

[24] *Women in Love,* 16; *The Decline of the German Mandarins,* 46: 'A government bill placed before the Prussian House of Deputies in 1910 proposed some slight reforms in the undemocratic electoral system of that state, among them one which would grant special privileges to those it labeled "bearers of culture" (*Kulturträger*).'

[25] *The Decline of the German Mandarins,* 90.

[26] See *Women in Love,* 430: 'It is a work of art . . . It has nothing to do with anything but itself, it has no relation with the everyday world of this and the other . . . they are two different and distinct planes of existence.'

an eminently high degree', and that the Jewish spirit is, like money, made up of two factors: 'desert and wandering, Saharaism and Nomadism. Money is as little concrete as the land from which the Jews sprang; money is only a mass, a lump, like the flock; it is mobile; it is seldom rooted in fruitful soil like the flower or the tree.'[27] Compare the descriptions of Loerke in *Women in Love*: 'Loerke, in his innermost soul, was detached from everything, for him there was neither heaven nor earth nor hell. He admitted no allegiance, he gave no adherence anywhere . . .'; elsewhere he is 'quick, detached' 'everywhere at once'. He is linked to the process of 'disintegrating the vital organic body of life' and frequently the terms associated with him are resonant of this disintegration: he mocks 'with an *acid* ridicule'; he is a 'mud-child', 'the very stuff of the underworld of life'; in his eyes he has 'the black look of inorganic misery'; he knows 'the subtle thrills of extreme sensation in reduction . . . the last subtle activities of analysis and breaking-down'. This is accounted for in terms of the fact that, as a Jew, Loerke has reached a more advanced stage of the racial life-cycle: he is 'further on than we are', 'the wizard rat that swims ahead'.[28] In attributing an 'acid ridicule' to Loerke, Lawrence is drawing on the imagery of disintegration which had become such a staple part of *völkisch* discourse.[29] Terms such as 'disintegration' (*Zersetzung*) and 'decomposition' (*Dekomposition*) were used to imply the erosion or crumbling of 'natural' bonds through industrial-ization, but also the penetrating, 'acid' forces of the intellect and critical analysis.[30]

The same kind of organicism is at work in Lawrence's reaction to Mark Gertler's painting *Merry-Go-Round*, in a letter dating from the same period as *Women in Love*:

You are all absorbed in the violent and lurid processes of inner decomposition: the same thing that makes leaves go scarlet and copper-green at this time of year . . . It would take a Jew to paint this picture. It would need your national history to get you here, without disintegrating you first. You are of an older race than I, and in these ultimate processes, you are beyond me, older than I am. But I think I am sufficiently the same, to be able to understand.[31]

---

[27] Werner Sombart, *The Jews and Modern Capitalism*, trans. M. Epstein (London and Leipzig, 1913), 206, 262, 271, 344. Just how enmeshed Lawrence was in this *völkisch* rhetoric is revealed by his use of exactly the same link between abstraction and the Sahara desert in a meditation on the disintegration of an organic culture. In *Women in Love* we read of 'the burning death-abstraction of the Sahara' (p. 254).

[28] *Women in Love*, 452, 405, 411, 452, 411 (my emphasis), 427, 422, 451, 428.

[29] Karl Alexander von Müller developed the imagery associated with *zersetzen* and *zerschwätzen* in a series of essays on 19th-cent. German history. See *The Decline of the German Mandarins*, 222.   [30] See *The Decline of the German Mandarins*, 221–2.

[31] *Letters*, ii, ed. George J. Zytaruk and James T. Boulton (1981), 660 (9 Oct. 1916).

Lawrence includes himself, and indeed the whole of Western civilization, in this process of decay, yet the consequences of his position hardly need underlining.

During the Weimar period, the links between anti-capitalism and anti-Semitism became more and more overt. The extent to which industrial capitalism and the Jewish race became synonymous is brought out in von Müller's *Deutsche Geschichte* (1926) in which he explicitly associates the emancipation of the Jews with the rise of iron and coal.[32] It was thought significant, for example, that Marx himself was Jewish. In what must be one of the most extraordinary ironies of history, Marx had used, indeed helped to forge, the anti-capitalist vocabulary which would in its turn be appropriated in the services of anti-Semitism. Hence a writer like Sombart concurs with Marx in seeing the monetary system as the very paradigm of idealism. It is well known that Marx himself made a detailed study of the aesthetics of Friedrich Vischer, and that his major economic works are permeated with the language of Romantic aesthetics.[33] Similarly, Lawrence's attack on Loerke (himself the proponent of an idealist aesthetic) is expressed in terms ('quick, detached'; 'everywhere at once'; 'he gave no adherence anywhere') which could just as easily be applied to *money*, and to a capitalistic, commodity-based culture. Marx in the *Economic and Philosophical Manuscripts of 1844* had used a language which anticipates Lawrence's descriptions of Loerke: 'Since money, as the existing and active concept of value, confounds and exchanges all things, it is the general *confounding* and *compounding* of all things—the world upside-down—the confounding and compounding of all natural and human qualities.' He had gone on: '[money] serves to exchange every property for every other, even contradictory, property and object: it is the fraternization of impossibilities. It makes contradictions embrace.'[34]

It is worth noting, however, that Lawrence significantly disrupts the neat equation of idealism, industrial capitalism, and the Jews by making the industrial magnate of *Women in Love* a blond, Nordic figure. Whilst he uses the rhetoric of his day in linking Loerke with idealism, he seems to see Loerke as part of a trend within Western civilization as a whole, a trend which Gerald, as much as Loerke, symptomatizes.

Lawrence, then, is curiously caught up in a rhetoric which looks forward to Nazism and backwards to Marx. His first sustained piece of literary criticism, the 'Study of Thomas Hardy', is saturated with monetary language,

[32] Karl Alexander von Müller, *Deutsche Geschichte und Deutscher Charakter* (Stuttgart, 1926), 158.   [33] See e.g. Eagleton, *The Ideology of the Aesthetic*, 208.
[34] *Economic and Philosophical Manuscripts of 1844*, ed. Dirk J. Struik, trans. Martin Milligan (London, 1970), 169.

explicitly opposing art to the network of exchange: art is the 'excess' or 'waste' symbolized in the poppy's extravagant flowering, that which cannot be recuperated, but falls outside the sway of exchange-value. Unlike the poppy, we, in a capitalist society, 'remain, like the regulation cabbage, hidebound, a bunch of leaves that may not go any further for fear of losing market value'.[35] Marx in the *Economic and Philosophical Manuscripts* had put forward a parallel argument to the effect that 'The care-burdened man in need has no sense for the finest play; the dealer in minerals sees only the commercial value but not the beauty and the unique nature of the mineral' (p. 141). Like Lawrence, he defines human creativity in terms of creating when there is no physical need to do so: '[An animal] produces only under the dominion of immediate physical need, whilst man produces even when he is free from physical need and only truly produces in freedom therefrom' (p. 113). In fact, the emphasis on the body inherent in Lawrence's aesthetics places him in a tradition which goes back beyond Marx to Saint-Simon and Feuerbach, and in particular to Feuerbach's bold reversal of the Hegelian aesthetic. For Hegel, the *Bildlichkeit* of Greek culture had shackled the Greeks to the physical world, and only with Christianity's cult of the spiritual had civilization been liberated from that physical bondage. Feuerbach reversed the argument: it was precisely in the sensuousness of Greek culture that its freedom consisted, while Christianity was restrictive and alienated humanity from the world of the senses. German idealist aesthetics, preoccupied as it was with the liberation of the subject *from* the senses, was seen by Feuerbach and Saint-Simon to be misguided: the goal should be the liberation of the senses themselves.[36]

Having looked in some detail at the organicism germane to *völkisch* ideology, I want to go on to retrieve from Lawrence's writings on art a concept of the organic very different from the Spenglerian brand, acting, in certain vitally important ways, as an antidote to it. To see how this could have been the case it is necessary to return briefly to Bourdieu's analysis of the *völkisch* cultural ethos.

3. A 'Semantic Disease'

One of the salient features, for Bourdieu, of the nebulous ideologies surrounding the Youth Movement, is the alarming pliability of their chief components. He is at pains to show that many of their key terms are flexible

---

[35] 'Study of Thomas Hardy', 12.

[36] For this account, I am indebted to Margaret A. Rose, *Marx's Lost Aesthetic: Karl Marx and the Visual Arts* (Cambridge, 1984), 32.

to the point of being practically indeterminate.[37] Here he draws heavily on the work of Fritz Ringer, who in *The Decline of the German Mandarins* explains how the German academics were 'perfectly content to blur any possible distinctions between various kinds of disintegration. They were at once the victims and the exploiters of an integral mood, an undifferentiated emotional reaction against the modern age' (pp. 223–4). Later in the book, Ringer elaborates on this:

The crisis of learning was like a semantic disease. The German language itself was affected by the passions of the day. Words became emotional stimuli. They trailed ever larger clouds of implicit meanings. Audiences were trained to respond to an expanding circle of vaguely antimodernist and antipositivist allusions. (p. 402)

He provides some concrete examples:

They never really distinguished between the fact of industrialization and the attitudinal changes with which they themselves identified it. They linked commerce with commercialism, machines with mechanistic conceptions, and the new economic organization with rationalism and utilitarianism. This confusion permitted them to trace everything disturbing in their modern environment to two different sorts of causes at once: to materialist or utilitarian theoreticians on the one hand, and to factories and parliamentary democracy on the other. (p. 221)

That this was indeed a *semantic* disease is clearly illustrated by various dictionary definitions of the period. See, for example, the following *Brockhaus* definitions of 'intellectualism' and 'wholeness' respectively:

intellectualism: the excessive emphasis upon the thought-out and reasoned as over against the will, practical action, and all [immediate] values of life . . . With the growth of civilization, there is always an increase of intellectualism, which many philosophers of culture consider destructive of vitality . . . For this reason, the pedagogy of the present has made it its goal to prevent the forces of the will and of practical action from being atrophied through intellectualism.

whole, wholeness [*Ganz, Ganzheit*]: in philosophy, the term for the substantive and meaningful coherence, completeness . . . integrity and . . . autonomy of objects of whatever kind . . . Wholeness can really be grasped and demonstrated only intuitively [*anschaulich*] and can barely be defined; the structure of a whole [*ganzheitlich*] object does not consist of isolated parts, is not a sum of parts [additive]; rather, it consists of members which are meaningfully interrelated moments of this whole, which form a unity. The concept whole is contrasted to the concepts sum, aggregate, mechanism, machine, and it has therefore become a basic concept in biology, psychology, in the humanistic disciplines, and in philosophy.[38]

[37] *L'Ontologie politique de Martin Heidegger*, 30–1.
[38] *Der Grosse Brockhaus*, 15th edn., cited in Ringer, *The Decline of the German Mandarins*, 417, 393.

Organicist metaphors and similes were two a penny, and their figurative status all but totally forgotten. A professor of forestry, for example, observed that a stand of trees was 'sociologically comparable to a living community'.[39] As an example of the semantic vagueness which seemed to have taken hold, Bourdieu cites the terms 'nature', showing how it can be opposed on the one hand to a cruel and dehumanizing industrialism, and on the other to democracy (in so far as the 'laws of nature' are not democratic): 'natural' in the sense of 'pre-industrial' and 'natural' in the context of a 'natural aristocracy' can have two completely different functions.[40] It is through a kind of semantic slippage or skewing that the one meaning is seen to entail the other. Bourdieu argues that the antitheses between totality and fragmentation, integration and disintegration, ontology and scientific rationalism, are not the sole property of conservative ideologies. The criticism of 'alienated labour', for example, was common to conservatives and Marxists alike (pp. 42–3). Apparently anodyne words like *Erlebnis*, 'experience' (the *Jugendbewegung* talked much of *Bunderlebnis*, a mystical communing), could assume a distinctly conservative colouring in certain political contexts; hidden links between technology and egalitarianism, or between utilitarianism and democracy, could be brought out where politically useful (p. 35). Similarly, Michael Löwy has shown, in *Georg Lukács: From Romanticism to Bolshevism* (1979), that Spengler's conservatism and early Western Marxism were propelled by many of the same impulses; that romantic anti-capitalism had both left-wing and right-wing potential (p. 30). A left-wing philosopher like Adorno, though he did not yearn to return to an organic *Gemeinschaft*, could none the less find Spengler's Culture–Civilization distinction useful.[41]

It is important to bear this indeterminacy in mind when analysing those texts which use the image of the organic. The concept of the organic, like that of nature, can be propelled by radically opposed motives, fulfilling different functions according to the different linguistic and historical configurations which shape it. Most importantly for Lawrence's aesthetics, it can be, and is, opposed to a totalizing instrumentalism, as later chapters will

[39] Heinrich Weber, *Das Sozialisierungsproblem in der Forstwirtschaft: Rektoratsrede* (Freiburg, 1931), 25, cited in Ringer, *The Decline of the German Mandarins*, 384.

[40] The antidemocratic tendency implicit in the term 'natural' is brought out in Ernst Troeltsch's 1923 lecture on 'Natural Law and Humanity in World Politics' as described by Ringer: 'Troeltsch said that . . . the German Romantic reaction against the French Revolution had been a revolt against "universal egalitarian morality", against the "whole mathematical-mechanistic West European scientific spirit", and against "the barren abstraction of a universal and equal humanity". The chief product of German Romanticism, according to Troeltsch, was a "new positive, ethical, and historical principle", namely the "concept of individuality".' See *The Decline of the German Mandarins*, 100.

[41] Theodor W. Adorno, 'Spengler After the Decline', in *Prisms*, trans. Samuel and Shierry Weber (London, 1967), 51–72.

show. It can also, if used differently, be opposed to democratic, rather than instrumental or totalitarian, 'levelling': homogenization can be both a flattening through instrumentalism and a democratic egalitarianism. In the discourse of writers like Spengler and Lawrence, organicism is opposed to both kinds of levelling, shifting imperceptibly from one position to another, but it seems to me important to distinguish between these different usages. Terry Eagleton, describing organicism, in what he sees to be its emphasis on the aloofness and autonomy of art, as 'a comfortingly absolute alternative to history itself', a dangerous forgetting, and a transcendental denial of the material, also shows how it can be interpreted as 'one of the few enclaves in which the creative values expunged from the face of English society by industrial capitalism can be celebrated and affirmed'; the Romantic theory of the imagination can be read as 'an image of non-alienated labour'.[42] The same, then, could be claimed for the organic that Eagleton claims for the aesthetic: 'Any account of this amphibious concept which either uncritically celebrates or unequivocally denounces it is . . . likely to overlook its real historical complexity.'[43] The next chapter looks at the organic as it manifests itself in Lawrence's writings on art and literature.

[42] *Literary Theory*, 20, 19.   [43] *The Ideology of the Aesthetic*, 9.

2

THE FRACTURED ORGANIC:
LAWRENCE'S AESTHETICS

The curious thing about art-speech is that it prevaricates so terribly.

(*Studies in Classic American Literature*)

We have thought and spoken till now in terms of likeness and one-ness. Now we must learn to think in terms of difference and otherness . . . We must get clear of the old oneness that imprisons our real divergence.

(*The Symbolic Meaning*)

The organic metaphor is, as I have already indicated, a particularly complex and confusing one because it aspires to transcend its own metaphoric status, suggesting that melding of language and the natural world which Paul de Man saw to be the characteristic strategy of ideology: 'What we call ideology is precisely the confusion of linguistic with natural reality, of reference with phenomenalism.'[1] To say that a poem is a rose seems to be very different from saying that a poem is organic, and yet on one level they are equivalent (i.e. metaphorical) statements. If all metaphors and symbols have, as Christopher Norris argues, an 'inbuilt appeal to organicist notions of an ultimate, transcendent rapport between mind, language and reality', the metaphor of the organic itself has an especially strong naturalizing tendency.[2] De Man argues, rightly in my view, that what we as literary critics need to do is to preserve at all costs the rational faculty which will enable us to unpick such 'phenomenalizing' or naturalizing structures. Yet it is easy to see how Lawrence can turn such an argument on its head, arguing that it is in fact rational or scientific discourse, with its pretensions to disinterested-ness, which employs what we would today call 'the ideology of the natural', which forgets its own rhetorical or metaphorical status and claims to be talking about the world *as it is*.

[1] Paul de Man, 'The Resistance to Theory', in Barbara Johnson (ed.), *The Pedagogical Imperative, Yale French Studies*, 63 (1982), 3–20 (p. 11).
[2] Christopher Norris, *The Contest of Faculties: Philosophy and Theory After Deconstruction* (London and New York, 1985), 41–2.

1. The Symbol

In the last chapter, I stressed the diversity of the uses to which the organic metaphor has been put. The original Romantic theorists of the organic did not, however, see their enterprise in such metaphoric terms. Coleridge said he 'would endeavour to destroy the old antithesis of *Words* & *Things*, elevating, as it were, words into Things, & Living Things too'. In *The Statesman's Manual* he explained further: 'By a symbol I mean, not a metaphor or allegory or any other figure of speech or form of fancy, but an actual and essential part of that, the whole of which it represents . . .'[3] Coleridge sounds here like Schelling, perhaps the most uncompromisingly organicist of the German Romantic aestheticians. For Schelling, the symbol both signified and vitally participated in the idea which it represented. It is this high Romantic version of the symbol to which Paul de Man, in *Blindness and Insight* (1971), would object. He repudiated the claims made by Romantics and post-Romantics for the symbol as a privileged trope, putting allegory in its place as a mode which acknowledged its distance from the phenomenal world instead of claiming some kind of reconciliation with it.[4]

We are usually told that Lawrence, like his Romantic predecessors, privileged the symbol over allegory, which, on the face of it, he did. 'Artspeech', he claimed, is 'a language of pure symbols', and he defined the symbol in full-blown organicist terms:

You can't give a great symbol a 'meaning', any more than you can give a cat a 'meaning'. Symbols are organic units of consciousness with a life of their own, and you can never explain them away, because their value is dynamic, emotional, belonging to the sense-consciousness of the body and soul, and not simply mental. An allegorical image has a *meaning*. Mr Facing-both-ways has a meaning. But I defy you to lay your finger on the full meaning of Janus, who is a symbol.[5]

But there is an ambiguity here: we are told on the one hand that 'Symbols *are* organic units of consciousness', and on the other that 'their *value* . . . belong[s] to the sense-consciousness', the term 'value' implicitly acknowledging a gap between language and nature. And at other points in the same essay, Lawrence argues that symbols '*stand for* units of human feeling, human experience' (p. 49). Already, then, the ontological status of the symbol

---

[3] Coleridge, *Collected Letters*, ed. E. L. Griggs (Oxford, 1956–71), i. 626; Appendix A, 'The Statesman's Manual', in *The Collected Works of Samuel Taylor Coleridge*, vi (*Lay Sermons*), ed. R. J. White (Princeton, NJ, and London, 1972), 79.

[4] 'The Rhetoric of Temporality', in *Blindness and Insight: Essays in the Rhetoric of Contemporary Criticism* (1971; 2nd edn. London, 1983), 187–228.

[5] *The Symbolic Meaning*, 19; 'Introduction to *The Dragon of the Apocalypse* by Frederick Carter', in *Apocalypse*, 48.

is unclear. Diane Bonds detects a similar ambiguity in Lawrence's views on language in general:

To the extent that he relies on metaphors of generation and organic growth in discussing consciousness, he promotes the fiction that the unconscious actually gives birth to the language through which it finds incarnation. This seeming denial of the preexistence of language, however, is actually a sign of Lawrence's deep awareness of the determinative power of the linguistic system. It is precisely this awareness that leads him to write in *Studies in Classic American Literature*, of the 'subterfuge' of art, for the writer's imprisonment in a moral or intellectual scheme that denies passional truth is to a large extent a result of such imprisonment in language.[6]

A close reading of Lawrence's writings on the symbol reveals, in fact, a discrepancy between theory and practice. For if in theory Lawrence's symbol *partakes* of the natural, material world in Schellingian fashion ('Symbols are organic units of consciousness with a life of their own'), in practice, Lawrence's symbol actually seems to cause a rift, a gap, between art-work and world. Indeed, Lawrence's privileging of the symbol stems from the fact that it does not make, in his view, the (instrumental) claim upon the world that other kinds of language make; instead, it openly acknowledges its disjunction from the material world. For if he defines the symbol in opposition to allegory, he also defines it in opposition to a 'realist' or 'mimetic' model of language, the kind of language which attempts to suppress or is unaware of its own rhetorical status, and which therefore *appropriates* the world as its own, refusing to acknowledge its disjunction from the real. Repeatedly throughout his career Lawrence attacks photographic or illusionistic art, criticizing what he calls the 'snapshot vision', because it naturalizes, or assumes an essential grip on the world, thus masking its own ideological intent: 'We . . . have learned to see ourselves for what we are, as the sun sees us. The kodak bears witness. We see as the All-seeing Eye sees, with the universal vision. And we *are* what is seen . . .'[7] Allegory, moreover, whilst it does not on the face of it attempt to naturalize in quite the way that realism does, is seen by Lawrence to naturalize at one remove, by implying that each of its elements has a corresponding element in the 'real' world (Lawrence calls this 'the algebraic tack; let X stand for sheep and Y for goats . . .').[8]

It will be clear, then, that, in at least one important sense, Lawrence's view of the distinction between symbol and allegory is the inverse of Paul de Man's. For de Man, as we have just seen, allegory is the mode which

[6] Diane S. Bonds, *Language and the Self in D. H. Lawrence* (Ann Arbor, Mich., 1987, 1978), 10–11.
[7] 'Art and Morality', in *Study of Thomas Hardy and Other Essays*, 165, 166.
[8] 'The Future of the Novel', in ibid. 149–155 (p. 155). This essay was first published as 'Surgery for the Novel—Or a Bomb' in *Literary Digest International Book Review* (Apr. 1923).

acknowledges its distance from the phenomenal, whilst the organic naturalizes the accidents of meaning. For Lawrence, on the other hand, it is allegory which, in establishing one-to-one links with the phenomenal world, appropriates it in a way in which symbolism does not. For while the organic has been used to imply a network of connections or 'fibres' within the art-work, or between the art-work and its creator, or again between the creator and his/her culture, there is also a strong sense in which the organic can imply something self-contained and separate.

The confusion arises here from the ambiguity inherent in speaking of the 'sensuousness' of the symbol. For many of the Romantic theorists of the symbol, 'sensuousness' referred primarily to the sensuousness of nature, so that the symbol *was* part of the natural world. A. W. Schlegel in his 1801 lectures argued that body and soul are one and the same substance, that '"organization" is merely the outward manifestation of *Geist*', so that the organisms of nature and the 'organisms' of art are both, literally, embodiments of this same *Geist* or life-spirit. At times Lawrence seems to come close to this position, particularly where he uses expressions like the 'living plasm' to describe poetry.[9] But at other times, 'sensuousness' refers to the sensuousness of the *signifier*; to the fact that language itself is constituted of material stuff (sound textures, paint, etc.). This is particularly true of Lawrence's writing on Cézanne and the Post-Impressionists, who, we are told, 'exploded the illusion, which fell back to the canvas of art in a chaos of lumps'.[10] Cézanne's art boldly asserts its own *materiality*, its painterliness. This last kind of materiality prevents the sign from being a transparent 'window' on to the real or the natural (one thinks of Adorno's claim that 'The density of its texture helps the thought to miss the mark').[11] Often the sensuous or bodily aspect of the symbol is such, for Lawrence, that the relationship between signifier and signified, far from being one of uninhibited transparency, is problematized. Cézanne's oil-painting, with its thick, impasted coats of pigment, proffers on one level 'a water pitcher that isn't very much like a water-pitcher, and apples which aren't very appley'.[12]

Paradoxically, then, Lawrence's symbol, in refusing to split the sign into a signifier inside the text or painting and a signified implicitly outside (as, in their different ways, both allegory and realism do), initiates a different kind of split *within* the sign, which problematizes the relationship between signifier

[9] 'Preface to the American edition of *New Poems*', in *Phoenix*, 218–22 (p. 219). This originally appeared as the preface to *New Poems* (New York, 1920).

[10] 'Introduction to These Paintings', 565.

[11] *Negative Dialectics*, trans. E. B. Ashton (London, 1973), 35.

[12] 'Art and Morality', First Version, in *Study of Thomas Hardy and Other Essays*, 231–7 (p. 233).

and signified. For to say that there is no specific or fixed signified outside art to which the signifier points is to leave two alternatives, one of which is far more idealist in tendency than the other. The more idealist one rests on the notion of some inarticulable, mysterious meaning which is in some way synonymous with the text or painting itself (the Schellingian position). Here the symbols of art are seen to indicate, tautologically, themselves, and through themselves to communicate some mystical notion of 'Being'. In other words, the organic is seen to unify the material signifiers of language (paintings/words) with some ultimate 'reality' beyond the material world (a reality roughly corresponding to the Kantian noumenon).[13] Poetry or painting becomes, in this aesthetic ideology, the *embodiment* of absolute truth, inseparable from it; the symbol is seen to be revelatory, a window on to 'Being' or 'reality'. Lawrence was quick to recognize in Clive Bell's 'significant form' an updated version of the symbol of German Romantic aesthetics, in which materiality both reveals itself as 'pure form' and simultaneously spirits itself away to reveal the 'ultimate reality' beyond.[14] Later, Heidegger was to complain that for Western metaphysics when it represents art aesthetically, 'The *aistheton*, what can be perceived by the senses, lets the *noeton*, the nonsensuous, shine through', implicitly privileging the latter over the former.[15]

The other version of the symbolic or organic empties the artefact of any such (transcendent) meaning, and opens up the rift between art-work and world I have just mentioned, which fractures and complicates meaning. There is an important sense, then, in which holistic theories of art, rather than unifying or totalizing signification and Being as the Romantic symbol does, can fulfil the opposite function of preventing any such identification. This rift between art-work and world opens up the way to semantic complexity, to a proliferation of meanings and ideologies which battle for attention, but none of which (so Lawrence argues) is given the final say. Lawrence gives the Book of Revelation as an example of this semantic inexhaustibility: the symbols of the Apocalypse 'have many meanings, and we only define one meaning in order to leave another undefined'.[16] Here the notion of the organic subverts the possibility of a single, apodictic 'right' reading of a text or painting.

Lawrence, then, did adopt the *terminology* of Romanticism by privileging the 'symbol', but his version of the organic in art was in practice very different from the more typically post-Romantic, transcendentalist one described by

[13] See below, pp. 96–7.   [14] See below, p. 88.

[15] 'A Dialogue on Language', in *On the Way to Language*, 14.

[16] 'A Review of *The Book of Revelation* by Dr John Oman', in *Apocalypse and the Writings on Revelation*, 39–42 (p. 42). The review of Oman's book first appeared in *Adelphi*, i (Apr. 1924), 1011–13, under the pseudonym of L. H. Davidson.

Eagleton in his book on Benjamin: 'Ineluctably idealizing, the symbol subdues the material object to a surge of spirit that illuminates it and redeems it from within. In a transfigurative flash, meaning and materiality are reconciled into one; for a fragile, irrationalist instant, being and signification become harmoniously totalized.'[17] Cézanne's oil-painting is characterized, for Lawrence, by a stubborn opacity rather than by transfiguration. Paradoxically, *realism*, in implicitly uniting the material signifiers of art with the signifieds of the phenomenal world, can be seen, and *is* seen by Lawrence, to approach more closely than the symbol to a position of spurious totalization.

These two models of the way in which a work of art might be interpreted, one materialist and one idealist in tendency, are, of course, two among many. A third account of the way in which a text or painting might be read, one which does *not* deploy the organic metaphor, argues that there *is* a 'right' reading to be decoded or deciphered if one looks closely enough. If organic models of art have been accused of right-wing mystification (their semantic inexhaustibility can, in conservative terms, become an ineffability which precludes rational critique), we find that this third account, one which does *not* rely on organicist metaphors, leads to the belief in a positivistic right reading which subsumes all others, and is also, therefore, a totalitarian position with very obvious right-wing potential. It is worth noticing that in the case of this third account, it is the notion of the organic which militates against that totalitarianism, by arguing that no reading is exhaustive. The organic becomes the stubborn, recalcitrant surplus which in Adorno's account of the aesthetic, for example, gives us a glimpse of alternative possibilities.

There is, however, a serious problem with Lawrence's notion of organic polysemy: it will militate blindly against *all* totalizing readings, unable to discriminate between them. Terry Eagleton has frequently made the point that the 'pure play of difference . . . would be quite as monotonous as the dreariest self-identity and indeed finally indistinguishable from it'.[18] In this sense, one can argue that Lawrence is using an ostensibly radical poetics to mask an essentially conservative politics. Such a charge has often been levelled against modernism as a whole. By refusing to attach any definitive meaning or voice to the text, by leaving the text as open as possible, the modernist author risks leaving the text in a vulnerable state, wide open to appropriation and misappropriation by others. Whilst the techniques of modernism serve a useful purpose in demystifying and unpicking those oppressive structures which had previously masqueraded as natural, we need to be on our guard against a situation in which any reading becomes as valid as any other.

[17] Terry Eagleton, *Walter Benjamin, or Towards a Revolutionary Criticism* (London and New York, 1981), 6. [18] *The Ideology of the Aesthetic*, 346.

The lack of discrimination implicit in the organic model of language comes out very clearly in Lawrence's apodictic statement that 'The ideal is *always* evil, no matter what ideal it be. No idea should ever be raised to a governing throne.'[19] Ultimately what is needed is a model of reading which is somewhere between the 'right reading' model on the one hand and the organicist models on the other. For, as Bakhtin argued in his later work, 'Both relativism and dogmatism equally exclude all argumentation, all authentic dialogue, by making it either unnecessary (relativism) or impossible (dogmatism).'[20] Genuine dialogue, Bakhtin argues, presupposes that something, but not everything, can be known. Juliet Sychrava, in her impressive analysis of idealism in aesthetics, expresses the same notion in different terms: 'We need to be able not only to show our post-Kantian awareness of the way in which texts are *relative* to contexts, but our naive awareness that contexts *determine* texts.'[21]

2. *Organicity* versus *Totality*

One of the most surprising parallels to emerge from a study of early twentieth-century aesthetic theory is that between Lawrence and the philosophers of the Frankfurt school, particularly Adorno. It stems from the cultural conservatism described in the last chapter, the romantic anti-capitalism and anti-technology which was so prevalent in Germany before and after the First World War, and which was a decisive influence on both Lawrence and Adorno. Adorno and Horkheimer's joint work, *Dialectic of Enlightenment* (1944), perhaps the key text of the Frankfurt school, is, after all, an attack on the 'culture industry' of commercial capitalism, and sees this culture industry to be the consummation of a degenerate technical rationality. Lawrence, of course, is by no means as circumspect or as philosophically rigorous as a thinker like Adorno, yet Eagleton's description of Adorno will undoubtedly strike a chord with Lawrence readers:

For Adorno as for Nietzsche, identificatory thought has its source in the eyes and stomach, the limbs and mouth. The pre-history of such violent appropriation of otherness is that of the early human predator out to devour the not-I. Dominative reason is 'the belly turned mind', and such atavistic rage against otherness is the hallmark of every high-minded idealism.[22]

---

[19] 'Fantasia of the Unconscious', 119.
[20] Mikhail Bakhtin, *Problems of Dostoevsky's Poetics*, ed. and trans. Caryl Emerson (Minneapolis, 1984), 69.
[21] Juliet Sychrava, *Schiller to Derrida: Idealism in Aesthetics* (Cambridge, 1989), 164.
[22] *The Ideology of the Aesthetic*, 345.

For Adorno and Horkheimer in their joint work, reason itself is not the object of attack so much as the Enlightenment concept of reason which, as Kant argued in the *Critique of Pure Reason*, makes 'a certain collective unity the aim of the operations of the understanding'. Citing Kant, Adorno and Horkheimer complain that 'The "systematization" of knowledge is "its coherence according to one principle" '.[23] Lawrence was not so discriminating in his condemnation of reason, though on occasions he too distinguishes between reason *per se* and reason as a reifying force: 'Though, if we pause to think about it, we shall realize that it is not Reason herself whom we have to defy, it is her myrmidons, our accepted ideas and thought-forms . . . Reason is a supple nymph, and slippery as a fish by nature.'[24]

An exploration of Frankfurt School aesthetics is beyond the scope of this study, though Adorno's work as a whole sheds interesting retrospective light on Lawrence's views on art, especially in view of recent attacks on the dangerous mystification of post-Romantic aesthetics. For no one could have been more acutely aware than Adorno that we were now living in a 'post-Auschwitz' era.[25] Yet Adorno insisted throughout his career that the only valid philosophy resisted paraphrase and that its content could not be extricated from its form.[26] His aesthetic theory was, like Lawrence's, one in which sensuous receptivity, the body, held in check the conceptual domination of nature.[27] He insisted on the importance of a holistic analysis, though by holistic he did not mean to prescribe any attempt at semantic reconciliation, or any intuitive grasp of a revealed 'truth'; he was acutely aware, like Lawrence, of the ironies and irreconcilable contradictions within the whole.[28] For Adorno, as for Lawrence in much of his art-criticism, the meanings of art were non-hierarchical. Hence Adorno's image of the 'constellation', which he borrowed from Benjamin to articulate the possibility of a cluster of elements existing in juxtaposition without those elements being reducible to a common denominator or originary first principle. In the same vein, Lawrence

---

[23] Max Horkheimer and Theodor W. Adorno, *Dialectic of Enlightenment*, trans. John Cumming (New York, 1978), 81.

[24] 'Introduction to *The Dragon of the Apocalypse*', 50.

[25] See Adorno's well-known declaration, 'To write poetry after Auschwitz is barbaric', 'Cultural Criticism and Society', in *Prisms*, 17–34 (p. 34).

[26] This is the first point that Martin Jay makes in *Adorno* (London, 1984), 11–12.

[27] See e.g. 'Spengler After the Decline', in *Prisms*, 67.

[28] Martin Jay (*Adorno*, 61–2) has pointed to the way in which Adorno's well-known and apodictic statement that 'the whole is the false' (*Minima Moralia*) has been widely misinterpreted by being taken out of context. By 'untrue', Adorno implied 'untrue for a (Utopian) future': his argument was that the sum total of things as they are is not the sum total of things *as they might be*. The implication here was that by looking out for recalcitrant fragments which did not blend in with the current whole, one might see glimmerings of an alternative future. See *Minima Moralia: Reflections from a Damaged Life*, trans. E. F. N. Jephcott (London, 1974), 50.

stated in 'Study of Thomas Hardy' that 'The business of art is never to solve, but only to declare', and, in a letter of the same period, he claimed that 'All vital truth contains the memory of all that for which it is not true: Ecstasy achieves itself by virtue of *exclusion* . . .' It is worth comparing this with Adorno's assertion in *Minima Moralia* that 'True thoughts are those alone which do not understand themselves'.[29]

In spite of their affinities with certain aspects of the conservative romanticism I described in the last chapter, neither Lawrence nor Adorno approved of totalistic thinking. They both repudiate instrumental reason in so far as it is, in their view, based on a totalitarian identity principle which reduces phenomena to its own pattern.

The point cannot be overemphasized that in much of Lawrence's writing on art, an organicist aesthetic does not imply that a work of art embodies a single, unifying, totalizing meaning. In his essay 'The Spirit of Place' in *Studies in Classic American Literature*, Lawrence explains that 'The artist usually sets out . . . to point a moral and adorn a tale. The tale, however, points the other way, as a rule', and in an earlier version of the same essay, he claims, 'We have thought and spoken till now in terms of likeness and oneness. Now we must learn to think in terms of difference and otherness . . . We must get clear of the old oneness that imprisons our real divergence.'[30] In his preface to the American edition of *New Poems*, he states that poetry should be 'without dénouement or close', characterized by 'inconclusiveness'; it is 'unrestful, ungraspable . . . unchainable'. He uses a fully fledged organic imagery:

The strands are all flying, quivering, intermingling into the web, the waters are shaking the moon. There is no round, consummate moon on the face of running water, nor on the face of the unfinished tide. There are no gems of the living plasm. The living plasm vibrates unspeakably, it inhales the future, it exhales the past, it is the quick of both, and yet it is neither. There is no plasmic finality, nothing crystal, permanent. If we try to fix the living tissue, as the biologists fix it with formation, we have only a hardened bit of the past, the bygone life under our observation.[31]

Here we confront another paradox inherent in the idea of the organic. I noted in the last chapter that it is frequently used within post-structuralist criticism to imply the fixed monolith against which deconstruction defines itself. Post-structuralists prefer to posit a mechanical model of language, in order, rightly in my view, to emphasize language's *constructedness*. But it is

---

[29] 'Study of Thomas Hardy', 72; *Letters*, ii (20 Dec. 1914), 247; Adorno, *Minima Moralia*, 192.   [30] *Studies in Classic American Literature*, 2; *The Symbolic Meaning*, 17.
[31] Preface to the American edition of *New Poems*, 220, 219.

easy to see how a *mechanical* model of language could, in a different lexicon, imply the very fixity which the organic is often seen to imply, and equally easy to see how the organic could be seen to be a more appropriate metaphor for the constant movement of *différance*.[32] If Gerald Crich in *Women in Love* is guilty of 'the substitution of the mechanical principle for the organic' (p. 231), we have to remember that the machine Gerald worships is logocentrism turned literal, the incarnation of the Logos, of verbal fixity. We should beware, then, of equating Lawrence's version of the organic in language with verbal fixity or totality. On the contrary, as in the writings of Frankfurt school philosophers like Adorno, the organic becomes an antidote to various kinds of totalizing.

In much of Lawrence's writing on art, then, the organic does not necessitate the suppression of heterogeneity in the name of identity; instead, it is linked to the production of conflicting and contradictory meanings. For Lawrence, as for Adorno, art is profoundly important as a repository of difference and non-identity. Adorno's celebrated declaration 'The whole is the false' is reminiscent of 'Study of Thomas Hardy', where Lawrence sees in the details of Gothic cathedrals a subversion of the 'monism' of the architectural whole: 'All the little figures, the gargoyles, the imps, the human faces, whilst subordinated within the Great Conclusion of the Whole, still, from their obscurity, jeered their mockery of the Absolute, and declared for multiplicity, polygeny' (p. 66). Lawrence elaborates on this in the 'Cathedral' chapter of *The Rainbow*:

They knew quite well, these little imps that retorted on man's own illusion, that the cathedral was not absolute. They winked and leered, giving suggestion of the many things that had been left out of the great concept of the church. 'However much there is inside here, there's a good deal they haven't got in,' the little faces mocked.

Apart from the lift and spring of the great impulse towards the altar, these little faces had separate wills, separate motions, separate knowledge, which rippled back in defiance of the tide, and laughed in triumph of their own very littleness. (p. 189)

Ruskin (whose links with Lawrence are explored in Chapter 7) had also seen in Gothic a valuable undercutting of a dangerously homogenizing instrumentalism, an antidote to the wrenching of the multifarious human spirit into the standardized shapes of the machine (we are told of Will Brangwen that 'the influence of Ruskin had stimulated him to a pleasure in the medieval

---

[32] Terry Eagleton, who read the typescript of this book, noted that the *impersonality* which Lawrence admires in the organic is also there in the mechanistic, its supposed antithesis. Both are anti-subjective modes. This deconstructs the opposition somewhat and perhaps accounts for what would seem to be a covert sympathy for the mechanical in some of the descriptions of Gerald Crich in *Women in Love*.

forms').[33] Skrebensky is savagely ironized in The Rainbow for assuming that 'The Whole mattered—but the unit, the person, had no importance, except as he represented the Whole' (p. 304). And in that same novel we are presented with a horrific picture of 'human bodies and lives subjected in slavery to that symmetric monster of the colliery' (p. 324).

Gothic art is treated ambivalently within the terms of The Rainbow. On the one hand, it is seen to live out the quirks and failings of the human body itself, unredeemed. We are told, for example, that Will Brangwen 'had always, all his life, had a secret dread of Absolute Beauty . . . So he had turned to the Gothic form, which always asserted the broken desire of mankind in its pointed arches, escaping the rolling, absolute beauty of the round arch' (p. 220). But whilst the narrative seems to endorse the creatureliness of Gothic, it also seems to recognize in this form of architecture an idealistic impulse, and to question the way in which the pointed arches of the cathedral reach away from the phenomenal world, striving towards the noumenal:

Here the stone leapt up from the plain of earth, leapt up in a manifold, clustered desire each time, up, away from the horizontal earth, through twilight and dusk and the whole range of desire, through the swerving, the declination, ah, to the ecstasy, the touch, to the meeting and the consummation, the meeting, the clasp, the close embrace, the neutrality, the perfect, swooning consummation, the timeless ecstasy. There his soul remained, at the apex of the arch, clinched in the timeless ecstasy, consummated. (pp. 187–8)

Whilst it would of course be reductive to see a passage from a novel as a piece of unqualified art-criticism on Lawrence's part, it is interesting to compare this section of The Rainbow with a passage from 'Study of Thomas Hardy', written at the same time, where Lawrence as art-critic is sceptical of aesthetic transcendence:

And Raphael, in reaching the pure symbolic solution, has surpassed art and become almost mathematics. Since the business of art is never to solve, but only to declare . . . And to single out one cycle, one moment, and to exclude from this moment all context, and to make this moment timeless, is what Raphael does, and what Plato does. So that their absolute Truth, their geometric Truth, is only true in timelessness. (p. 72)

It is quite typical of Lawrence that he should use the same term, 'symbolic', to describe a totalizing 'mathematics' which he distinguishes from art, and, as we saw earlier in the chapter, to describe 'art-speech' itself. For, as we shall see shortly, this kind of semantic instability, the way in which signifiers

[33] The Rainbow, ed. Mark Kinkead-Weekes (Cambridge, 1989), 105; see below, pp. 134–6.

constantly shift their position, is arguably the mark of Lawrence's own 'art-speech'.

Lawrence, then, like Adorno, recognized that the repudiation of difference, the eliminating of 'otherness', had very dangerous implications. In his essay on Franklin, Lawrence is critical of a 'negative, destructive form of oneness . . . a oneness attained by destroying all incompatible elements in each individual, leaving the pattern or standard man'.[34] For Adorno, anti-Semitism and totalistic thinking are linked: the Jew represented non-identity and difference for totalitarian Germany.[35] For Lawrence in his study of the Etruscans, the Etruscan art, characterized by 'the odd spontaneous forms that are never to be standardized', subverts the totalizing impulses of Roman imperialism.[36] For both of them, art is characterized by plurality, heterogeneity, contradiction, and not by consensus or by the unity posited through intentionalist theories of art. The Book of Revelation, which Lawrence uses as a paradigm for the work of art, exemplifies 'Not meaning *within* meaning: but rather, meaning against meaning'.[37] The American classics become, in Lawrence's study of them, a series of fissured texts, exemplifying 'perfect duplicity', as I investigate more fully later on.[38]

3. *Mimetic* versus *Differential Models of Language*

One way in which to interpret Lawrence's project as art-critic, and indeed the project of modernist aesthetics generally, is to see it repeating moves which were being made quite independently in Continental linguistic philosophy at around the same time. Both philosophers of language and philosophers of art were reacting against what they perceived to be a naïvely logocentric model of signification. Though they had never heard of Saussure, many modernist art-critics were attempting to articulate what was essentially the distinction between a pre-Saussurean and a post-Saussurean model of language. In drawing attention to the arbitrary nature of the linguistic sign, Saussure had dispelled the myth of a mimetic model of language, whereby signifiers unproblematically stood for signifieds which existed outside language, showing how language generated the meanings produced by its own rhetoric, its system of differences (I shall call this the 'differential' model of language). Because the elements of the language were no longer seen to have

---

[34] *The Symbolic Meaning*, 41.   [35] See Adorno, *Negative Dialectics*, 362.
[36] 'Etruscan Places', in *Mornings in Mexico and Etruscan Places*, 32. See also below, pp. 184–6.
[37] 'Introduction to *The Dragon of the Apocalypse* by Frederick Carter', 48.
[38] *Studies in Classic American Literature*, 94.

the one-to-one correspondence with things outside themselves upon which the age-old concept of pictorial mimesis had been based, they could be made to generate multiple meanings.[39] Ironically, language first had to be recognized as a self-contained structure (and, in this sense, as 'organic'), before the notion of a purely differential meaning, and its post-structuralist legacy, could come into being.

Saussure and his successors set up the myth of a purely mimetic language only to destroy it. For the implication of Saussure's theory was that *all* discourses could now be seen to generate the meanings produced by their own rhetoric, and to be subsumed, therefore, by the differential, as opposed to the mimetic, model of language. Yet the distinction between mimetic and differential models of language is, in some shape or form, one to which even the most subtle of critical theorists seem to cling. Lacan, whilst boldly asserting that there is no metalanguage, none the less seems *in practice* to favour a particular *kind* of language which in its uncontrolled polysemy manifests a kind of textual stress. Malcolm Bowie, in *Freud, Proust and Lacan: Theory as Fiction* (1987), raises the very relevant question, 'Why . . . is a sumptuously polyvalent language to be preferred to the one-thing-at-a-time languages of logic, or conceptual analysis, or empirical description or traditional psychoanalytic theory?' 'Is it', he ventures, 'that such a language, having more goals for desire visibly on the move within it, may be thought to maintain a closer, more robust contact with the matrix of desire?' (pp. 129–30). Yet such a distinction between two kinds of language can surely only apply to the text *as it is read*. The language of logic can also be *read* (or *written*, in Derrida's sense) as uncontrollably polyvalent. But it is less likely *in practice* to be read as such, and it is this which gives the distinction its validity.

Saussure, then, set up the essential–differential distinction only to collapse it. In parallel fashion, the modernist art theorists, Lawrence included, used the shibboleth of a naïvely mimetic realism against which to define their own views on language. In retrospect, it now seems that they presented realism in crude and reductive terms. It is unlikely that unproblematic, one-to-one correspondence between elements of language and world was ever really assumed by realist art, that art ever aspired to *be* the world, rendering itself curiously redundant, in the way that many modernist art theorists suggest. But this is what Lawrence would have us believe, and it is also what

---

[39] Susanne Langer, working within an Anglo-American rather than Continental tradition, articulated what is basically the same distinction in terms of 'discursive' and 'non-discursive' symbolism. 'Discursive symbolism', for Langer, denotes language as the term is ordinarily understood (i.e. words with relatively 'fixed' meanings arranged in sequence according to established conventions); in 'non-discursive symbolism', on the other hand, images derive their meanings from their relations to one another in the total pattern. See *Philosophy in a New Key* (Cambridge, Mass., 1942), 79–102.

his Bloomsbury contemporaries tried to argue (this common link between Lawrence and Bloomsbury is examined more fully in Chapter 5). The move by which Lawrence and his Bloomsbury contemporaries set up realism as the naïve Other of their own enterprise parallels the one which Juliet Sychrava detects in the Romantic art theorists, who set up a model of 'naive' poetry in order to validate sentimentalism: 'Writers like Schlegel retain the naïve principle to provide a contrast and a foil for sentimentalism. This is . . . illogical, because it involves sustaining two contrasting aesthetic principles—the realist and idealist, or pre- and post-Kantian, within one theory as though they were characteristic of different kinds of poetry rather than philosophical perspectives.' 'Mimesis', Sychrava goes on to argue, 'is an aesthetic, theoretical label, and not a poetic act'. There is, she asserts, no epistemological or structural difference between eighteenth-century 'descriptive' and nineteenth-century 'Romantic' verse.[40] What we are dealing with instead are different *models* or *theories* of language. Stephen Land, in his analysis of eighteenth-century semantic theory, seeks to explain this shift from one model to the other through the concept of the sublime. He argues that 'The concept of the sublime provided perhaps the most important single path from representationalism to alternative theories of linguistic signs'.[41] One could argue that twentieth-century post-structuralism enacts a different version of the sublime: the disjunction between language and a recalcitrant Nature brings about the endless spawning and proliferating of the signifier, where language tautologically celebrates its own processes.

Mimetic language is posited, then, by Lawrence and other modernist art-theorists, as a coinage or currency in which terms are used and reused to represent a relatively fixed value within society. This fixed value, the product of a closed-circuit language system, is the 'sameness' which Nietzsche complains about, and which moves Rilke, following Nietzsche's Zarathustra, to declare his faith in the 'not yet said'.[42] The theme of language as coinage is a constant theme of modernist literature. For Miriam in Dorothy Richardson's *Pilgrimage*, language sets things 'in a mould that was apt to come up again',[43] and in *Women in Love*, Birkin is oppressed by the same sense of being trapped in the old terms: ' "The point about love . . . is that we hate the word because we have vulgarised it. It ought to be proscribed, tabooed from utterance, for many years, till we get a new, better idea . . . Let the old meanings go" '

---

[40] *Schiller to Derrida: Idealism in Aesthetics*, 46, 66–7.

[41] *From Signs to Propositions: The Concept of Form in Eighteenth-Century Semantic Theory* (London, 1974). Cited in Sychrava, *Schiller to Derrida*, 117.

[42] Nietzsche, 'Twilight of the Idols', 82–3; Rilke ('Ich glaube an alles noch nie Gesagte'), *Ausgewählte Werke* (Leipzig, 1938), i. 14.

[43] *Deadlock* (1921), in *Pilgrimage*, 4 vols. (London, 1979), iii. 10.

(p. 130). No writer was more aware of the problems of linguistic reification than Lawrence:

Man must wrap himself in a vision, make a house of apparent form and stability, fixity. In his terror of chaos he begins by putting up an umbrella between himself and the everlasting whirl. Then he paints the under-side of his umbrella like a firmament. Then he parades around, lives and dies under his umbrella. Bequeathed to his descendants, the umbrella becomes a dome, a vault, and men at last begin to feel that something is wrong.

Man fixes some wonderful erection of his own between himself and the wild chaos, and gradually goes bleached and stifled under his parasol. Then comes a poet, enemy of convention, and makes a slit in the umbrella; and lo! the glimpse of chaos is a vision, a window to the sun. But after a while, getting used to the vision, and not liking the genuine draught from chaos, commonplace man daubs a simulacrum of the window that opens onto chaos, and patches the umbrella with the painted patch of the simulacrum. That is, he has got used to the vision; it is part of his house-decoration.[44]

Unlike mimetic language, the holistic or differential language of art or creativity is seen by Lawrence to ascribe new values to the terms it uses, and so in effect to initiate the viewer or reader into new languages, languages specific to each particular work of art or literature. More recently, Ad Reinhardt has expressed the same idea in terms of 'a sign which refuses to signify', by which he seems to mean that the signs of art signify *themselves*, in a way that all linguistic terms must before they become coinage, or before, as Derrida expresses it in *Writing and Difference*, image and mark have been held apart by a *logic* of representation.[45] For Heidegger, the act of naming does not 'hand out titles' or 'apply terms'; it 'calls into the word'.[46] And for Michael Phillipson, art is 'Language before languages' or 'the opening of relation itself'.[47] But, as Phillipson explains, such Language will always risk becoming language, becoming fixed coinage in its turn.

Lawrence's protestations on the need for semantic fluidity beg the question whether he himself, as artist, puts theory into practice. And yet if, as I have just argued, the two models of language collapse into the 'differential' model, the question is, in a way, beside the point: Lawrence can have no access to a special *kind* of language, no matter what he may claim about 'art-speech'.

---

[44] 'Review of *Chariot of the Sun* by Harry Crosby', in *Phoenix*, 255–62 (pp. 255–6). This review first appeared in a slightly different version in *Exchanges* (Dec. 1929), as 'Chaos in Poetry'.

[45] Ad Reinhardt, cited in Barbara Rose, *Art-as-Art* . . . (New York, 1975), 111. Heidegger also remarked that 'Dictionaries have little to report about what words, spoken thoughtfully, say' ('The Thing', in *Poetry, Language, Thought*, 163–86 (p. 175)).

[46] 'Language', in *Poetry, Language, Thought*, 187–210 (p. 198).

[47] *Painting, Language and Modernity* (London, 1985), 16, 17.

In my view, Lawrence's theory of art-speech only really makes sense as a theory of *reading*, and indeed Lawrence seems to acknowledge this when he claims that it is the *critic's* task to 'save the tale from the artist who created it'.[48] Ultimately, it makes little sense to argue that some kinds of language are logocentric where others are not; it is rather that language can be *read* logocentrically or 'differentially'. An illustration of this would be the fact that so-called realist art *can* be made, in practice, to yield just as much polyvalence as experimental art, provided that it is *read* in a particular way. It need not be read as a 'closed' form imposing single, transparent meanings.

Yet, as we saw with Lacan, there *are* ways in which the *writer* can attempt to foreground polyvalence, inviting a particular kind of reading, and it seems to me that this is what Lawrence does wherever we find the insistent repetition with variation which is such a hallmark of his style. Many critics have noted the way in which words interrogate themselves in a novel like *Women in Love*, so that even Birkin, who denounces the 'dead letter' of modern culture, is denied any privileged access to language, but can only partake in the same 'unredeemed' though ever-shifting lexicon. His words are no more sacred than any others, and every word he uses positively is found in debased form in the mouths of other characters. How is it, one wonders, that Birkin wants a relationship based on something 'inhuman' (p. 146), while Gerald bases his industry on an 'inhuman principle' (p. 228)? Many critics have asked this and similar questions. Leo Bersani, for example, has noted that 'singleness' is a quality Birkin shares with Loerke and Winifred Crich, while Diane Bonds has produced an intricate analysis of the way in which a simple word like 'go' mutates in this novel. Michael Ragussis produces analyses of terms like 'knowledge', 'equal', etc., and points out that Lawrence often plays off against each other words with the same root (organic/organization, equal/ equilibrium), thus further dispelling the idea of an essential link between word and referent.[49] There has, moreover, been a resurgence of interest in the later fiction, where Bakhtin provides the critical terminology for an analysis of the dialogic qualities of novels like *Aaron's Rod* and *Kangaroo*.[50] On the other hand, Diane Bonds, in the conclusion to her study, suggests that the later, leadership works might be seen as 'sublimations of the longing to restore an Absolute—some transcendental signified—the very idea of which has largely been discredited by Lawrence's earlier writings'.[51]

[48] *Studies in Classic American Literature*, 2.

[49] Leo Bersani, *A Future for Astyanax: Character and Desire in the Novel* (Boston, 1976), 176; *Language and the Self*, 82–8; *The Subterfuge of Art: Language and the Romantic Tradition* (Baltimore and London, 1978), 172–97 (p. 183).

[50] See e.g. Avrom Fleishman, 'He Do the Polis in Different Voices: Lawrence's Later Style', in *D. H. Lawrence: A Centenary Consideration*, ed. Peter Balbert and Phillip Marcus (Ithaca, NY, 1985), 162–79.   [51] *Language and the Self*, 112.

To prevent reification, Lawrence seems, in *Women in Love*, to be engaged in a process of endless semantic deferral. Bonds produces a very convincing reading of *Women in Love* in terms of acting out the *mise en abîme* of language:

The narrative generated by the figure of the abyss is offered up in *Women in Love* by words that through their own movements suggest what we might mean in speaking of the abyss of language. The interplay of figurative and literal produces the effect of 'sinking' that I have mentioned, and the tendency, with many terms, for meanings to proliferate then polarize may create in the reader a sense of never getting to the 'bottom' of meaning in *Women in Love*.[52]

As an illustration of this 'sinking' effect, I want to explore the image of 'labour' in *The Rainbow* and *Women in Love*.[53]

4. The Labour of Language in The Rainbow and Women in Love

Artistic labour, industrial labour, and the labour of childbirth form an intricate mesh in *The Rainbow* and *Women in Love*. In *The Rainbow*, there are still traces of what Lawrence (together with Marx and Ruskin) sees to be an 'integrated' labour, where mind and body are wholly involved in work, and where the expression of self makes the analogy with birth appropriate. Hence the description of Will Brangwen in later life 'gradually coming to a knowledge of beauty in the plain labours' and rekindling some of his old enthusiasm for wood-carving, seeing the carvings, in an analogy with the labour of childbearing, as 'utterances of himself'. The imagery at this point is overtly that of the infant emerging from the womb:

He was a man of ceaseless activity. Blindly, like a mole, he pushed his way out of the earth that covered him, working always away from the physical element in which his life was captured. Slowly, blindly, gropingly, with what initiative was left to him, he made his way towards individual expression and individual form. (p. 330)

There are other instances in this novel of a positive, life-giving kind of labour: Tom Brangwen back on the farm, 'glad of the active labour and the smell of the land' (p. 19); Anna and Will gathering the corn-harvest during their own courtship, the prelude to a fecund marriage; or the labour of the little Ursula and her father setting potatoes in the ground. Or, again, we see Anna rearing her new child: 'She threw herself into the labour, the child was

---

[52] Ibid. 91.

[53] Michael Ragussis also discusses the use of 'labour' in *Women in Love* and some of his points overlap with mine, though he does not explore the Marxian connotations of the term. See *The Subterfuge of Art*, 193–7.

everything' (p. 92). But even within the terms of *this* novel, labour is capable of becoming its own antithesis. The labour of Will's wood-carving is set up in opposition to the labour of his daytime, office job, itself alienated labour. For while we are told that Will 'laboured cleaning the stone-work, repairing the wood-work, restoring the organ', he finds that 'During the day, at his work in the office, he kept himself suspended. He did not exist. He worked automatically till it was time to go home' (p. 193). Compare Marx's answer to the question 'What is the alienation of labour?':

First, the fact that labour is *external* to the worker, i.e., it does not belong to his essential being; that in his work, therefore, he does not affirm himself but denies himself . . . The worker therefore only feels himself outside his work, and in his work feels outside himself. He is at home when he is not working, and when he is working he is not at home.[54]

As *The Rainbow* proceeds, these intimations of an alienated labour obtrude more. What more graphic image of this 'disintegration' than Lawrence's description of Wiggiston ('There was no meeting place, no centre, no artery, no organic formation', p. 320), or of the colliers as buds unable to germinate: 'It was as if a hard, horny shell enclosed them all' (p. 321). Increasingly, labour is given over to what Marx terms 'the sense of having'; it is subsumed by what Adam Smith called 'production', though Marx saw this to be a grim distortion of the term. The labour of the miners now distorts the human shape but panders to 'the sense of having': 'They believe they must alter themselves to fit the pits and the place, rather than alter the pits and the place. . . . The men die of consumption fairly often. But they earn good wages' (p. 322). To pursue the analogy with childbirth, the 'perfect womb' of the cathedral (p. 186), which nurtured Will's artistic impulses, has been replaced by a travesty of nurturing maternity, the 'great mistress' of the pit (p. 324).

One could say that, with *Women in Love*, integrated labour gives way completely to alienated labour, and art to aestheticism, or to its inverse, technology. But this would be to overlook the highly complex dialectic going on within *Women in Love* itself, where the term 'labour' seems to be more and more subtly nuanced as the novel progresses. 'Labour' in this novel partakes of a nexus of imagery of materialism, disintegration, and solipsism. At one level, labour has become a commodity. One thinks of Marx's question 'What is capital?', in answer to which he quotes Adam Smith in *The Wealth of Nations*: 'A certain quantity of *labour stocked* and stored up to be employed'.[55] And Gerald's 'fight with matter' (p. 227) is reminiscent of

[54] *Economic and Philosophic Manuscripts of 1844*, 110.
[55] Ibid. 78, citing Adam Smith, *The Wealth of Nations*, i. 295.

Pécqueur as quoted by Marx: 'The element of *matter*, which is quite incapable of creating wealth without the other element, *labour*, acquires the magical virtue of being fertile for them [who own this matter] as if by their own action they had placed there this indispensable element.'[56] Ultimately, of course, Gerald *becomes* the mute matter he has been fighting.

The alienated labour of the miners is the labour which Loerke finds so aesthetically gratifying: speaking of the factory-workers in Cologne for whom he has sculpted a granite frieze, he remarks that 'machinery and the acts of labour are extremely, maddeningly beautiful' (p. 424). The frieze itself depicts a fairground scene, a 'frenzy of chaotic motion'. Loerke explains that the fairground reveller is in fact fulfilling 'the counterpart of labour—the machine works him, instead of he the machine' (p. 424). Loerke's version of labour entails a frightening loss of autonomy, a reversion to a regressive, infantile state, just as Loerke himself is described as a 'mud-child' (p. 427).

Deploring the materialistic culture which Loerke finds so inspiring, Birkin complains that 'life is a blotch of labour, like insects scurrying in filth' (p. 55). The labour which underpins this materialism must become another kind of labour, more akin to that of childbirth, as Birkin's remark to Gerald suggests: 'We've got to bust it completely, or shrivel inside it, as in a tight skin' (p. 54). Insect imagery in Lawrence's work, and particularly in this novel, seems to suggest the mind–body split and a subsequent self-enclosure or solipsism. Hermione is 'like an insect in its skin' (p. 42) and Gudrun is 'like a beetle toiling in the dust' (p. 11), in a possible inversion of the lilies of the field of Matthew 6: 28, which 'toil not, neither do they spin'. The labour of toiling beetles is linked at various points in the novel to disintegration, the same disintegration ('division') of labour which infantilizes Gerald's workers, in that it forces them into a position of abject dependence on the industrial machine. The link is made, for example, through the African fetish of the beetle-like woman in labour in whom, in Birkin's eyes, 'the relation between the senses and the outspoken mind had broken' (p. 253). The African woman's labour in some ways parallels the industrial labour which is Gerald's concern, and which is also evoked in terms of the mind–body split, 'pure organic disintegration' (p. 231).

Birkin's reference to tight skins, as I have already remarked, also connects to that more positive version of labour, the labour of childbirth, hinted at towards the novel's opening with reference to Ursula: 'If only she could break through the last integuments! She seemed to try to put her hands out, like an infant in the womb' (p. 9). But even the creative labour of childbirth

---

[56] Marx cites Constantin Pécqueur, *Théorie nouvelle d'économie sociale et politique, ou Étude sur l'organisation des Sociétés* (Paris, 1842), 411–12.

has for the most part been debased in this novel. Where Will Brangwen had created 'utterances of himself' in a labour analogous to giving birth, Crich's workers are *themselves* the children, held in perpetual subjection. Gerald's relationship with his employees is a grim parody of the father–child relationship, in that the miners are never allowed to 'grow up', to assume a position of paternalistic responsibility in their turn.

Ideas of pregnancy and childbirth are dealt with more explicitly through the Pussum. On two occasions, the Pussum (herself pregnant) is closely juxtaposed, and implicitly associated, with the African fetish of the woman in labour.[57] But she is also associated with labour in the other sense of 'work': she has the 'inchoate look of a violated slave' (p. 79), subservient to Gerald in a kind of parody of the slavery of his mineworkers: 'he felt, she must relinquish herself into his hands, and be subject to him. She was so profane, slave-like . . .' (p. 67). There is a strong hint, then, that pregnancy or maternity, which, like labour, should be a mark of mature adulthood and self-responsibility, has become symptom instead of self-alienation and loss of control. The Pussum is more child than parent, 'so young and so far in spirit from any child-bearing' (p. 68). Like Gerald's industrial slaves, and like the 'savages' he has encountered on his travels, whom he describes as 'not born yet' (p. 66), the Pussum has been infantilized by Gerald: she is 'small and childish and vulnerable' (p. 76), and her posture, as she lies in bed with him, is foetus-like, 'small and curled up and defenceless'. This topsy-turviness casts us back again to the African fetish, which reminds Gerald of a foetus even though it depicts a woman who is herself in labour. The infantilization of the workers is of course one of the recurrent themes of Marx's writing. Alienated labour turns everything upside down; it is, as Marx explains, 'activity as suffering, strength as weakness, begetting as emasculating, the worker's *own* physical and mental energy . . . as an activity which is turned against him, independent of him and not belonging to him'.[58] So topsy-turvy is this world that the slave-master Gerald finds himself afraid of 'being shut up, locked up anywhere—or being fastened. I'm afraid of being bound hand and foot' (p. 67). He fears becoming a slave, or a child, himself. And the idea of childbirth is picked up yet again in the 'cradle of silent snow' (p. 398) of the Alps, a cradle which proves to be Gerald's burial-ground.

Thus Lawrence, in a kind of linguistic labour, chips away at a given signified, changing its shape little by little, but never letting it settle into a final form. His is the verbal labour described in 'Water-Party':

There was always confusion in speech. Yet it must be spoken. Whichever way one moved, if one were to move forwards, one must break a way through. And to know,

---

[57] See pp. 74 and 78–80.   [58] *Economic and Philosophical Manuscripts of 1844*, 111–12.

to give utterance, was to break a way through the walls of the prison, as the infant in labour strives through the walls of the womb. (p. 186)

To be infantilized is to be denied this utterance (*infans* = 'dumb, unable to speak'), to be denied the verbal labour of self-expression and, by extension, self-determination. But even on this issue, closure is withheld from the reader. Lawrence, characteristically, gives things a final twist, refusing to allow the idea of 'art-speech' itself to reify into something unequivocally positive. For though he, as writer/narrator, engages in the kind of verbal play I have just described, he attributes the same skill to Gudrun and Loerke, both figures who are subjected to fierce criticism within the terms of the novel. In this sense, Lawrence turns art-speech against itself. For if Lawrence fears linguistic reification, he also fears the implications of an arcane babble. Words for Loerke are supple and flexible; he is 'a chatterer, a mag-pie, a maker of mischievous word-jokes' (p. 422). With Gudrun he shares 'polyglot fancies', 'tossing about the little coloured balls of verbal humour and whimsicality' (p. 468). It is as though Lawrence were making an oblique attack on the very modernist literary techniques that he himself practises. This is made all the more striking by the fact that Loerke picks on the very term 'labour' with which Lawrence-as-narrator has been juggling. He articulates the idea of 'labour' in a mixture of Italian and French, as if to underscore the instability of the signifier–signified link: ' "Travaillé— lavorato?" he cried, "E che lavoro—che lavoro? Quel travail est-ce que vous avez fait?" ' (p. 425). Loerke is, then, a curious parody of Lawrence-as-narrator, both of them working on 'the plane of suggestion' (p. 448). Long before Derrida, we find ourselves in a *mise en abîme*, a semantic abyss which is quite typical of Lawrence's writing.

5. *The Semiotic*

The idea of linguistic 'labour', with its implicit reference to the mother–child bond, leads me on to Julia Kristeva's idea of the 'semiotic', a concept connected to the close mother–child relationship which exists before the child has acquired the dominant language. Loerke's 'polyglot fancies' suggest the avant-garde techniques of a writer like Joyce, whose *Finnegans Wake* (1939) takes the idea of the polyglot text to its logical extreme. It was through her study of such modernist and avant-garde writers as Joyce and Artaud, Lautréamont and Mallarmé, that Kristeva illustrated her theory of the 'semiotic'. Lawrence's interest in linguistic textures, in verbal play, and the style he felt he had to defend in his Foreword to *Women in Love* (the 'continual, slightly modified repetition' or 'pulsing, frictional to-and-fro'), suggest that he could plausibly have been included in Kristeva's study.[59]

In *Desire in Language*, Kristeva defined the 'semiotic' as 'a *heterogeneousness* to meaning and signification . . . detected . . . in the first echolalias of infants as rhythms and intonations anterior to the first phonemes, morphemes, lexemes, and sentences'.[60] The 'semiotic', then, designates a pre-linguistic realm of communication inhabited by mother and child before the child enters into the dominant language and culture, into the realm of the 'Symbolic' (Lacan's term), a realm of law and separation and categorization. As I noted in the Introduction, Kristeva draws heavily on Lacan's work because it represents, among other things, a monumental attack on the Cartesian *cogito ergo sum*, on the idea of the unified subject as the given. Lacan exposes this belief in one's unity and self-knowledge as an illusion of mastery. Like Freud before him (and like Lawrence), he posits a situation in which consciousness is continually betrayed and disrupted by the unconscious. But it is specifically Lacan's notion of the mirror phase which Kristeva uses in order to formulate her idea of the semiotic. In the very early stages of the child's life, according to Lacan, the child cannot distinguish between itself and its environment; it has no awareness of its corporeal boundaries, perceiving itself to be in a state of seamless unity with the mother. The mirror phase is initiated by the child's recognition that she or he *is* separate from the mother, and from the rest of the world, and this is registered as a sudden loss or lack. In other words, the child's recognition of itself as a (potential) totality, a subject in its own right, is inseparable from its recognition that the world as a whole is *not* its own. In saying 'I am', the child is also saying, 'I am *not* the mother, *not* the other, *not* the rest of the world.' The bond with the mother, then, has to be repressed in order for the child to say 'I am', and to enter into language and culture, into the Symbolic Order, which is itself posited on splitting and separation (here Lacan is directly indebted to Saussure, who showed how language and meaning arise from difference and separation). From now on, lack, gap, splitting, will be the child's mode of being.

Kristeva is primarily interested in the period *before* the mirror phase, the pre-Oedipal phase, which she speaks of in terms of the semiotic *chora*. Along Lacanian lines, she argues that this semiotic continuum must be split if signification is to be produced. The subject must be able to attribute differences and thus signification to what was the heterogeneous babble of the *chora*. Following Lacan, Kristeva posits the mirror phase as the phase which initiates this splitting, and the Oedipal phase with its threat of castration as the

---

[59] 'Foreword' to *Women in Love*, 485–6 (p. 486).

[60] *Desire in Language: A Semiotic Approach to Literature and Art*, trans. Thomas Gora, Alice Jardine, and Leon S. Roudiez (New York, 1980), 133.

moment in which the splitting process is completed, the (now incestuous) desire for unity with the mother repressed, and the phallus, or the law of language, accepted. Once the subject has entered into the Symbolic Order, the *chora* is more or less successfully repressed and can be perceived only as a *pressure* upon or within symbolic language; a pressure which exerts itself through contradictions, fissures, absences, and silences. From now on the *chora* constitutes the heterogeneous, illogical, disruptive dimension of language.

Kristeva's concept of the semiotic is of relevance here because she identifies its survival into adulthood via poetic language. Poetic language, she argues, is more open to the semiotic, and 'posits its own process as an undecidable process between sense and nonsense, between *language* and *rhythm* . . . between the symbolic and semiotic'. The semiotic 'introduces wandering . . . into language'.[61] This linguistic 'wandering' seems to correspond to Lawrence's own writerly practice in novels like *The Rainbow* and *Women in Love*, as well as to Loerke's conversation, which, we are told, 'was full of odd, fantastic expression, of double meanings, of evasions, of suggestive vagueness' (p. 453). Moreover, just as, for Lawrence, such 'wandering' undermines any fixed or static signifier–signified link, so for Kristeva the semiotic shows 'not only that the Saussurean cleavage (signifier–signified) is forever unbridgeable, but also that it is reinforced by another, even more radical one between an instinctual, semioticizing body, heterogeneous to signification, and this very signification based on prohibition (of incest), sign, and thetic signification establishing signified object and transcendental ego' (p. 139). Kristeva urges the same fracturing of the unified subject in favour of plurality and multivocality which so fascinates Lawrence in critical works like 'Study of Thomas Hardy' and *Studies in Classic American Literature*, where he searches for what he calls the 'marvellous under-meanings' of texts.[62] Like Lawrence's 'art-speech' as described in *Studies*, Kristeva's semiotic bears witness to what she calls 'the constraints of a civilization dominated by transcendental rationality' (p. 139). And just as Kristeva suggests that certain kinds of writing have been able to evade the seemingly monolithic control of the Symbolic, so Lawrence argues in his study of the American classics that art is 'a sort of subterfuge', evading the artist's attempts at censorship:

And the American art-speech reveals what the American plain speech almost deliberately conceals. What Hawthorne deliberately says in *The Scarlet Letter* is on the whole a falsification of what he unconsciously says in his art-language. And this, again, is one of the outstanding qualities of American literature: that the deliberate ideas of the man veil, conceal, obscure that which the artist has to reveal. This

---

[61] Ibid. 135, 136.   [62] *Studies in Classic American Literature*, 94.

quality of duplicity which runs through so much of the art of the modern world is almost inevitable in an American book. The author is unconscious of it himself. He is sincere in his own intention. And yet, all the time, the artist, who writes as a somnambulist, in the spell of pure truth as in a dream, is contravened and contradicted by the wakeful man and moralist who sits at the desk.[63]

If the Lacanian Symbolic is a reworking of the Freudian superego which censors and categorizes, for Kristeva the semiotic constitutes a challenge to the law of patriarchy. Those texts which are produced from the rhythms and pulsions of the semiotic *chora*—the pre-linguistic, pre-Oedipal experience—and which are in this sense antecedent to representation, offer the possibility of a non-patriarchal expression. Along with other prominent feminist theorists like Luce Irigaray and Hélène Cixous, Kristeva links the notion of polyvalence, of plural meanings, to femininity. For Irigaray with her famous 'two lips' theory, there will always be plurality in feminine language.[64] These plural meanings are not arranged into any kind of hierarchy: there is not one primary or dominant meaning and various secondary meanings; on the contrary, in a feminine language there is no dominant, official, or 'proper' meaning. 'Proper' for Irigaray, as for Cixous and Kristeva, has resonances of the proprietorial, of property and patriarchy, of legality and restriction. If we translate these concerns from gender to race, the parallels with Lawrence soon become clear. In his study of the American classics, Lawrence is not so much concerned with patriarchy as with what he calls 'the old parenthood of Europe' (p. 4), with a repressive Europeanism which stifles the voices of aboriginal America. But in Lawrence's readings of the works of Melville, Hawthorne, and others, these aboriginal voices are heard as a powerful undercurrent; they mingle and clash with the voices of authority and conformity. No voice is given priority over any other; the competing meanings are not reconciled and then transcended in one, single, overarching meaning.

Although Kristeva links 'semiotic' writing to feminist concerns, she stresses that this mode of writing is available to male and female writers alike: 'If the feminine *exists*', she argues, 'it only exists in the order of significance or signifying process, and it is only in relation to meaning and signification, positioned as their excessive or transgressive other, that it *exists*, *speaks*, *thinks* (itself) and *writes* (itself) for both sexes.'[65] If we share this view, we are forced into a paradoxical situation whereby writers who, on a discursive

[63] *The Symbolic Meaning*, 18.
[64] See e.g. *This Sex Which Is Not One*, trans Catherine Porter with Carolyn Burke (Ithaca, NY, 1985).
[65] 'Il n'y a pas de maître à langage', *Nouvelle Revue de psychanalyse*, xx (Autumn 1979), 119–40 (p. 135), cited in Toril Moi (ed.), *A Kristeva Reader* (Oxford, 1986), 11.

level, express startlingly misogynistic views can none the less be seen to be practitioners of this 'feminine' discourse. For many contemporary feminists, it is not so much that certain styles or structures in literature and art can be classified as inherently masculine or feminine; it is rather that any art which deconstructs or defamiliarizes, which forces us to recognize the constructedness of those forms which we had taken for granted or seen as natural, will be suited to a feminist politics, as indeed to any progressive politics. This is a view taken by, among others, Catherine Belsey and Rosalind Coward, who, by the same token, see realism as inherently reactionary, drawing as it does on the idea of the natural, of the way things are, have always been, and, by implication, always will be.[66] For if avant-garde modes of writing bring us back into contact with the semiotic, realist modes are, for critics like Belsey and Coward, more entrenched in the Symbolic Order, the realm in which logocentrism prevails. And, as is well known, for many feminist post-structuralists, this logocentrism is also a phallogocentrism, uniting the phallus and the logos, since it presents the world in terms of binary oppositions (active–passive, man–woman, reason–passion) which implicitly privilege the masculine term. There is a sense, then, in which realist art, with its implicit logocentrism, can be said to be a 'masculine' practice. It can be seen to rest on the notion of a bounded, coherent self separated from, and in mastery of, an objective outer world. Modernist writing, on the other hand, with its foregrounding of the pre-Oedipal or aural features of language, its formal decentredness, indeterminacy, multiplicity, and fragmentation, is seen to be compatible with a feminine aesthetic. In the Introduction I cited Kristeva's claim that 'in a culture where the speaking subjects are conceived of as masters of their speech, they have what is called a "phallic" position. The fragmentation of language in a text calls into question the very posture of this mastery.'[67] It is, as I have already stressed, precisely this posture of mastery which Lawrence attacks in his own critical writing.

In spite of all this, Lawrence's attitude towards polyvalence and word-play remains deeply ambivalent. As we have already seen, the narrator in *Women in Love* shares a propensity for word-play with Gudrun and Loerke. It is interesting in this regard that Kristeva explicitly links the semiotic to what is taboo in society, and the Symbolic to legality, but in particular she links the semiotic to the taboo of incest: 'because it utters incest', she argues, 'poetic language is linked with "evil" ' (p. 137). Gudrun's relationship with

[66] Catherine Belsey, *Critical Practice* (London, 1980), 51; Rosalind Coward, ' "This Novel Changes Lives": Are Women's Novels Feminist Novels? A Response to Rebecca O'Rourke's Article "Summer Reading" ', *Feminist Review*, v (1980), 53–64 (p. 60).

[67] 'Oscillation Between Power and Denial', in Marks and Courtivron, *New French Feminisms*, 165.

Loerke is nothing if not 'illegitimate', and this illegitimacy is expressed through linguistic promiscuity:

They had a curious game with each other, Gudrun and Loerke, of infinite suggestivity, strange and leering, as if they had some esoteric understanding of life, that they alone were initiated into the fearful central secrets, that the world dared not know. Their whole correspondence was in a strange, barely comprehensible suggestivity, they kindled themselves at the subtle lusts of the Egyptians or the Mexicans. The whole game was one of subtle inter-suggestivity, and they wanted to keep it on the plane of suggestion. From their verbal and physical *nuances* they got the highest satisfaction in the nerves, from a queer interchange of half-suggested ideas, looks, expressions and gestures, which were quite intolerable, though incomprehensible, to Gerald. He had no terms in which to think of their commerce, his terms were much too gross. (p. 448)

Incest is the ultimate blurring of that which should be kept separate; it violates the most sacred of social taboos. Lawrence himself vociferously opposed Freud's suggestion that the incest-wish was one of the most fundamental of human drives. Yet, as we have just seen, the 'illegitimate' language-games that Gudrun and Loerke play are only one step away from Lawrence's own literary technique in a work like *Women in Love*, where words such as 'labour', 'knowledge', 'experience', and 'inhuman' are constantly on the move. How odd it seems, then, that at so many other points in his work (and particularly in discursive works such as 'Study of Thomas Hardy'), Lawrence seems to offer us what is almost a parody of the Lacanian Symbolic Order, with his rigid binaries and hierarchies of Love/Law, Will-to-Motion/Will-to-Inertia, etc., all of which point, ultimately, to the man–woman polarity. For theorists like Kristeva, Irigaray, and Cixous, the main function of the Symbolic Order is to uphold patriarchy by keeping the male–female distinction intact, with its privileging of the male term. Correspondingly, Loerke's 'semiotic' babble seems to be linked to a certain blurring of gender distinctions: Loerke is described as 'an odd creature, like a child' (p. 405), and Gudrun ponders, 'there were no more *men*, there were only creatures, little, ultimate creatures like Loerke' (p. 452). Sandra Gilbert and Susan Gubar have interpreted Lawrence's depiction of Loerke in terms of his fear of the 'nomanhood', the feminization of men, fostered by the Great War.[68] Not only does Loerke confound male–female and adult–child distinctions, he also blurs the subject–object division: he is both 'craftsman' and 'creature' (p. 452). Similarly, one of Lawrence's war-poems, 'New Heaven and Earth',

---

[68] Sandra M. Gilbert and Susan Gubar, *No Man's Land: The Place of the Woman Writer in the Twentieth Century*, 3 vols. (New Haven, Conn., and London, 1988–), i: *The War of the Words* (1988), 89.

charts the violation of the distinctions between self and other, lover and beloved, murderer and murdered, even the eschatological distinctions between creator and created, God and man:

> . . . I was the author and the result
> I was the God and the creation at once;
> creator, I looked at my creation;
> created, I looked at myself, the creator:
> it was a maniacal horror in the end.
>
> I was a lover, I kissed the woman I loved,
> and God of horror, I was kissing also myself.
> I was a father and a begetter of children,
> and oh, oh horror, I was begetting and conceiving in my
> own body.[69]

Yet, as I have tried to show throughout this chapter, it is the indeterminacy and multiplicity of the semiotic, rather than the mastery of the Symbolic, 'dominated by transcendental rationality', which, for Lawrence, is the distinguishing mark of 'art-speech'.

Lawrence's interest in the unconscious, and in the ruptures, contradictions, absences, and meaninglessness which betray consciousness, is countered, then, by a strong urge to control. As I have already suggested, it is as though Lawrence's anti-authoritarian aesthetics, his request that we should attend to the unconscious 'under-meanings' of texts, emerges out of a need to counter his own authoritarian tendencies. And if Lawrence clings on, ultimately, to the repressive posture he so vehemently criticizes, it is interesting that he detects exactly the same contradiction in Freud. For Lawrence, as we shall see in the next chapter, Freud presents a curious paradox: he sets out to diagnose repression, yet he is nothing if not repressive himself, engaging in the repressive interpretation of the psychic text. The very same charge could be levelled against Lawrence in some of his critical writing. In a parody of the Hegelian master–slave dialectic employed so frequently by Freud, Lawrence sees the ego's mastery to be a horrifying mental tyranny, yet it is a tyranny of which he himself is guilty.

It seems appropriate at this point to look more closely at the role of the unconscious in Lawrence's aesthetics. Lawrence's antipathy to Freudian theory is well known, though the relationship between their various 'models' of the unconscious has not really been examined on more than a superficial level. Perhaps Lawrence's extraordinarily hostile reaction to Freud was triggered by self-recognition.

---

[69] 'New Heaven and Earth', in *The Complete Poems*, ed. Vivian de Sola Pinto and F. Warren Roberts (London, 1964), 256–61 (p. 257).

3

ANALYSING THE ANALYST:
LAWRENCE'S CLASH WITH FREUD

1. Freud as Conquistador

During the period 1913–18, Lawrence was preoccupied with various anthro-pological works.[1] One of these was *The Voice of Africa* (1913), Leo Frobenius's record of his attempts to 'unriddle the surface' of a continent inhabited by aboriginal peoples with 'no recorded history'. Frobenius's voyage was pre-cipitated by what he described as the 'European thirst for investigating the unknown', and sustained by the expectation of 'wresting some relics of antiquity every now and again from the lap of the earth'.[2] During the same period, Freud had been concerning himself, in his 1915 paper 'The Un-conscious', with the 'aboriginal population' inhabiting what he would later call, in his *New Introductory Lectures on Psycho-Analysis* (1933), the 'internal foreign territory' of the mind;[3] and he likened his researches, in a well-known analogy, to the unearthing of the long-buried relics of Pompeii:

I then made some observations upon the psychological differences between the conscious and the unconscious, and upon the fact that everything conscious was subject to a process of wearing away, while what was unconscious was relatively unchangeable; and I illustrated my remarks by pointing to the antiques standing about in my room. They were, in fact, I said, only objects found in a tomb, and their burial had been their preservation: the destruction of Pompeii was beginning only now that it had been dug up.[4]

For Freud, Pompeii's destruction denotes cure, an unearthing of the re-pressed wishes which have been causing the patient's neurosis or hysteria.

---

[1] Between 1913 and 1918, Lawrence read anthropological works by Harrison, Frazer, Murray, Frobenius, and others. See *Letters*, ii. 90, 470, 556; iii. 233.
[2] Leo Frobenius, *The Voice of Africa*, trans. Rudolf Blind, 2 vols. (London, 1913), i. 4; i, p. xiii; i. 5; i. 2.
[3] *The Standard Edition of the Complete Psychological Works of Sigmund Freud*, trans. from the German under the General Editorship of James Strachey, in collaboration with Anna Freud, 24 vols. (London, 1953–74), xiv. 195; xxii. 57. All further Freud citations will refer to this edition.   [4] 'Notes upon a Case of Obsessional Neurosis', x. 176.

For Lawrence, the image of plundered tombs would, one suspects, have had a very different resonance. In 1921 Lawrence published his bitter indictment of Freud, *Psychoanalysis and the Unconscious*, written 'to establish the smallest foothold in the swamp of vagueness which now goes by the name of the unconscious' (p. 241), and not long afterwards came *Fantasia of the Unconscious* (1922), for which Lawrence cites Frobenius as one of his sources. Finally, *Studies in Classic American Literature* (1923) was one of the earliest examples of an extended work of psychoanalytic criticism. If, as I have argued, some notion of 'the unconscious' was central to Lawrence's aesthetics, it is necessary to ask why Lawrence was so hostile towards Freudian theory.

Frobenius entitles his preface to *The Voice of Africa* 'Fiat Lux': he sets out to shed light, as he phrases it, over Stanley's 'dark continent' (p. xiv). Freud's parallel project is that of reclaiming land from the primordial chaos of the unconscious mind, and again the opening of Genesis provides the analogue: 'Where id was, there ego shall be. It is a work of culture—not unlike the draining of the Zuider Zee.'[5] While Frobenius and his co-imperialists scar the African earth with their 'spades' and 'picks', Freud, the self-styled '*conquistador*',[6] engages in his colonization of the human psyche. These geo-political and psychic models merge in Lawrence's *Studies in Classic American Literature*. Here, the hunting down of the whale in Melville's *Moby Dick* becomes, in Lawrence's reading of it, both the tracking down and subduing of unconscious forces, and the symbol of an insidious process of Europeanization. The capture of Moby Dick himself, a gleaming white trophy, symbolizes 'the last attainment of extended consciousness', the triumph of Lawrence's 'white' consciousness, his own idiosyncratic version of the Freudian ego.[7]

Lawrence probably first became acquainted with American literature as a child, through *The International Library of Famous Literature*, which was kept in the Lawrences' home. Francis Bret Harte, in his introduction to the volume covering 'The Rise of the "Short Story" ', depicts the American pioneers managing to 'shake off the English yoke' in all matters except literary ones; they prove unable to free themselves from 'the trammels of literary precedent'.[8] There is as yet, Bret Harte argues, no real 'Americanism' in art. The Old World legacy exerts itself in terms of trite sentiment and rigidly conventional plots, of 'blameless virgins of the North—heroines

[5] *New Introductory Lectures on Psycho-Analysis*, xxii. 80.
[6] Cited in Ernest Jones, *Sigmund Freud: Life and Work*, 3 vols. (London, 1953–7), i. 382.
[7] *The Symbolic Meaning*, 249.
[8] Francis Bret Harte, 'The Rise of the "Short Story" ', in *The International Library of Famous Literature*, ed. Richard Garnett, 20 vols. (London, 1899), xv, pp. xi–xix (p. xiii).

or fashionable belles—habited as hospital nurses, bearing away the deeply wounded but more deeply understood Harvard or Yale graduate lover who had rushed to bury his broken heart in the conflict' (p. xv). In Lawrence's study of the American classics, the sense of an oppressive conventionalism in American literature is equally strong, but it is seen to be in conflict with other, more subversive forces. Nathaniel Hawthorne is described as 'a master of serpent subtility', and this intrusion of the serpent into Eden is accounted for in terms of Hawthorne's self-division, a division which the American texts themselves embody or enact.[9] Lawrence goes on to develop the idea psychoanalytically, identifying the European conformism with the author's *conscious* mind, and suggesting that the creative process itself, which involves the unconscious mind, is capable of subverting that conformism. Just as, for Lawrence, the body is the submerged subtext of all conscious life, so he detects in these apparently conservative American texts, 'unconscious' subtexts telling quite different tales. The French–American writer Crèvecoeur, for instance, 'invents from his own ego' as a European, while his 'rudimentary', 'aboriginal' vision enables him to see 'insects, birds, and snakes in their own pristine being'.[10]

Lawrence's attack on Freud, in the opening paragraph of *Psychoanalysis and the Unconscious*, as 'the psychiatric quack who vehemently demonstrated the serpent of sex coiled round the root of all our actions' is well known. The biblical allusion, which is typical of Lawrence's references to psychoanalysis, suggests more than a simple puritanical distaste: Freud, in seeking to 're-deem' humanity through the 'civilizing' powers of the ego, has, in Lawrence's view, only reinscribed the fall. The image of the serpent connects Freud with the post-Cartesian philosophical tradition which was seen by Lawrence (and, as we shall see later, by Heidegger) to be symptomatic of this fall.[11] Lawrence's reading of Freud was unusual for its period, in that Freud was more commonly seen by his own contemporaries to have subverted, not reinforced, this rationalist tradition.

Here Nietzsche provides a clue to the cause of Freud's 'postlapsarian' condition, somewhat ironically, in view of the fact that Nietzsche is seen by Lawrence (and later by Heidegger) to manifest the symptoms of this 'fall' at their most advanced stage. Nietzsche was one of the philosophers to familiarize Lawrence with the unconscious long before he had even heard of the Freudian model. Readings in Hegel, Schopenhauer, and Herbart are

---

[9] *The Symbolic Meaning*, 141.   [10] Ibid. 63, 61.

[11] See e.g. 'Apocalypse', in *Apocalypse and the Writings on Revelation*, 57–149 (p. 126): 'The Logos which was like the great green breath of spring-time is now the grey stinging of myriads of deadening little serpents.' 'Apocalypse' was first published in Florence, 1931, as a book.

all recorded as early as 1908 (William James's *Some Varieties of Religious Experience* is added to the list in 1909);[12] but it was Nietzsche, to whose works Lawrence had access during the Croydon years, who saw the overdeveloped consciousness of the European psyche as a 'sickness', and who provided the link between self-analysis or 'clarity about oneself', and uncleanliness.[13] Lawrence's study of the American classics becomes the story of the 'fallen Puritan psyche', fallen in the sense that sex has been severed from the spirit which alone, for Lawrence, validates it.[14] The instrument of the fall is seen to have been an insatiable *intellectual* curiosity, synonymous for Lawrence with an insatiable lust for power. In the opening sentence of his *Genealogy of Morals* (1887), Nietzsche provides a salutary reminder that 'we knowers are unknown to ourselves'. From Lawrence's point of view, Freud's epistemo-logical project can be seen as both presumption and cruelty, in so far as Freud is guilty of what Nietzsche describes as 'cheerfully and curiously splitting open the soul, while the body still breathes'.[15]

At the root, then, of Lawrence's objection to Freud is the concept of the ego as a coercive occupying force. As I noted in the last chapter, Freud's emphasis on the ego's mastery of the id and his use of the Hegelian master-slave dialectic becomes for Lawrence a horrifying mental tyranny, a subjec-tion of the spontaneous sources of being to the 'psychic-mechanical law'.[16] In a striking reversal of Freud's equation of the 'primitive' with something 'older in time' and 'nearer to the perceptual end' in psychical topography, Lawrence witnesses a rampant intellectual barbarism, a taking over of 'the remnants of the once civilised world-people, who had their splendour and their being for countless centuries in the way of sensual knowledge . . . It is we from the North, starting new centres of life in ourselves, who have become young.'[17] This can be seen very clearly in the character of Clifford

---

[12] See 'Art and the Individual', in *Study of Thomas Hardy and Other Essays*, 133–42. This essay was written in 1908 and first published as 'Early Work' in *Young Lorenzo: The Early Life of D. H. Lawrence* (Florence, 1932). See also Jessie Chambers, *D. H. Lawrence: A Personal Record* (1935; Cambridge, 1980), 98, 111, 113.

[13] See e.g. *Ecce Homo*, 122–3. This idea was developed into a more fully fledged critique of psychoanalysis and the 'soul-doctors' by Karl Kraus, famous in his own day for arguing that psychoanalysis is the disease for which it masquerades as the cure. See Thomas Szasz, *Karl Kraus and the Soul-Doctors* (London and Henley, 1977), 103.

[14] *The Symbolic Meaning*, 168.

[15] 'The Genealogy of Morals', in *The Birth of Tragedy and The Genealogy of Morals*, trans. Francis Golffing (New York, 1956), 249. Carlyle's attitude towards scientific knowledge as a kind of fatal vivisection, which inevitably kills the object of its researches, fed directly into Lawrence; for Carlyle, no aspect of human existence had escaped being 'probed, dissected, distilled, desiccated, and scientifically decomposed' (*Sartor Resartus*, in *The Works of Thomas Carlyle*, 30 vols. (London, 1896–9), i. 4). Compare *Studies in Classic American Literature*, 66.

[16] *The Symbolic Meaning*, 59.

[17] *The Interpretation of Dreams*, v. 548; *The Symbolic Meaning*, 223.

Chatterley, who, whilst in his professional life 'a *real* businessman', supposedly the embodiment of responsible adulthood, in a paternal relation to the miners working under him, is in his emotional life a 'child-man', in thrall to the 'Magna Mater' Mrs Bolton.[18] He is a 'child' in the double sense of emotionally regressive and intellectually hypertrophied. This emphasis on an *intellectual* brutality leads to Lawrence's reversal of the Freudian teleology regarding the Oedipus complex.

2. *Versions of the Oedipus Complex*

Lawrence probably first encountered Freudian theory (in a diluted and distorted form) on meeting Frieda Weekley in 1912, and subsequently through discussions with the Freudian analysts David Eder and Barbara Low in 1914.[19] Frieda, who was by her own account 'full of undigested theories' about Freud on meeting Lawrence (she had been introduced to them through the Freudian disciple Otto Gross), undoubtedly left her mark on the final revision of *Sons and Lovers* (1913).[20] None the less, Lawrence's first novel, *The White Peacock* (1911), together with some of the early short stories ('The Shades of Spring', 'A Modern Lover'), makes it clear that at least some of his views on 'the unconscious', and in particular his critique of the 'self-consciousness' of modern civilization, were already firmly established before any recorded knowledge of Freud.[21] Those critics who greeted *Sons and Lovers* as a 'Freudian' novel failed to take into account the fact that Paul Morel's predicament differed from Freud's Oedipus complex in certain crucial respects.[22]

In a 1912 paper entitled 'On the Universal Tendency to Debasement in the Sphere of Love', Freud distinguished between two libidinal currents, the 'affectionate' and the 'sensual'.[23] The 'affectionate' current goes back to the earliest years of infancy and directs itself in the first instance towards those people who minister to the child's basic needs. It does, however, carry along with it certain 'components of erotic interest', which are, in the case of the male child, usually directed towards the mother or mother-surrogates and

---

[18] *Lady Chatterley's Lover*, 314.

[19] See *Letters*, ii, esp. pp. 258, 279 (15 Jan. 1915; [11 Feb. 1915]).

[20] Frieda Lawrence, *Not I but the Wind* (New York, 1934), 3.

[21] 'The Shades of Spring', in *The Prussian Officer and Other Stories*, ed. John Worthen (Cambridge, 1983), 98–112; 'A Modern Lover', in *Love Among the Haystacks and Other Stories*, ed. John Worthen (Cambridge, 1987), 28–48. 'The Shades of Spring' first appeared in *Forum*, Mar. 1913, as 'The Soiled Rose'; 'A Modern Lover' was first published in *Life and Letters*, Sept.–Nov. 1933.

[22] See *Letters*, i. 476 (19 Nov. 1912).   [23] xi. 177–90.

are accompanied by hostility towards and fear of the father. This fear represents itself in the child's mind as the threat of castration, and leads to the
suppression of the incestuous wishes. With the onset of puberty, however,
the affectionate current is joined by the 'sensual' current, cathecting the
object or objects of the primary infantile choice with quotas of libido which
are now far stronger, but in the meantime a barrier against incest has been
erected. If the child's attachment to his infantile object-choices is too great
(and this, Freud stresses, is directly connected to the amount of 'affection'
shown by those caring for the child), the libido retreats into a realm of
imaginative activity and becomes fixated to those first object-choices. In
cases of what Freud terms 'psychical impotence', the adolescent's 'sensual'
current manages to find *some* outlet, but in a severely restricted way, seeking
only those objects which do not recall the incestuous figures forbidden to it.
Freud goes on to argue that 'if someone makes an impression that might lead
to a high psychical estimation of her, this impression does not find an issue
in any sensual excitation but in affection which has no erotic effect. The
whole sphere of love in such people remains divided in the two directions
personified in art as sacred and profane (animal) love' (pp. 182–3).

The symptoms of Freud's hypothetical complex bear a striking resemblance to Paul Morel's situation in *Sons and Lovers* (Paul's 'spiritual' love is
directed towards Miriam Leivers, who has obvious affinities with Mrs Morel,
while Clara Dawes corresponds to the 'harlot' figure of Freudian fantasy),
and resembles still more closely the predicament of, say, Halliday in *Women
in Love*, who is described as 'split mad. He wants a pure lily, another girl,
with a baby face,—the good old chaste love—and at the same time he *must*
have the Pussum, just to defile himself with her' (p. 95).[24] It should be borne
in mind, however, that when Lawrence finally came to formulate his ideas on
the cause of such problems, in his two treatises on the unconscious, his
account differed radically from Freud's. Lawrence does not make Freud's
distinction between 'affectionate' and 'sensual' currents; rather, he explains
his own version of the Oedipus complex in terms which correspond more
closely to the Freudian ego and id. He divides the child's responses into two
main categories, the 'sympathetic' (roughly corresponding to a spiritual
response, uncontaminated by sexuality), and the 'voluntary' (indicating a
passional or sexual response). Where for Freud the child's libidinal impulses

---

[24] Another example of this occurs in the 'Prologue' chapter of *Women in Love*, where Birkin
turns away from the overcerebral Hermione towards 'the other, the dark, sensual, almost
bestial woman [as if] thoroughly and fully to degrade himself' (p. 499). Lawrence may have
derived his ideas on this syndrome from Jung's *Psychology of the Unconscious*, especially the
chapter entitled 'The Battle of Deliverance from the Mother'. See Daniel A. Weiss, *Oedipus
in Nottingham: D. H. Lawrence* (Seattle, 1962), 17.

towards its parents exist as it were from the beginning, constituting a part of the 'cauldron of seething excitement' which is the Freudian id, for Lawrence the Oedipal situation originates in a kind of *invasion* of the id by the ego. More specifically, it originates in the excessive parental fostering of the child's 'sympathetic' centres, in what is a kind of '*spiritual*' incest'.[25] This sparks off a corresponding activity in the child's 'lower', 'voluntary' centres, which, however, refuses to connect with the mother (or, one might infer, with anyone resembling the mother). We are back on a more domestic level to the excessive emphasis on the intellect, on what Lawrence terms the 'ideal', which he attributes to the psychoanalytic enterprise as a whole: 'This motivizing of the passional sphere from the ideal', Lawrence warns, 'is the final peril of human consciousness. It is the death of all spontaneous, creative life, and the substituting of the mechanical principle.'[26]

3. Freud's 'Fallen' Text

In Lawrence's view, the domination of the ego which he sees to be central to Freud's project stems from a complicity between scientific method and coercion. As Lawrence sees it, Freud's mistake is that he attempts to approach the unconscious through a scientific discourse which is premissed on the 'mimetic' or 'logocentric' model of language I discussed in the last chapter. As I shall try to show later in the book, Lawrence sees the same complicity between logocentrism and coercion in technology, and indeed Freud represents for Lawrence a kind of technologist himself: 'The mind is the instrument of instruments; it is not a creative reality.'[27] It is not difficult to see why Lawrence's attack on Freud takes on such a peculiar force: in an important sense, for Lawrence, Freud is worse than the technologists who are his 'external' counterpart, in that he attempts to systematize the one area of the psyche (the unconscious) which has hitherto been immune to, or capable of subverting, system. To use an analogy which Lawrence could not have used, Freud is the equivalent on the psychological plane of a disease like Aids on the physical, in that he attacks the one thing which might have warded off attack; for the unconscious, in a culture which is characterized for Lawrence by psychic sickness, is the immune system itself. But the parallel can only be taken so far, in that Freud's weapon, scientific 'method', fails, in Lawrence's view, to reach its object of attack. In attempting to 'frame' the unconscious, Freud fails to respect what Lawrence calls its 'untranslatable

[25] 'Fantasia of the Unconscious', 118.
[26] 'Psychoanalysis and the Unconscious', in *Fantasia of the Unconscious and Psychoanalysis of the Unconscious*, 207.   [27] Ibid. 246.

otherness'.[28] Long before Lacan and Derrida, Lawrence argues that, since there is no metalanguage, Freud's hermeneutic enterprise is misguided.

For Lawrence, then, psychoanalysis is not only an epistemology of the unknowable, but it is, in medical terms, a 'symptom' of the sicknesses, the psychic imbalances, it claims to cure. For Freud, in Lawrence's view, is nothing if not repressive himself, engaging in the repressive interpretation of the psychic text. Dispensing with conscious or surface intention, he becomes intentionalist in a new way; indeed, he becomes, for Lawrence, the archetypal intentionalist critic in his semantic precision, his determination to decipher the elements of the text and to trace them back to a solid bedrock of psychoanalytic 'truth'.

J. Hillis Miller, in his essay 'Stevens' Rock and Criticism as Cure, II', conflates Nietzschean and Freudian terminologies by dividing critics into two groups: 'Socratic, theoretical or canny critics on the one hand, and Apollonian/Dionysian, tragic, or uncanny critics on the other'. Miller alludes here to Section XV of *The Birth of Tragedy* (1872), where Nietzsche speaks of Socrates in connection with 'the illusion that thought, guided by the thread of causation, might plumb the farthest abysses of being and even *correct* it.'[29] Freud's obsession with causality would seem at first sight to place him in Miller's 'Socratic' category; it becomes clear, however, that Freud has admitted elements into his procedure which are subversive of the causal chain when he repudiates the notion that it is possible to *predict* whether a person will develop a neurosis or not. It becomes apparent that his enterprise is more hermeneutical than strictly 'scientific', more a question of *reading* and *interpreting* than of *proving*. Moreover, his analyses can only be retrospective. Lawrence is one of the first to draw attention to this 'retrospective teleology' in Freud. The analyst, Lawrence suggests, provides a view of the patient's history which the patient projects back on to reality and then experiences. He gives the incest-desire as an example: 'The mind', he argues, 'transfers the idea of incest into the affective-passional psyche, and keeps it there as a repressed motive.' It is in this sense that, for Lawrence, 'the Freudian unconscious is the cellar in which the mind keeps its own bastard spawn'.[30]

In Lawrence's view, then, Freud's quest for the unconscious in its pristine form is a hopeless one if it is to be conducted along the signifying chains of discursive or 'mimetic' language. This model of language, as I noted in the

---

[28] *The Symbolic Meaning*, 17.
[29] 'Stevens' Rock and Criticism as Cure, II', *Georgia Review*, xxx/2 (Summer 1976), 335–8 (p. 335); 'The Birth of Tragedy' in *The Birth of Tragedy and The Genealogy of Morals*, 93. For the larger part of his article, Miller uses the term 'uncanny' in connection with the notion of intellectual uncertainty, rather than in the strictly Freudian sense of 'that class of the frightening which leads back to what is known of old and long familiar' (*The Uncanny*, xvii. 222).   [30] 'Psychoanalysis and the Unconscious', 203, 204.

last chapter, assumes a neat one-to-one signifier–signified correspondence. Indeed, Freud's descriptions of the unconscious, as if in acknowledgement of the fact that it will forever remain recalcitrant to the constraints of a 'fallen' language, are pervaded by the imagery of the *signifier*: he compares the interpretation of dreams to 'the decipherment of an ancient pictographic script such as Egyptian hieroglyphs', and informs his readers that 'the unconscious speaks more than one dialect'. Whether these 'dialects' are 'gesture-languages' (hysteria), 'picture-languages' (dreams), or 'thought-languages' (obsessional neuroses), there is a sense that none of them can quite penetrate to this stubbornly elusive 'signified'.[31]

Freud seems, then, to be aware of the quixotic no man's land in which psychoanalysis resides: his essay on Leonardo is, he confesses, 'partly fiction',[32] yet at the same time he grants a paradoxical validity to the insights of literature as a supplementary form of 'scientific' evidence.[33] He explains that he is obliged to operate with 'the figurative language peculiar to psychology' and points out that even if he were able to use physiological and chemical terms, they too would be figurative, not the mimetic discourse of a positivist science.[34] Time and again, his pursuit leads him into alogical and absurd situations; his notion of *regression* to some origin or bedrock of truth seems only to lead to infinite *regress*, to the point at which, in Nietzsche's words, 'logic . . . curls about itself and bites its own tail'.[35]

Derrida's well-known deconstruction of Freud, in *Writing and Difference*, has shown how in any meditation on origins (if 'origin' is to denote some kind of authenticity or essence), the object of the interpretative quest is always deferred. In a startling adumbration of Derrida's celebrated description of the unconscious text as 'a text nowhere present, consisting of archives which are *always already* transcriptions' in which 'Everything begins with reproduction',[36] Lawrence dismisses the contents of the Freudian unconscious as 'spawn produced by secondary propagation from the mental consciousness itself'.[37] The reverse side of the coin here is that when psychoanalysts supposedly 'translate' the terms of the unconscious into conscious terms, all they have, as opposed to a derived origin, is an originary secondariness, as Derrida points out: 'Since the transition to consciousness is not a derivative or repetitive writing, a transcription duplicating an unconscious writing, it occurs in an original manner, and, in its very secondariness, is originary and

---

[31] 'The Claims of Psycho-Analysis to Scientific Interest', xiii. 177–8.

[32] *Letters of Sigmund Freud, 1873–1939*, ed. Ernst L. Freud (London, 1961), 312 (7 Nov. 1914).   [33] *Delusions and Dreams in Jensen's Gradiva*, ix. 8.

[34] *Beyond the Pleasure Principle*, xviii. 60.   [35] 'The Birth of Tragedy', 95.

[36] 'Freud and the Scene of Writing', in *Writing and Difference* trans. Alan Bass (Chicago, 1978), 196–250 (p. 211).   [37] 'Psychoanalysis and the Unconscious', 204.

irreducible.'[38] In other words, where some psychoanalysts might choose to see their discipline as a bridge, it can more pessimistically be seen to articulate a gap.

Like Darwin, whose relevance for Lawrence is explored later in the book, Freud is criticized by Lawrence on grounds of *plot*. By insisting on a teleology or history of sexuality, Freud is forced into adopting the enabling fiction of the 'primal repression', in which the unconscious both initiates the repression and is constituted as repression; without it his story of the psyche could not begin.[39] For Harold Bloom in 'Freud and the Poetic Sublime', primal repression is the model for the structure of literary reference itself (and one might extend this to all reference): the retroactive installation of a referent, which language situates, through rhetoric, outside itself.[40] Lawrence is acutely aware of such problems, and therefore anxious to separate his own 'unconscious' from Freud's implicit plotting: 'When we postulate a beginning, we only do so to fix a starting-point for our thought. There never was a beginning . . .'[41] Where, according to Derrida's reading of the Freudian unconscious, psychoanalysts are dealing 'not with horizons of modified presents—past or future—but with a "past" that has never been present, and which never will be, whose future to come will never be a *production* or a reproduction in the form of presence',[42] for Lawrence the unconscious *is* 'the pure present, and the pure Presence, of the soul—present beyond all knowing or willing. Knowing and willing . . . are as it were the reflex or *afterwards* of being.'[43] Lawrence posits an unconscious which *is* pristine, raw, primary, uncorrupted by bias or teleology, and he does so by placing it outside and beyond any 'fallen' epistemological enterprise: 'The supreme lesson of human consciousness is to learn how *not to know*. That is, how not to *interfere*. That is, how to live dynamically, from the great Source, and not statically, like machines driven by ideas and principles from the head, or automatically, from one fixed desire.'[44] This is the only escape from the circular and self-deconstructing traps which Freud lays for himself. Ideas, principles, fixed desires, all imply some kind of reification, where the Lawrentian unconscious is a *mode* of existence (of being and acting), not an essence. Charles Rycroft articulates what must be Lawrence's basic objection to Freud when he speaks of 'the fallacy of reifying a *quality*': 'Consciousness and unconsciousness can only be qualities or attributes of something else, in this case of the actions (including the thinking activity) of

---

[38] 'Freud and the Scene of Writing', 162.   [39] 'Repression', xiv. 148.
[40] 'Freud and the Poetic Sublime', *Antaeus* (Spring 1978), 355–77.
[41] *The Symbolic Meaning*, 176.
[42] 'Différance', in *Margins of Philosophy*, trans. Alan Bass (Chicago, 1982), 1–27 (p. 21).
[43] *The Symbolic Meaning*, 37.   [44] 'Fantasia of the Unconscious', 72.

an agent.'[45] Freud, it seems, has put too much cognitive emphasis on isolable entities.

For Lawrence, then, the unconscious operates 'beyond, where there is no speech and no terms of agreement . . . It is quite inhuman,—so there can be no calling to book, in any form whatsoever—because one is outside the pale of all that is accepted, and nothing known applies.'[46] Elsewhere, he refers to it as 'blood-consciousness . . . the nearest thing in us to pure material consciousness'.[47] This is, of course, a *religious* affirmation of the unconscious; its 'verification' through the signifying chains of logic would be worthless. Indeed, for Lawrence, the deconstruction of a metaphysics of perfect presence is a dubious enterprise, in so far as such deconstruction can itself only come from a metaphysical standpoint.

4. Art as Palimpsest

Lawrence objects to the command of the subject which psychoanalysis seems to foster, to the dominance of what he refers to, in explicitly Freudian terms, as the 'old stable ego'. It should not, he argues, in his frequently quoted letter to Edward Garnett, be allowed to predominate in art.[48] But Freud, too, connects creativity with the attenuation of the powers of the ego. In his book on jokes, he suggests that it is the *form* of jokes which is the key to their success, in that their economy of wordplay seems to prevent their being paraphrased; he thus connects form and its tapping of the unconscious with the escape from discursivity.[49] Elsewhere, he suggests that the artist has what he calls a 'flexibility of repression', a greater freedom at his disposal owing to his ability to relax the controls of reason. He quotes Schiller: 'Where there's a creative mind, Reason . . . relaxes its watch upon the gates, and the ideas rush in pell-mell.'[50] There is an obvious parallel here with Lawrence's claim in *Studies in Classic American Literature* that 'the American art-speech reveals what the American plain speech almost deliberately conceals', and that 'the deliberate ideas of the man veil, conceal, obscure that which the artist has to reveal'.[51] Freud analyses Jensen's novella *Gradiva* in the following terms:

The author directs his attention to the unconscious in his own mind, he listens to its possible developments and lends them artistic expression instead of suppressing them by conscious criticism. Thus he experiences from himself what we learn from

---

[45] 'The Freudian Slip', in *Psychoanalysis and Beyond* (London, 1985), 81–91 (p. 90).
[46] *Women in Love*, 146.   [47] 'Fantasia of the Unconscious', 171.
[48] *Letters*, ii. 183 (5 June 1914).
[49] *Jokes and Their Relation to the Unconscious*, viii. 16–17.
[50] *The Interpretation of Dreams*, iv. 103.   [51] *The Symbolic Meaning*, 18.

others—the laws which the activities of the unconscious must obey. But he need not state these laws, nor even be clearly aware of them; as a result of the tolerance of his intelligence, they are incorporated within his creations.[52]

In Jensen's tale itself, the hero Norbert Hanold's world becomes a palimpsestic one in which misreading and cross-reading seem inevitable: Zoe Bertgang's name (the first part of which is the Greek for 'life') is overwritten (as a result of Hanold's *repression* of his desires for her) by that of the dead Gradiva (a Greek translation of the German 'Bertgang'), just as Zoe's living flesh is overlaid with antique marble. Hanold's childhood is repeatedly re-articulated in the terms of the classical past, and the repression of his desires is equated by Zoe to the burial of Pompeii by the Vesuvian ashes. Towards the end of his analysis of *Gradiva*, Freud extends his discussion of the 'burying over' and 'uncovering' activities of Jensen's plot into a more general observation of the way in which literary works themselves are many-layered: they are never the 'innocent' works their authors may take them to be.[53]

I have already suggested that, for Lawrence too, literary texts are palimpsestic. In the 'Study of Thomas Hardy', we find the dictum that 'The degree to which the system of morality . . . of any work of art is submitted to criticism within the work of art makes the lasting value and satisfaction of that work' (p. 89). He finds a good example of the fissured text in the Book of Revelation, which is of course a literal palimpsest, but which he uses as a paradigm for the work of art:

It is one book, in several layers: like layers of civilisation as you dig deeper and deeper to excavate an old city. Down at the bottom is a pagan substratum, probably one of the ancient books of the Aegean civilisation: some sort of a book of a pagan Mystery. This has been written over by Jewish apocalyptists, then extended, and then finally written over by the Jewish-Christian apocalyptist John: and then, after his day, expurgated and corrected and pruned down and added to by Christian editors who wanted to make of it a Christian work.[54]

In other words, art must in some sense deconstruct itself. Lawrence finds a perfect example of this self-deconstructing art in Shelley's 'Ode to a Skylark': 'Shelley wishes to say, the skylark is a pure, untrammelled spirit, a pure motion. But the very "Bird thou never wert", admits that the skylark is in very fact a bird, a concrete, momentary thing.'[55] The 'Study of Thomas Hardy' is scattered with such thumbnail deconstructive readings. At the level of 'metaphysic', Hardy's Alec d'Urberville is 'a vulgar intriguer', while at the level of art he is 'a rare man who seeks and seeks among women for one of such character and intrinsic female being as Tess' (p. 101). Hardy as

---

[52] *Delusions and Dreams in Jensen's Gradiva*, ix. 92.   [53] Ibid. 91.
[54] 'Apocalypse', 81.   [55] 'Study of Thomas Hardy', 91.

intentionalist author is 'something of an Angel Clare' who will try to make things conform to his preconceptions, but as an artist he gives us a far more complex picture (p. 101). This is what Lawrence calls 'the supreme justice of the artist' (p. 99); art 'must give fair play all round' (p. 89).

The problem with the American writers, according to Lawrence's study of them, would appear to be that they are not endowed with quite enough of Freud's 'flexibility of repression': they 'give tight mental allegiance to a morality which all their passion goes to destroy'.[56] 'What Hawthorne deliberately says in *The Scarlet Letter*', we are told, 'is on the whole a falsification of what he unconsciously says in his art-language'.[57] *The Scarlet Letter* is, then, one of those novels against which Lawrence would warn in *Lady Chatterley's Lover* (p. 105), which are 'always ostensibly on the side of the angels'. But the 'double language' or 'perfect duplicity' of the American writers is seen to be preferable to the kind of writing which masquerades as monolithic 'truth'.

It is possible, as I suggested in the last chapter, to apply Lawrence's analysis to his own works. For the critic Tony Pinkney, *Women in Love* is a riven text, in that Birkin, whilst professing allegiance to organic spontaneity and integration, uses and is described in 'a phraseology which is shot through with intimations of modernity, of its shifting cosmopolitan deracinatedness'. This novel is, Pinkney argues, simultaneously a critique of modernism and 'a modernist artefact in its own right, formally enacting the polyglottism of Eliot's *Waste Land* or Ezra Pound's *Cantos*'.[58] And I have tried to show how Lawrence chips away at any fixed link between signifier and signified, rendering meaning mobile and unstable. One could say that Lawrence's own prose-style represents an attempt to render palpable the energies of the unconscious through the relaxation of the control of the 'old stable ego'. The modified repetition in Lawrence is inseparable from an endless *semantic* modification; we are never allowed to feel that a final 'signified' has been reached. In addition, supposedly 'key' words prove alarmingly polysemous, sometimes even turning themselves inside out to become their polar opposites. In the last chapter I focused on the term 'labour', and in later chapters I will see the terms 'experience' and 'complete' as examples of this.[59] Another example would be the way in which 'abstraction' is used in *Women in Love*. It is used in connection with the African fetishes to connote, among other things, an overdevelopment of the sensual centres at the expense of the intellect: the face of the African woman in labour is 'abstracted in utter physical stress', 'abstracted almost into meaninglessness by the weight of

[56] *Studies in Classic American Literature*, 162.   [57] *The Symbolic Meaning*, 18.
[58] *D. H. Lawrence*, 91, 82.   [59] See below, pp. 115, 169.

sensation beneath' (p. 79). Yet in the same novel 'abstraction' is repeatedly associated with Gerald Crich, who epitomizes the overdevelopment of the intellect in the white races who 'having the arctic north behind them, the vast abstraction of ice and snow', are about to 'fulfil a mystery of ice-destructive knowledge, snow-abstract annihilation' (p. 254). 'Abstraction' is both the regression to an 'uncreate' state of physical mindlessness, and the assertion of Gerald's hypertrophied, mechanizing will.

For Lawrence, then, there is no absolute or final 'meaning' to which a work of art points; rather, an endless number of meanings are generated by the ever-shifting relations between the elements of the art-work, its system of differences. In therapeutic practice, Freud, too, laid stress on free association, on a 'proportional' mode of interpretation which derived the 'meaning' of symbols from the context provided by the patient: 'My procedure', he claims, 'is not so convenient as the popular decoding of dreams which translates any given piece of a dream's content by a fixed key. I, on the contrary, am prepared to find that the same piece of content may concede a different meaning when it occurs in various people in various contexts.'[60] It has been argued by Paul Ricoeur in this connection that the clue to Freud's aesthetic is to be found in the essay on Michelangelo's *Moses*, where the focus is on the *overdetermination* of the various features of the statue; far from reducing the enigma, Ricoeur suggests, Freud multiplies it.[61] On the other hand, and rather tellingly, music, which of all art-forms would most firmly be categorized as non-discursive, which as the most formalistic of the arts paradoxically allows the unconscious freest play, had little appeal for Freud, precisely because he felt unable to *explain* its effect upon him.[62] Often, Freud seems to wish to ground art in *legibility*. 'Only with the greatest reluctance', he confesses, could he bring himself to believe that 'intellectual bewilderment' is a necessary component of the aesthetic experience. In this emphasis on deciphering and decoding, art simply becomes a passageway, a lure, to an unconscious 'reality', an 'incentive bonus' ('*bestechende Lustprämien*'), which enables the viewer to enter into enjoyment of the fantasies covertly offered, such fantasies being the semantic bedrock of art.[63] To return to the mimetic

---

[60] *The Interpretation of Dreams*, iv. 105. Kenneth Burke speaks of Freud's 'essentializing strategy' in terms of 'his tendency, when dealing with a group of motives, to single out one as the causal ancestor of the others, where the "proportionalist" strategy would be to study the various factors as a cluster, the motivation being synonymous with the interrelationships among them' ('Freud—and the Analysis of Poetry', in *The Philosophy of Literary Form: Studies in Symbolic Action*, 3rd edn. (Berkeley, Calif., and Los Angeles, 1973), 258–92).
[61] *Freud and Philosophy: An Essay on Interpretation*, trans. Denis Savage (New Haven, Conn., and London, 1970), 170.   [62] 'The Moses of Michelangelo', xiii. 211.
[63] 'Creative Writers and Day-Dreaming', ix. 153.

and differential models of language examined in the last chapter, it can be seen that Freud interprets art in terms of the mimetic or essentialist model, premissed on a neat signifier–signified correspondence; it consists of 'decorative' pictograms, where the meaning has been 'softened' or 'concealed' by form.[64] Freud's categories of 'word-presentation' and 'thing-presentation', and his designation of the unconscious as the domain of thing-presentations detached from their word counterparts ('the unconscious presentation is the presentation of the thing alone'), assume this same unproblematic signifier/ signified link.[65]

In spite of his denunciation of the 'Logos', Lawrence reminds his readers in the 'Foreword' to *Women in Love* that the 'struggle for verbal consciousness should not be left out in art. It is not superimposition of a theory. *It is the passionate struggle into conscious being*' (p. 486). This is a problem with which Ursula and Birkin struggle, and which, as we saw in the last chapter, *Women in Love* articulates in terms of the need for verbal 'labour':

> She listened, making out what he said. She knew, as well as he knew, that words themselves do not convey meaning, that they are but a gesture we make, a dumbshow like any other . . . He turned in confusion. There was always confusion in speech. Yet it must be spoken. Whichever way one moved, if one were to move forwards, one must break a way through. And to know, to give utterance, was to break a way through the walls of the prison, as the infant in labour strives through the walls of the womb. There is no new movement now, without the breaking through of the old body, deliberately, in knowledge, in the struggle to get out.[66]

And in a 1928 letter to Earl Brewster, Lawrence writes of *Lady Chatterley's Lover*, 'it's a novel of the phallic consciousness: or the phallic consciousness *versus* the mental spiritual consciousness: and of course you know which side I take. The *versus* is not my fault: there should be no *versus*. The two things must be reconciled in is. But now they're daggers drawn.'[67] In *Women in Love* we see Rupert Birkin's ambivalence towards the African fetishes with their 'impulse for knowledge all in one sort, mindless progressive knowledge through the senses . . . knowledge in dissolution and corruption' (p. 253). Loerke, the Dresden sculptor in the same novel, is described as a 'mud-child' (p. 427), both 'mud' and 'child' connoting an 'uncreate' regression from which the narrator seems to dissociate himself. Michael Ragussis, in *The Subterfuge of Art*, places Lawrence in a Romantic tradition which, though it has so often been associated with both primitivism and transcendentalism, is

---

[64] 'The Claims of Psycho–Analysis to Scientific Interest', xiii. 187.
[65] 'The Unconscious', xiv. 201, 228.   [66] *Women in Love*, 186.
[67] Moore (ed.), *Collected Letters*, ii. 1044 (11 Mar. 1928).

in fact a criticism of both: it 'refuses the myths of the child and of the god as models for the man' (p. 11). If, in *The Symbolic Meaning*, Lawrence asserts that in the highest art, the primary mind 'expresses itself direct, in direct pulsating communication', he qualifies this by adding that 'this expression is harmonious with the outer or cerebral consciousness'. In psychoanalytic terms, art becomes both symptom and cure in a celebrated comment of Lawrence's of which the first half alone is usually quoted: 'One sheds one's sicknesses in books—repeats and presents again one's emotions to be master of them.'[68]

Freud himself is notoriously confusing on this question of the regressiveness of art. For each of his comments to the effect that art is an 'illusion', a 'substitute gratification', a 'narcotic', there are others which seem to link art with some effort of control over reality.[69] In *Beyond the Pleasure Principle*, Freud relates his speculative discovery that there are dreams whose purpose is not hallucinatory but which are attempts to master a stimulus retroactively by first developing the anxiety.[70] This has been developed into a theory of creativity by, among others, Harold Bloom in his 'Freud and the Poetic Sublime'. For Paul Ricoeur, too, Freud presents art as both symptom and cure in that, where instincts as such are unreachable, inaccessible, traceable only in their 'psychical derivatives', the psychical derivative of art involves an element of production or creation, a making present and palpable: 'Leonardo's brush does not recreate the memory of the mother; it creates it as a work of art.'[71] Certainly Freud himself would seem to place art on a scale somewhere between complete conscious control (the assertion of Lawrence's 'old stable ego') and a complete surrender to unconscious forces, when he remarks, in connection with surrealism and other experimental art-forms, that 'the notion of art defies expansion as long as the quantitative proportion of unconscious material and preconscious treatment does not remain within definite limits'.[72] Ernst Kris develops this in his designation of the artist's ability to tap unconscious sources without losing control as 'regression in the service of the ego'.[73]

Birkin's words to Ursula about the need to give utterance suggest that art and creativity, for Lawrence, far from involving an unwholesome regression to an infantile state, provide a route to healthy, integrated living. It is at this point that Lawrence's connections with the psychoanalytic tradition of the British Object-Relations School should be explored.

---

[68] *Letters*. ii. 90 (26 Oct. 1913).
[69] See e.g. xi. 50; xii. 224; xiii. 188; xvi. 375–7; xx. 64.   [70] xviii. 32.
[71] *Freud and Philosophy*, 174.   [72] Freud, *Letters*, 444 (20 July 1938).
[73] *Psychoanalytic Explorations in Art* (New York, 1952), 60.

5. Lawrence and the British Object-Relations School

Marion Milner's book *On Not Being Able to Paint* (1950) records the attempts of a practising psychoanalyst to draw without the help of conventional textbooks on the subject. Milner expresses the same dissatisfaction with and distrust of orthodox art-teaching methods found in Lawrence's work (such methods are parodied at length towards the end of his 'Introduction to These Paintings').[74] Milner, like Lawrence, finds that the rules of perspective, of light and shade, of grouping, and so on, somehow miss the point of art:

It was as if one's mind could want to express the feelings that come from the sense of touch and muscular movement rather than from the sense of sight. In fact it was almost as if one might not want to be concerned, in drawing, with those facts of detachment and separation that are introduced when an observing eye is perched upon a sketching stool, with all the attendant facts of a single view-point and fixed eye-level and horizontal lines that vanish. It seemed one might want some kind of relation to objects in which one was much more mixed up with them than that.[75]

This is reminiscent of the 1925 essay 'Art and Morality', where Lawrence criticizes the artist who attempts to present a still-life of an apple photographically; an artist who is 'more mixed up' in the apple might take into account 'the vast moist wall through which the insect bores to lay her eggs in the middle, and the untasted unknown quality which Eve saw hanging on a tree. Add to this the glaucous glimpse that the mackerel gets as he comes to the surface, and Fantin Latour's apples are no more to you than enamelled rissoles' (pp. 166–7). It is striking in this regard that Milner should speak in the same terms of 'curving round to the other side, to the back of presented appearance' that Lawrence had used in his writings on Cézanne:

Certainly seeing with one's own eyes, whether in painting or in living, seeing the truth of people and events and things needed an act of the imagination; for the truth was never presented whole to one's senses at any particular moment, direct sensory experience was always fragmentary and had to be combined into a whole by the creative imagination. Even the perception of a chair or a carrot was an imaginative act, one had to create imaginatively, out of one's past experience of walking round things or holding them in one's hand, *the unseen other side of the chair or the carrot.* And how much more did one have to create the insides of things.[76]

One of Milner's first discoveries in her attempt to paint is that the outlines of things, which she had always assumed to be real, are, in the words of

[74] *On Not Being Able to Paint*, 2nd edn. (London, 1957), 582–3.   [75] Ibid. 10.
[76] 'Introduction to These Paintings', 579; *On Not Being Able to Paint*, 14, my emphases.

a traditional textbook on the subject, 'the one fundamentally unrealistic non-imitative thing in this whole job of painting'.[77] It is worth recalling that Paul Morel, the artist of *Sons and Lovers* (1913), distrusts outline; pondering one of his botanical sketches, he considers that 'it's . . . as if I'd painted the shimmering protoplasm in the leaves and everywhere, and not the stiffness of the shape. That seems dead to me. Only this shimmeriness is the real living. The shape is a dead crust.'[78] Milner comes to associate outline with 'the emotional need to imprison objects rigidly within themselves', to *control* them.[79]

Milner draws a connection between these *spatial* problems (of outline, distance, and so on) and 'problems of being a separate body in a world of other bodies which occupy different bits of space: in fact it [painting] must be deeply concerned with ideas of distance and separation and having and losing'.[80] She sheds light on Lawrence's art-criticism, in that she goes on to make the very connections between art and our relationship to others/ the outside world which Lawrence makes. Milner is one of the British 'Middle School' of psychoanalysts, otherwise known as the 'Object-Relations' theorists, who were to some extent influenced by Melanie Klein but departed from Kleinian theory on certain important issues. They extricated themselves from a Freudian impasse by assuming that human beings are not naturally unintegrated but innately whole and already adapted to their environment (an assumption which Lawrence also makes), and that various psychic splits occur only in so far as they have experienced frustration, separation, or loss. For Charles Rycroft, for example, in his 1975 essay 'Psychoanalysis and the Literary Imagination', the primary and secondary processes coexist in the individual psyche from the beginning and may continue to function in harmony, especially through art: creative people retain into adult life something of the imaginative freedom of healthy children. For Rycroft, wish-fulfilment is seen as a product of the psychic split (just as, for Lawrence, Crèvecoeur's letters enact a conflict between 'wish-fulfilment' and 'a primal, dark veracity'):[81] 'In so far as . . . the state of primary relatedness is disrupted, dissociation occurs in such a way that wishful thinking and adaptive adjustment come to operate in different psychic realms.'[82] For D. W. Winnicott, health and creativity depend on the establishment of a third 'intermediate' realm (he locates art in this realm) in which objects are felt to be parts of both external and internal reality, to possess both

---

[77] Cited in ibid. 15.

[78] *Sons and Lovers*, ed. Helen Baron and Carl Baron (Cambridge, 1992), 183.

[79] *On Not Being Able to Paint*, 16.   [80] Ibid. 12.

[81] *Studies in Classic American Literature*, 30, 28.

[82] Cited in Peter Fuller's introduction to Charles Rycroft, *Psychoanalysis and Beyond*, 25.

selfhood and otherness, and in which activities are both wish-fulfilling and adaptive.[83] Similarly, for Adrian Stokes, art evokes a sense of 'entity', of a lapidary wholeness, whilst being at the same time 'a contagion that spreads and spreads'.[84] The paradox of Winnicott's 'intermediate living' is something he wishes 'to be accepted and tolerated and respected . . . not to be resolved. By flight to split-off intellectual functioning it is possible to resolve the paradox, but the price of this is the loss of the value of the paradox itself.'[85] He links the intermediate realm to the point in the infant's life when s/he becomes dimly aware of the mother's 'otherness', of the fact that mother and baby do not flow seamlessly into one another. The baby posits the idea of a 'potential space', situated 'at the interplay between there being nothing but me and there being objects and phenomena outside omnipotent control'.[86]

This connection between art and the earliest mother–child relationship is characteristic of the Object-Relations theorists. For Stokes, the artist re-creates 'the sensation of oneness with the satisfying breast no less than an acceptance of the whole mother as a separate person'.[87] Lawrence can be found describing art in precisely the same terms: art displays 'the living conjunction or communion between the self and its context',[88] a conjunction which he sees to involve both the solar plexus as the centre of 'sympathy' or the impulse to merge, and the lumbar ganglion as the 'voluntary' centre of separate identity (and hence of the recognition of 'object-otherness'). For Lawrence, art and love are frequently interchangeable, and he describes love in terms which sound very like those of the art-models put forward by Stokes, Segal, and Winnicott, of both 'the sense of union, communion, at-oneness with the beloved' and 'the complementary objective *realization* of the beloved, the realization of that which is apart, different'. Lawrence also uses the mother–child paradigm: the child both 'drinks in . . . the contiguous universe', and asserts its own separate identity.[89] Art is likewise a form of 'meaning-at-oneness, the state of being at one with the object', in which the sense of an *object* is as important as the sense of fusion.[90] Van Gogh's painted sunflowers are a 'third thing, utterly intangible and inexplicable, the off-spring of the sunflower itself and Van Gogh himself'.[91]

[83] *Playing and Reality* (London, 1971), 1–25.

[84] 'Form in Art: A Psychoanalytic Interpretation', *Journal of Aesthetics and Art Criticism*, 2 (1959), 193–203 (p. 193). [85] *Playing and Reality*, 1–25.

[86] *Through Paediatrics to Psycho-Analysis* (London, 1975), p. xx.

[87] 'Form in Art', 197. [88] *The Symbolic Meaning*, 117.

[89] 'Psychoanalysis and the Unconscious', 239, 224.

[90] 'Making Pictures', in *Phoenix II*, 602–7 (p. 605). This essay first appeared in *Creative Art*, 5 (July 1929), 466–71.

[91] 'Morality and the Novel', in *Study of Thomas Hardy and Other Essays*, 171.

In 'Apocalypse', true knowledge is equated with our awareness of 'the other thing':

Man has two supreme forms of consciousness, the consciousness that I AM, and that I am full of power; then the other way of consciousness, the awareness that IT IS, and that IT, which is the objective universe or the other person, has a separate existence from mine, even preponderant over mine. This latter is the way of knowledge: the loss of the sense of I AM, and the gaining of knowledge, or awareness, of the other thing, the other creature. (p. 168)

But, as Lawrence makes clear on so many occasions, the self must not be sacrificed in the pursuit of this knowledge; both self and other are essential.[92]

It is at this point that my argument brings me to the Bloomsbury aesthetics of the next three chapters; for Peter Fuller, who has done much to reinterpret aesthetics in the light of this infant–mother relationship, sees Clive Bell's 'aesthetic emotion' to derive from precisely this same emotional nexus. In *Art and Psychoanalysis*, Fuller argues that modernism is poised between, or partakes of both, the traditional notions of the 'beautiful' and the 'sublime': the aesthetic emotion is concerned with 'the submergence of self into the environment, and the differentiation of self out from it . . . The "sublime" (romantic, colour) emphasises one aspect of this nexus—that of mergence and union; "beauty" (classical, outline) and its derivatives stresses the other—that of separation'.[93] For Fuller, it is no coincidence that Bell should evoke aesthetic rapture in terms of standing on the 'cold white peaks' of art, for 'Bell found in the modern movement, and enjoyed there, a capacity of painting to revive something of the spatial sensations and accompanying "good" emotions which the infant feels at his mother's breast' (p. 157). Fuller follows Gombrich in finding an academic painting of *The Three Graces* by Bonnencontre considerably improved by being photographed through rolled glass.[94] Fuller's explanation for this, though, is very different from Gombrich's; it relates again to the point in the child's development 'when the existence of the boundaries (outlines) or limiting membranes of the self and of its objects are at once perceived and imaginatively ruptured' (p. 171). Fuller concludes from this that 'those spatial organisations constructed

---

[92] In 'Study of Thomas Hardy', Lawrence expresses this merging and separateness in art in terms of the Will-to-Motion and the Will-to-Inertia (p. 59) and in terms of male and female principles (pp. 64–5). Much of the study is devoted to an analysis of the male–female ratio in the work of different artists. Compare Adorno's description of negative dialectics as a procedure which acknowledges 'the preponderance of the object', something which, although to some extent mediated by an active subjectivity, cannot be reduced to it (*Negative Dialectics*, 183).

[93] Peter Fuller, *Art and Psychoanalysis*, 2nd edn. (London, 1988), 199.

[94] Ibid. 167–71, citing Ernst Gombrich, 'Psycho-Analysis and the History of Art', in *Meditations on a Hobby Horse* (London, 1963), 30–44.

by the early modernists are not merely enrichments of nostalgic fantasy life, but also potentially of our relation to the world itself' (p. 172). Lawrence's description of the Etruscan world fits the self/notself pattern perfectly:

It must have been a wonderful world, that old world where everything appeared alive and shining in the dusk of contact with all things, not merely an isolated individual thing played upon by daylight; where each thing had a clear outline, visually, but in its very clarity was related emotionally or vitally to strange other things, one thing springing from another, things mentally contradictory fusing together emotionally, so that a lion could be at the same moment also a goat, and not a goat.[95]

This relationship between the individual and the environment ('environment' including other human beings), between microcosm and macrocosm, was one of Lawrence's constant preoccupations, and finds many different articulations in his work. Lawrence never ceases to remind us that art *connects* us with the world:

. . . the point of every work of art is that it achieves a state of feeling which becomes true experience, and so is religious. Everything that puts us into connection, into vivid touch, is religious. And this would apply to Dickens or Rabelais or *Alice in Wonderland* even, as much as to *Macbeth* or Keats. Every one of them puts us curiously into touch with life . . .[96]

The 'third thing' which microcosm and macrocosm constitute is symbolized in Lawrence's work by, among other things, the Crown, the Rainbow, and the Holy Ghost; but it finds a concrete embodiment in art. Art provides a locus in which merging and separating, engagement and autonomy, are simultaneously possible;[97] but art can only do this if both artist and viewer/reader renounce the kind of psychic subjugation in which Freud (according to Lawrence) is engaged. This assertion of the ego in art and art-criticism is the psychic equivalent of Gerald Crich's solipsistic will-to-power and mechanization, which leads only to *production*, not *creation*. It is easy to see how, in another light, Freud is like the Christian editor of the Apocalypse, the expurgator, the destroyer of heretical works.

---

[95] 'Etruscan Places', 68.   [96] 'Apocalypse', 155.

[97] Heidegger's aesthetic theory, and his epistemology generally, are closely bound up with this same reciprocity between merging and separateness. The following passage from 'Origin of the Work of Art' sounds like a description of the model Lawrentian relationship (*Poetry, Language, Thought*, 47): 'All things of earth, and the earth itself as a whole, flow together into a reciprocal accord. But this confluence is not a blurring of their outlines. Here there flows the stream, restful within itself, of the setting of bounds, which delimits everything present within its presence. Thus in each of the self-secluding things there is the same not-knowing-of-one-another.' He also goes on to speak of the striving between world and earth in the artwork, in which 'the opponents raise each other into the self-assertion of their natures' (p. 49).

Although the aesthetics of Lawrence and Freud, then, can be seen to coincide at several important junctures, Freud remains for Lawrence a Gerald Crich of the psyche. Lawrence's readers are faced with an antithesis between the unconscious (and art) on the one hand, and a kind of imperialism on the other. The 'anti-imperialism' of Lawrence's aesthetics is examined in more detail in Chapter 10. Just as, for Lawrence, it is important to recognize the 'otherness' of the art-object, to concede the art-image in all its semantic instability, and not subject it to the external control, or imperialism, of a fixed, logocentric discourse, so, for Lawrence, Freud must renounce a form of therapy in which the powers of the ego are pitted against the subversive forces of the id in 'the old struggle for dominancy'.[98]

[98] 'Review of *The Social Basis of Consciousness*, by Trigant Burrow', in *Phoenix*, 377–82 (p. 379). This review was first published in *Bookman* (American), Nov. 1927.

4

LAWRENCE AND BLOOMSBURY I:
SIGNIFICANT FORM

Clive Bell's *Art* (1914), one of the key texts of Bloomsbury art-criticism, is at best an incoherent, at worst a disturbingly élitist work. Peter Fuller, in *Art and Psychoanalysis*, is harshly critical of it in ways which few people would wish to question, attacking Bell as 'opinionated, arrogant, ultimately downright reactionary', yet none the less finding in Bell's theory 'kernels of truth' which can shed light on his own (psychoanalytical and materialist) arguments (p. 146). In spite of its faults, Bell's *Art* is an important text for the student of Lawrence's art-criticism. Lawrence had many direct and indirect connections with Bloomsbury, and Bell and Fry are two of the very few art-critics he takes the trouble to criticize overtly. In fact, his attack on Bloomsbury aesthetics is vociferous and uncompromising. As a result, literary history has generally defined Lawrence's views on art in opposition to those of Bloomsbury, which is not the most fruitful way of approaching the art-criticism of either camp.

That literary history should have chosen to polarize Lawrence and Bloomsbury, taking Lawrence's attack at face value, seems odd as soon as one takes even the most cursory glance at their common interests and concerns. Roger Fry was, like Lawrence, a champion of the African art and sculpture which had begun to permeate the European art world, partly through its impact on artists like Gauguin, Picasso, and Kirchner, partly through the work of a number of prominent anthropologists. Like Lawrence, moreover, both Fry and Bell took a stand against the 'illusionist' art which had begun with Renaissance quattrocento painting and had been given a further impetus in the nineteenth century from the invention of photography itself (in the next chapter I look in more detail at this hostility towards the pseudo-photographic). In a 1920 review of a Chelsea Book Club exhibition of thirty pieces of African sculpture, Fry contrasted the African sculptors' 'profound imaginative understanding of form' with 'our cheapest illusionist art'. Lawrence, who had first-hand experience of African carvings through his friends Philip Heseltine and Mark Gertler, also found in them an exhilarating freedom from the limitations imposed upon pseudo-photographic art. He wrote in his essay 'Art and Morality' in 1925 that the African fetish statue 'stirs more than all the Parthenon frieze. It sits in the place where no kodak can snap it.'[1] Further, both Lawrence and Fry, like Bell, singled out Cézanne as the most important painter for the modern age, an issue I explore at length in Chapter 6. These surface similarities between Lawrence and Bloomsbury are, I think, borne out by a closer comparison of their respective writings on art. Such a comparison reveals that Lawrence's attack on Bloomsbury aesthetics is in certain important ways both superficial and misleading, and that Lawrence is in fact united with Bloomsbury, wittingly or unwittingly, on a number of vital issues.

None the less, it is repeatedly claimed by literary critics and art-historians alike that Lawrence and the Bloomsbury artists and art-critics were poles apart.[2] As evidence, they usually cite Lawrence's 'Introduction to These Paintings', the long essay written towards the end of his life, in January 1929, for the Mandrake Press edition of his own paintings. The essay contains a remorseless attack on 'significant form', the catch-phrase of Bloomsbury aesthetics, and the keystone of the theory put forward in Bell's *Art*. One of the chief exponents of a Lawrence–Bloomsbury opposition was of course F. R. Leavis, who in his last full-scale study of Lawrence identified the art theories of Loerke, the Dresden sculptor in *Women in Love*, with Bell's doctrine of significant form; Leavis dismisses Bell's theory as 'the sophisticated fatuity that Lawrence dispatches with such witty conclusiveness in *Introduction*'.[3] Loerke, it is worth recalling, puts forward a theory of absolute aesthetic autonomy, claiming of one of his sculptures that 'It is a work of art, it is a picture of nothing . . . It has nothing to do with anything but itself.'[4]

Like Leavis, most readers of the 'Introduction' see Lawrence's attitude towards Bloomsbury art-criticism as a confirmation of something in which they already believed: it reinforces the myth of Bloomsbury's detached rationalism, a myth propagated by, among others, J. M. Keynes in his memoir *My Early Beliefs* (1949). Keynes's image of himself and his Cambridge/ Bloomsbury friends as 'water-spiders, gracefully skimming, as light and reasonable as air', has had an immense influence on Bloomsbury studies.[5] The image suggests insubstantiality, a mind unburdened of its corporeal limitations. In the introduction to Keynes's memoir, David Garnett writes of

---

[1] Fry, 'Negro Sculpture', in *Vision and Design* (London, 1920), 70–3 (p. 73). This essay was first published in the *Athenaeum* (16 Apr. 1920), 56; Lawrence, 'Art and Morality', in *Study of Thomas Hardy and Other Essays*, 168.

[2] See e.g. Claudia C. Morrison, *Freud and the Critic* (Chapel Hill, NC, 1968), 209–10; Keith Alldritt, *The Visual Imagination of D. H. Lawrence* (London, 1971), 153; Jeffrey Meyers, *Painting and the Novel* (Manchester, 1975), 77; J. B. Bullen, introduction to *Art* by Clive Bell (Oxford, 1987), pp. xxi–l (p. xli).

[3] *Thought, Words and Creativity: Art and Thought in Lawrence* (London, 1976), 75.

[4] *Women in Love*, 430.

[5] John Maynard Keynes, *Two Memoirs, Dr Melchior: A Defeated Enemy and My Early Beliefs* (London, 1949), 103.

his great admiration for Lawrence, with the reservation that, as a rationalist and a scientist himself, he opposed 'Lawrence's intuitive and dogmatic philosophy', finding the ideas of his Cambridge friends more congenial (p. 76). Keith Alldritt, in *The Visual Imagination of D. H. Lawrence*, writes of 'the characteristic Bloomsbury predilection for the eighteenth century', and sees Lytton Strachey's 'respect for reason and detachment' to inform, among other Bloomsbury works, Bell's *Art*.[6] And while Quentin Bell draws attention to a more intuitive strain in Bloomsbury, he does so only in passing.[7] Yet Clive Bell's aesthetic, as this chapter will attempt to show, is based solidly on the (bodily) intuition which Lawrence so relentlessly defends. Far from being in a tradition of dispassionate rational enquiry, Bell's *Art* is bound up in the same post-Romantic quest for the organic which characterizes Lawrence's work. It becomes apparent that for any meaning at all to be attached to the concept of 'Bloomsbury', a clear distinction must be made between Bloomsbury aesthetics and other aspects of Bloomsbury thought.

1. Significant Form and 'Disintegration'

There is an evocative scene in *Sons and Lovers* in which Miriam leads Paul into the wood to show him some wild roses: 'They were white, some incurved and holy, others expanded in an ecstasy' (p. 96). This is one of a series of episodes in which Paul blunderingly attempts to commit himself to Miriam, repeatedly baulking at what he sees to be her 'overspiritual' nature (their friendship is described as 'all thought and weary struggle into consciousness', p. 209). The conjunction of the colour white with the term 'ecstasy' was one which Lawrence was to use time and time again; its reference is to the mythical severance of mind from body, to a postlapsarian world blighted by 'the collapse of the white psyche'.[8] The terms 'ecstasy' and 'thrill' (which recur in descriptions of Miriam's inner life) are almost always associated by Lawrence with the mind–body split ('disintegration') and with characters who best exemplify it. In *Women in Love*, Hermione Roddice, a high priestess of culture, has 'the face of an almost demoniacal ecstatic' (p. 21); her relationship with Birkin is enacted in 'a transcendent white ecstasy' (p. 495); towards the end of the novel, Gudrun, Loerke, Gerald, and others spend the time in 'an ecstasy of physical motion' on the Tyrolean ski-slopes (p. 421). The theme of an oppressive 'white-consciousness' is conveyed through the Alpine snow itself, which provides a fitting backdrop to Gerald's

---

[6] Alldritt, *The Visual Imagination of D. H. Lawrence*, 181.
[7] Quentin Bell, *Bloomsbury* (London, 1968), 40.
[8] *Studies in Classic American Literature*, 59.

self-destruction on the mountainside; for Gerald exemplifies the overconscious Northern spirit: he possesses 'frost-knowledge' (p. 254).

It is in this context that Lawrence's reaction to Bloomsbury art-criticism must be assessed. For it was very late in life, in the winter of 1928–9, that Lawrence read Bell's *Art*, just before writing his own 'Introduction to These Paintings'.[9] By this time, his own version of the 'postlapsarian' rhetoric so prevalent at this period was fully developed. Reading *Art* in January 1929, Lawrence could only have felt he was encountering a 'fallen' text, for Bell's imagery suggests the language of disintegration that Lawrence himself had used in *Women in Love* and elsewhere. Bell, putting himself in the category of those who have been privileged enough to experience the 'aesthetic emotion', addresses himself to those of us who are less privileged: 'And let no one imagine . . . that he can even guess at the austere and thrilling raptures of those who have climbed the cold, white peaks of art'; deploring the inadequacies of Gothic, he warns his readers that before a Gothic cathedral, they 'will not be strung to austere ecstasy . . . do not expect the thrill that answers the perception of sheer rightness of form'. The aesthetic emotion, he argues, transports us beyond the concerns of day-to-day living: it 'springs, inhuman or super-human, from the heart of an abstract science'.[10] Such expressions are reminiscent of Lawrence's response to Gertler's *Merry-Go-Round*, which he believed to have been painted 'in an ecstasy of destructive sensation',[11] but they are also immediately suggestive of certain passages in *Women in Love*, and in particular the scenes in Halliday's flat, where Birkin contemplates the African fetishes, the product of 'thousands of years of purely sensual, purely unspiritual knowledge' (p. 253). Birkin compares this form of 'disintegration' with the European form: 'The white races, having the arctic north behind them, the vast abstraction of ice and snow, would fulfil a mystery of ice-destructive knowledge, snow-abstract annihilation' (p. 254). Lawrence must have found Bell's 'cold white peaks' reminiscent of this, and of the final chapters of *Women in Love*, set against the alpine snow, the 'terrible waste of whiteness' (p. 400) which is Loerke's, and Gerald's, element. Lawrence's description of the snowscape brings to mind Bell's transcendent realm of 'austere ecstasy': 'The first days passed in an ecstasy of physical motion, sleighing, ski-ing, skating, moving in an intensity of speed and white light that surpassed life itself, and carried the souls of the human beings beyond into an inhuman abstraction of velocity and weight and eternal, frozen snow' (p. 421). And Gudrun seems to have reached Bell's peaks of aesthetic exaltation:

[9] See Moore (ed.), *Collected Letters*, ii. 1118 (11 Jan. 1929), where Lawrence writes that he has received Bell's *Art* and Fry's *Cézanne*. Lawrence had met Bell much earlier, in Nov. 1915, and had probably heard about 'significant form' at that time. See *Letters*, ii. 435–6 (15 Nov. 1915).   [10] *Art*, 32–3, 145, 25.   [11] *Letters*, ii. 660 (9 Oct. 1916).

Gudrun was driven by a strange desire. She wanted to plunge on and on, till she came to the end of the valley of snow. Then she wanted to climb the wall of white finality, climb over, into the peaks that sprang up like sharp petals in the heart of the frozen, mysterious navel of the world. She felt that there, over the strange, blind, terrible wall of rocky snow, there in the navel of the mystic world, among the final cluster of peaks, there, in the infolded navel of it all, was her consummation. If she could but come there, alone, and pass into the infolded navel of eternal snow and of uprising, immortal peaks of snow and rock, she would be a oneness with all, she would be herself the eternal, infinite silence, the sleeping, timeless, frozen centre of the All. (p. 410)

A few pages on, and Gudrun's transcendent state is phrased in the terms which Lawrence would later use to attack Bell ('The ego . . . shuts itself up and paints the inside of the walls sky-blue, and thinks it is in heaven'): 'For Gudrun herself, she seemed to pass altogether into the whiteness of the snow, she became a pure, thoughtless crystal. When she reached the top of the slope, in the wind, she looked round, and saw peak beyond peak of rock and snow, bluish, transcendent in heaven.'[12]

In 'Introduction to These Paintings', Lawrence's mock-evangelical tones parody the language of *Art* so closely as to establish beyond doubt (even if there were no other evidence) that he had read Bell's work very shortly before embarking upon his own essay. Not only do catch-phrases like 'aesthetic ecstasy' reverberate both through *Art* and through Lawrence's own attack on contemporary art-criticism: some of Lawrence's allusions are far more pointed and precise. He refers to the defenders of Post-Impressionism as the 'Primitive Methodists' of art-criticism, whose chapels are built 'in a Romanesque or Byzantine shape'.[13] This corresponds to Bell's characteristically sweeping claim in the opening chapter of *Art* that 'Most people who care much about art find that of the work that moves them most the greater part is what scholars call "Primitive" ' (p. 22). Romanesque and Byzantine art are among the types of primitive art Bell mentions specifically. On these pages of *Art*, too, we find the reiterated praise of the absence of representation in the best primitive works, inciting Lawrence's mock-pious declaration that the 'elect' 'had renounced the mammon of "subject" in pictures, they went whoring no more after the Babylon of painted "interest", nor did they hanker after the flesh-pots of artistic "representation" '.[14] The exhortation which follows, 'Oh, purify yourselves, ye who would know the aesthetic ecstasy, and be lifted up to the "white peaks of artistic inspiration" ', is a direct allusion to Bell's 'cold, white peaks of

---

[12] 'Introduction to These Paintings', in *Phoenix*, 567; *Women in Love*, 420.
[13] 'Introduction to These Paintings', 565. For Lawrence's views on Primitive Methodism and the evangelical preoccupation with the 'elect', see 'Apocalypse', in *Apocalypse and the Writings on Revelation*, 63–5.   [14] 'Introduction to These Paintings', 565.

art'.[15] Lawrence goes on to refer directly to significant form, evoking it, with incantatory insistence, through a characteristic cluster of absolutes:

Purify yourselves, and know the one supreme way, the way of Significant Form. I am the revelation and the way! I am Significant Form, and my unutterable name is Reality. Lo, I am Form and I am Pure, behold, I am Pure Form. I am the revelation of Spiritual Life, moving behind the veil.[16]

Here Lawrence is parodying the third chapter of *Art*, entitled 'The Metaphysical Hypothesis', in which Bell ventures to speculate that the artistic vision enables us to see 'that which lies behind the appearance of all things— that which gives to all things their individual significance, the thing in itself, the ultimate reality' (pp. 69–70). And so the parallels continue.[17]

As Lawrence sees it, Bell's 'language of salvation' is nothing more than self-glorification. Certainly there is a disquieting element of élitism in *Art*, which Bell's terminology betrays on practically every page: 'The gross herd', he regrets, 'still clamours for a likeness'; 'the vulgar' cannot be made to understand that the artist's aim is not necessarily to 'catch a likeness' (pp. 39, 66). In the 'Introduction', this becomes the 'low lust for likenesses' from which Lawrence pretends to dissociate himself (p. 565). Bell goes on to make an alarming pseudo-medical diagnosis to the effect that 'in the spectator a tendency to seek, behind form, the emotions of life is a sign of defective sensibility always. It means that his aesthetic emotions are weak or, at any rate, imperfect.' These unfortunates are 'deaf men at a concert': 'They know that they are in the presence of something great, but they lack the power of apprehending it' (pp. 28–9). This élitism stems from the assumption that 'only artists and educated people of extraordinary sensibility and some savages and children' are sufficiently sensitive to the significance of form (pp. 80–1). Beneath Bell's class-ridden language, then, lies an anti-intellectualist argument inherited from Romantic aesthetics, to the effect that the least sensitive to significant form are those in whom an excessively intellectual culture has induced a visual atrophy. This does not sound so very different from 'Introduction', where Lawrence shows, moreover, that he is equally capable of a condescending 'pity' for those denied the arcane pleasures of art: 'So those

---

[15] Ibid. 565; *Art*, 33.   [16] Ibid. 565–6.

[17] As if the reader were not already sure of the target of Lawrence's attack, he goes on to tell us that the prophets of the new era in art 'will revive the Primitive Method-brethren, the Byzantines, the Ravennese, the early Italian and French primitives' ('Introduction', 566). This is undoubtedly a reference to a footnote on p. 36 of *Art*, where Bell informs us that a certain Mr Okakura, Government editor of *The Temple Treasures of Japan*, whilst immediately understanding 'the Byzantine masters and the French and Italian primitives', could see nothing but 'vulgarity and muddle' in the Renaissance painters, as a result of their 'descriptive pre-occupations' and their 'literary and anecdotal interests'.

poor English and Americans in front of the Botticelli Venus. They stare so hard; they do so want to see. And their eyesight is perfect. But all they can see is a sort of nude woman on a sort of shell on a sort of pretty greenish water' (p. 557). This is reminiscent of the scene in *Women in Love* in which Hermione Roddice forces a party of guests to stare at a bank of wild daffodils, deliberately making it into an object of aesthetic contemplation: 'The daffodils were pretty', the narrator comments, 'but who could see them?' (p. 87).[18]

Bell claims that those uncorrupted by civilization 'see, because they see emotionally'; 'civilised' people, in the pejorative sense, 'use their eyes only to collect information': 'The habit of recognising the label and overlooking the thing, of seeing intellectually instead of seeing emotionally', he argues, 'accounts for the amazing blindness, or rather visual shallowness, of most civilised adults'.[19] Bell's labels approximate to Lawrence's 'mental concepts', described in the 'Introduction' as the product of 'the mental consciousness stuffed full of clichés that intervene like a complete screen between us and life' (p. 582). Lawrence had explored exactly this issue in chapter VIII of *Fantasia of the Unconscious* (1922), in which he had denounced an education-system which encourages the child to see conceptually and to draw 'correctly':

> The image on his retina is not the image of his consciousness . . . His consciousness is filled with a strong, dark, vague prescience of a powerful presence, a two-eyed, four-legged long-maned presence looming imminent. And to force the boy to see a correct one-eyed horse-profile is just like pasting a placard in front of his vision. It simply kills his inward seeing.[20]

What Lawrence apparently fails to recognize is this 'primitivist' strain running through so much modern art theory. It had manifested itself in Ruskin in the notion of the 'innocent eye', of vision uncorrupted by knowledge,[21] but it is far more prominent in Bloomsbury aesthetics. In Lawrentian tones, Roger Fry explains how the greater intellectual power of Neolithic, as opposed to Palaeolithic, man, 'manifested itself in his desire to classify phenomena, and the conceptual view of nature began to predominate. And it was this habit of thinking of things in terms of concepts which deprived him for ages of the power to see what they looked like . . . when he tried to reproduce his sensations, his habits of thought intervened . . .'[22]

---

[18] There may be an echo of Ruskin here. See *Modern Painters*, in *The Works of John Ruskin*, ed. E. T. Cook and Alexander Wedderburn, 36 vols. (London, 1903–12), v. 333: 'The more I think of it I find this conclusion more impressed upon me,—that the greatest thing a human soul ever does in this world is to see something, and tell what it *saw* in a plain way. Hundreds of people can talk for one who can think, but thousands can think for one who can see.' All further Ruskin citations will refer to this edition.

[19] *Art*, 81, 79.   [20] 'Fantasia of the Unconscious', 86–7.

[21] 'The Elements of Drawing', *Works*, xv. 25–228 (p. 27 n.).

[22] 'The Art of the Bushmen', *in Vision and Design*, 56–64 (p. 62).

Fry's views were to receive support from ·Herbert Read, who was of course a great admirer of Lawrence, and contributed an essay to Mervyn Levy's edition of Lawrence's paintings.[23] Read argued that aesthetic perception preceded conceptual knowledge in human development; he traced modern art back to Romantic aesthetics and to Vico's belief that poetry represents an early stage in human development and can be produced in the present only by those who are able to suspend the operations of the rational intellect, reverting to a pre-conceptual mode of expression. Read accounts for what he sees to be the creative atrophy of modern civilization in terms of the mind–body split, the 'disintegration' which is so central to Lawrence's vision of the civilized world:

Civilisation produces a split consciousness, a world made up of discordant forces, a world of images divorced from reality, of concepts divorced from sensation, of logic divorced from life. At best we can recover an integrated consciousness in our art, but even our art has been invaded by intellectual attitudes which destroy its organic vitality . . . The purpose of education, as of art, should be to preserve the organic wholeness of man and of his mental faculties, so that as he passes from childhood to manhood, from savagery to civilisation, he nevertheless retains the unity of consciousness which is the only source of social harmony and individual happiness.[24]

Lawrence's main objection to significant form is that, as he sees it, it is the product of this split consciousness, a manifestation of the dualism which the whole of his critical output is directed against, and, what is worse, of a quasi-Platonic dualism, exalting the spirit: Plato is an 'arch-priest' of 'the crucifixion of the procreative body for the glorification of the spirit, the mental consciousness'.[25] Lawrence fails to see that it was precisely this dualistic split which Bell's theory of significant form was attempting to heal.

2. Aesthetic Emotion

Although Lawrence writes disparagingly of Bell's 'aesthetic emotion', he rather puzzlingly uses the term himself in a piece entitled 'Pictures on the Walls', written at about the same time as the 'Introduction': 'The value of a picture', he declares, 'lies in the aesthetic emotion it brings . . . The aesthetic emotion dead, the picture is a piece of ugly litter.'[26] And the essay 'Making

---

[23] 'Lawrence as a Painter', in *The Paintings of D. H. Lawrence*, ed. Mervyn Levy (London, 1964), 55–64.   [24] Herbert Read, *Education Through Art* (London, 1943), 69–70.

[25] 'Introduction to These Paintings', 569. One of the central paradoxes of Lawrence's work is, of course, that it is deeply informed by the very dualism it attacks.

[26] 'Pictures on the Walls', in *Phoenix II*, 608–15 (p. 611). This essay first appeared in *Vanity Fair*, 3 (Dec. 1929), as 'Dead Pictures on the Wall'.

Pictures', of the same period, contains what is virtually a plagiarism of *Art*. Here 'thrill', 'exaltation', 'purity of spirit', are used positively, and Lawrence proves to be just as capable as Bell of separating the 'true' art-lover from the 'herd', from those who remain embedded in the mire of the instinctive, everyday life: to appreciate art, he states apparently quite without irony, the viewer needs 'a purity of spirit, a sloughing of vulgar sensation and vulgar interest, and above all, vulgar contact, that few people know how to perform'.[27] These pieces, with their emphasis on 'aesthetic emotion', provide a clue to Lawrence's connections with Bloomsbury.

In the essay 'John Galsworthy', Lawrence claims that, in art-criticism, 'the touch-stone is emotion, not reason. We judge a work of art by its effect on our sincere and vital emotion, and nothing else.'[28] Here Lawrence is unwittingly arguing Bell's case for him. That Bell is equally antagonistic to rigid theory is made clear in the first chapter of *Art*, where he argues that 'it is useless for a critic to tell me that something is a work of art; he must make me feel it for myself. This he can do only by making me see; he must get at my emotions through my eyes.'[29] In other words, as William G. Bywater demonstrates in *Clive Bell's Eye*, Bell does not make G. E. Moore's distinction between cognition and emotion.[30] Moore's *Principia Ethica* (1903) has commonly been held to be the 'Bible' of Bloomsbury, and the textual support for Bloomsbury rationalism. Yet Bell explicitly dissociates himself from Moore on the question of aesthetics.[31] In this regard, it is surprising to read in a study as recent as Victor Burgin's *The End of Art Theory* (1986) yet another equation of Bell's aesthetic with Moore's philosophy.[32] In collapsing the distinction between cognition and emotion, Bell in fact closes the gap which Lawrence's own aesthetics seeks to bridge.

A close reading of *Art* reveals that significant form comes into being as a result of the emotional encounter between painting and viewer; it enforces participation rather than simple acquiescence, in that *how* the viewer looks affects what s/he sees. The contents of an aesthetic space cannot, as Bell sees it, be passively catalogued; on the contrary, the viewer of the painting must be in an emotionally receptive state to be able to recognize significant form. Lawrence, like many other art-historians after him, presents Bloomsbury aesthetics in terms of a passive, quasi-scientific cataloguing of aesthetic data,

[27] 'Making Pictures', in *Phoenix II*, 605.

[28] 'John Galsworthy', in *Study of Thomas Hardy and Other Essays*, 207–20 (p. 209). This essay first appeared in *Scrutinies*, collected by Edgell Rickword (London, 1982), 51–72.

[29] *Art*, 9. This emphasis on 'seeing and feeling' can be traced to Ruskin, who in *The Stones of Venice* argues that the artist's work is 'two-fold only; to see, to feel' (*Works*, xi. 49).

[30] William G. Bywater Jr., *Clive Bell's Eye* (Detroit, 1975), 35. See G. E. Moore, *Principia Ethica* (Cambridge, 1971), 189–94.   [31] *Art*, 88.

[32] Victor Burgin, *The End of Art Theory* (Basingstoke and London, 1986), 31.

of colour values, tensions, and so on. Historians of significant form have not, in general, taken into account the emotional vector involved: they have seen Bell's theory in terms of an austere and dehumanized concern for line and colour. Bell's own preference for the 'purer' forms of Romanesque and Byzantine art (as opposed to Gothic) has reinforced this view of his aesthetic theory. But a vital part of what constitutes significant form, for Bell, must inhere in the viewers themselves. If this were not the case, there would be no need to place so much emphasis, as Bell does, on adequate and inadequate responses to art. Bell's preference for Romanesque and Byzantine is not, in other words, at odds with an organicist emphasis on the sensuous or bodily element in the aesthetic response.

Lawrence is misguided, then, to see 'aesthetic ecstasy' in terms of a purely cerebral state, to read into Bell's discourse the same divorce from the sensuous which he sees in the statistics of scientific textbooks.[33] Bell's aesthetic response, as Bywater shows, corresponds not to the mental assimilation of 'facts', but to the intuitive grasp of the 'truth' that significant form simply *is* present. That it is present is incapable of proof; it cannot be supported by logical reasoning.[34] In the last piece Lawrence wrote, a review of Eric Gill's *Art Nonsense and Other Essays*, he made a final plea against the abstracting process which he saw to be fundamental to modern art-criticism, against the extrapolation of concepts, and the translation (and hence diminishing) of these concepts into other concepts: terms like 'Art' and 'Beauty', he argues, are 'words which represent deep emotional states in us . . . incapable of definition'.[35] The implication is that art-criticism *per se* is to be deplored, and this refusal to subject art to critical analysis means that Lawrence's position is not so very far from Bell's, even though he attacks significant form, in the 'Introduction', as a theory that revolves entirely around such unverifiable absolutes as 'rightness' and 'reality': 'I am Significant Form, and my unutterable name is Reality' (p. 566). For both Lawrence and Bell, then, the aesthetic is a kind of anti-aesthetic, cutting through theory. It becomes clear that Bell's aesthetic is far more relativistic than Lawrence suggests, and that, far from being a product of the mind–body split, it roots itself in the 'integrated' perception so central to Lawrence's philosophy.

That this emphasis on form does not imply the intellectuality which is often assumed to be intrinsic to the 'formalism' of Bell and Fry, is borne out by Read's views concerning the intuitive basis of form:

Form, though it can be analysed into intellectual terms like measure, balance, rhythm and harmony, is really intuitive in origin; it is not in the actual practice of

[33] 'Introduction to These Paintings', 574.   [34] Bywater, *Clive Bell's Eye*, 33.
[35] 'Review of *Art Nonsense and Other Essays* by Eric Gill', in *Phoenix*, 393–7 (p. 397). This review first appeared in *Book Collector's Quarterly*, 12 (Oct.–Dec. 1933), 1–7.

artists an intellectual product. It is rather emotion directed and defined . . . When we describe art as 'the will to form', we are not imagining an exclusively intellectual activity, but rather an exclusively instinctive one . . . Frankly, I do not know how we are to judge form except by the same instinct that creates it.[36]

The aesthetic act for Read, as for the Bloomsbury art-critics, is identifiable with the experience of the integrated self.

Both Lawrence and Bell, then, base their aesthetics on an organicist notion of intuition. There are, however, important differences between their particular versions of the organic. The main difference, as I indicated in the Introduction, is that significant form, like the Romantic concept of the symbol, but unlike Lawrence's concept of art, is based on an idealist notion of absolute spiritual truth. Bell takes a step which Lawrence tries not to take, from the integration of the cognitive and the sensuous within the aesthetic response, to a more spurious kind of integration, the identification of form in art with a transcendentalist notion of 'Being'.

3. The Life–Form Opposition: Bloomsbury and Expressionism

Claudia Morrison voices a characteristic response to Lawrence's aesthetics when she remarks that Lawrence 'only rarely commented on style and form, which was of far less importance than the art work's ultimate moral meaning, its relevance to and significance for life'.[37] She goes on to argue that 'The definition of art in terms of its content, the equation of its worth with its didactic message, was quite typical of Lawrence, and was one of the basic assumptions behind all his criticism' (p. 210). This life–form dichotomy has been central to accounts of modernist art theory generally, as well as to accounts of a Lawrence–Bloomsbury opposition. While Lawrence is seen to be the upholder of 'life', Bell and Fry are generally labelled 'formalists' in the sense of adherents to the autotelic or self-referential nature of art.[38] A typical instance of this, as we saw earlier in the chapter, is the conflation of Loerke, the sculptor in *Women in Love*, with the Bloomsbury art-critics, on account of his defence of an absolute aesthetic autonomy: 'It is a work of art, it is a picture of nothing, of absolutely nothing . . . *I* and my art, they have *nothing* to do with each other. My art stands in another world, I am in this world' (pp. 430–1).

Bloomsbury's most extreme asseveration of aesthetic autonomy occurs on page 25 of *Art*, where Bell claims that 'to appreciate a work of art we need

---

[36] *The Meaning of Art* (London, 1931), 8.   [37] Morrison, *Freud and the Critic*, 209.
[38] See. n. 2; in addition, see Bullen, introduction to *Art*, p. xxii, and Fuller, *Art and Psychoanalysis*, 146.

bring with us nothing from life, no knowledge of its ideas and affairs, no familiarity with its emotions'. The aesthetic emotion, he argues, 'springs, inhuman or super-human, from the heart of an abstract science'. Bell's idiom here, it must be conceded, sounds anti-Lawrentian in the extreme, yet for this single assertion there are a hundred others to contradict it. The book as a whole repeatedly betrays the fact that art for Bell never had the autonomy which this statement claims for it.

What numerous critics seem to have overlooked but Lawrence himself clearly recognized is that, although Bell is anxious to dissociate himself from an expressionistic theory of art according to which a painting might be seen to convey the artist's 'message', an expressionism of a quite different kind permeates his work through and through. The Expressionist movement, largely German, was at its height when Bell's *Art* was written, and much of what is found in the Continental Expressionist manifestos of this period is paralleled in Bell's so-called 'formalist' manifesto, on the levels both of argument and of detailed imagery. Kandinsky, for example, whose *Concerning the Spiritual in Art* was published in 1911 and appeared in English in 1914, directed his aesthetic wholly against representation, against illusionism and anecdote, as Bell does.[39] So much is not incompatible with a rigid formalism. But Bell also, like Kandinsky, assigns great importance in his work to the creating consciousness of the artist, and for him as for the Expressionists the creative impulse springs from a primal source within the individual which is uncontaminated by any academic knowledge of art, and which finds its way into the art-work without any rational mediation. So little has reason or willed construction to do with the creation of form for Kandinsky that he sees the artist as the divinely inspired copier of the forms which seem to spawn within him from some source that can never be plummeted:

I have never been able to bring myself to use a form which came to me by some logical way, which had not arisen purely within my feelings. I was unable to invent forms, and the sight of such forms always disgusts me. All the forms I ever used came of their own accord, they presented themselves to me already shaped, and all I had to do was to copy them . . .[40]

For Bell, as for the Expressionists, the creative impulse, the form, and the audience's response all cohere in a single, shared insight; for both, the emotion associated with this insight is one of 'ecstasy'; and for both, the insight has something to do with the noumenal. Bell's emphasis on 'that which lies behind the appearance of all things . . . the thing in itself, the ultimate reality' takes him a long way from a strictly formalist position. It can

---

[39] Wassily Kandinsky, *Concerning the Spiritual in Art*, trans. M. T. H. Sadler (London, 1977), 1–5.   [40] Cited in Wolf-Dieter Dube, *The Expressionists* (London, 1972), 112.

be found practically verbatim in many of the Expressionist documents. Franz Marc, co-editor with Kandinsky of the *Blue Rider Almanac* (1912), speaks of 'things as they really are, behind appearances',[41] and for another of the Expressionists, Alexej von Jawlensky, art offers 'that fleeting contact with the soul of things, with that Something, unsuspected and ignored by all, which trembles in every object of the material world'.[42] This preoccupation with the noumenal derives from Kant, and points to a certain strain of post-Romantic thought with which Lawrence could not comply. For here he saw evidence of another split, this time between the phenomenal and the noumenal, which again, like the mind–body split, prioritized the non-material. In this case, moreover, Lawrence was right to see such a split in Bell's aesthetic. The very circularity of Bell's theory of significant form (significant form is that which induces aesthetic emotion; aesthetic emotion is the emotion induced by significant form) implies a self-enclosed insulation from the phenomenal world. This kind of circularity is associated at several points in Lawrence's work with a spurious feeling of 'ecstasy' ('ecstasy', argues Birkin in *Women in Love*, 'is like going round in a squirrel-cage', p. 251) and therefore, implicitly, with idealism.

Lawrence's first encounter with 'ecstasy' in aesthetics was probably in 1909, when he read Arthur Machen's *Hieroglyphics: A Note upon Ecstasy in Literature* (1902).[43] Machen's treatise, though dealing with literature rather than painting, is so similar in every particular to Bell's *Art* that it is tempting to believe Bell had read it. For Machen, as for Bell, ecstasy is 'the touchstone which will infallibly separate the higher from the lower in literature'. For both writers, the crucial question is 'Is the incident significant or insignificant?', and for both of them, young children and 'primitive man before he was defiled by the horrors of civilisation' are the most susceptible to aesthetic emotion.[44] Machen describes Milton's *Lycidas* in the virtually apocalyptic terms which characterize Bell's work: 'Its austere and exquisite rapture

---

[41] Cited in Roger Cardinal, *Expressionism* (London, 1984), 67.

[42] Cited in Dube, *The Expressionists*, 115.

[43] See *Letters*, i. 107 (20 Jan. 1909), where Lawrence's response to Machen's emphasis on 'ecstasy' is somewhat sceptical. Lawrence was already, at this early stage, pinpointing an idealist tendency in aesthetics to which he objected: 'I say, all mysteries and possibilities lie in the things and happenings, so give us the things and happenings, and try just to show the flush of mystery in them, but don't begin with a mystery . . .'. But there is also in Machen an emphasis on the unconscious nature of literary creativity which probably influenced Lawrence. See Arthur Machen, *Hieroglyphics: A Note Upon Ecstasy in Literature* (London, 1960), 120: 'I am strangely inclined to think that all the quintessence of art is distilled from the subconscious and not from the conscious self; or, in other words, that the artificer seldom or never understands the ends and designs and spirit of the artist.' Compare Lawrence's views in *Studies in Classic American Literature*, examined in Chs. 2–3.

[44] *Hieroglyphics*, 21, 86, 90.

thrills one so that I could almost say: He who understands the mystery and the beauty of *Lycidas* understands also the final and eternal secret of art and life and man.' The emphasis, in Machen as in Bell, is on withdrawal from the 'common life', and Machen claims, as Bell does, that 'Art and Life are two different spheres'.[45]

These similarities between Machen and Bell may stem less from a direct influence of one upon the other than from the fact that both works are steeped in the quest for the noumenal which informed German Expressionism. For Kant, we are permanently screened off from the noumenal, in that the 'thing-in-itself' (*Ding-an-sich*) does not fulfil the conditions necessary to our being able to experience it: it is not characterized by the space and time which are the ineluctable features of the phenomenal world. Things-in-themselves cannot be mediated either by the Forms of our Sensibility or by the Forms of our Understanding.[46] The 'thing-in-itself' of Expressionism modified Kant's *Ding-an-sich* in that it allowed itself to be revealed through art; for the Expressionists (and Bell), art tears a rent in the veil of the phenomenal universe to reveal the reality beyond (art, declares Marc, is like 'tearing the veil from the face of a mysterious person'; it allows us to 'peep through the cracks in the world's surface').[47] Similarly for Machen, art deals not with the 'outward show' but with the 'inward spirit'; it is 'essential' rather than 'accidental'. Later in Machen's study we find the typically post-Romantic privileging of the symbol as a reconciliation of the concrete and temporal with the eternal and spiritual: 'No mere making of the likeness of the external shape will be our art, no veracious document will be our truth; but to us, initiated, the Symbol will be offered, and we shall take the Sign and adore, beneath the outward and perhaps unlovely accidents, the very Presence and eternal indwelling of God.'[48]

This version of the symbol, in supposedly 'redeeming' matter, implicitly subdues it before the Kantian noumenon, as I suggested in Chapter 2. The same is true of the images of light and crystal (another vestige of Romanticism) so prevalent in Expressionist documents (for Kandinsky, the 'white ray' of the spirit will bring about the regeneration of art).[49] In the work of the German Romantic Novalis, the crystal had been the quintessentially Romantic image, as the embodiment of the organic and the revelatory.[50] In

[45] Ibid. 83, 57, 30.

[46] Kant, *Prolegomena to Any Future Metaphysics*, trans. P. G. Lucas (Manchester, 1953), 75–9.

[47] Cited in V. H. Miesel (ed.), *Voices of German Expressionism* (London, 1973), 93.

[48] *Hieroglyphics*, 84, 153.

[49] Kandinsky, 'On the Question of Form', in *The Blaue Reiter Almanac*, ed. Wassily Kandinsky and Franz Marc, trans. H. Falkenstein (London, 1974), 147–87 (p. 147).

[50] See Bruce Haywood, *Novalis: The Veil of Imagery: A Study of the Poetic Works of Friedrich von Hardenberg (1772–1801)* (The Hague, 1959), 109, 114–15, 149.

Lawrence, on the other hand, the crystal is always a negative image, precisely because its transparency suggests a Kantian (or Platonic) denigration of the material world. It almost always occurs in 'disintegrative' contexts, as in the description of Gerald Crich, whose 'fair hair was a glisten like cold sunshine refracted through crystals of ice'.[51] Lawrence could not subscribe to the Kantian notion of an inaccessible ontological plane, still less to the Schopenhauerian modification of Kant which assumed that since time and space are necessary to difference, the noumenal must be one and undifferentiated.[52] A great deal of modernist writing expresses an impulse towards the unity underlying diversity, and indeed works such as Virginia Woolf's *The Waves* (1931) and *Between the Acts* (1941) are a sustained investigation of this theme. Modernism's preoccupation with the epiphanic moment (Woolf's 'moments of being', Joyce's 'epiphanies', and so on) implies this same unity underlying the heterogeneous, phenomenal, time-ridden world. But such epiphanic moments are conspicuously absent from Lawrence's discussions of art, in which heterogeneity and difference are all-important (as they had been for Nietzsche). For Lawrence, the material world in which we live is *already revealed*.[53]

It is the belief in the penetration to an 'ultimate reality' as the eternal and essential feature of art that can, for Bell, unite primitive art with Cézanne, and for the editors of the *Blue Rider Almanac* unite works by Cézanne, Van Gogh, or Picasso with tribal carvings, Alaskan textiles, Bavarian glass-pictures, and children's drawings, in what Kandinsky calls a 'synthesized' book.[54] For the Expressionists take the same radically anti-theoretical stance as Bell: 'Theory', announces Kandinsky, 'is the lamp which sheds light on

---

[51] *Women in Love*, 14. See also Lawrence's 'Review of *A Second Contemporary Verse Anthology*', in *Phoenix*, 322–6 (p. 324), where he describes an idealist culture in terms of living in a 'dome of crystal'. This review first appeared in the *New York Evening Post Literary Review*, 29 Sept. 1923.

[52] Arthur Schopenhauer, *The World as Will and Representation*, trans. E. F. J. Payne, 2 vols. (New York, 1969), i. 113: 'Again, the will is one not as a concept is one, for a concept originates only through abstraction from plurality; but it is one as that which lies outside time and space, outside the *principium individuationis*.'

[53] Lawrence's view of Bloomsbury Expressionism can be articulated in the terms of Worringer's distinction, in *Abstraction and Empathy*, between abstraction and empathy, and between geometrical and organic forms. Worringer's classification, like Lawrence's aesthetics, is based on the premiss that style is both psychological and social in origin, deriving from society's attitude towards Nature. Worringer's views corroborate Lawrence's theory that abstract, geometrical forms are favoured by societies preoccupied with non-material, i.e. spiritual, reality, whilst organic forms are adopted by societies finding spiritual satisfaction in the visible, material world. Lawrence's religiosity (and, in spite of his criticisms of Bell's *Art*, he is far from incapable of sounding evangelical himself), is of course of the second kind, bound to the phenomenal world. See Wilhelm Robert Worringer, *Abstraction and Empathy: A Contribution to the Psychology of Style*, trans. M. Bullock (London, 1953). This work was first published as *Abstraktion und Einfühlung* (Munich, 1908).

[54] Cited by Klaus Lankheit in the introduction to *The Blaue Reiter Almanac*, 11–48 (p. 37).

the petrified ideas of yesterday and of the more distant past.'[55] As in Bell, this anti-intellectualism leads to a disturbing élitism for the Expressionists (a position of 'either you appreciate art or you don't'), for the consequence of any aesthetic which rejects theory (i.e. which rejects aesthetic laws) is the notion that taste cannot be coerced. These critics all use a messianic language of exaltation, of peaks and heights and apexes and spiritual pyramids: Bell's 'superb peaks of aesthetic exaltation' and 'cold, white peaks of art' are paralleled by Kandinsky's acute-angled triangle, at the apex of which stands the solitary but privileged artist, while the 'vulgar herd' mills around the base.[56] These comparisons show that Bell's work, far from articulating the absolute formal autonomy which so many art-historians have attributed to it, and which is traceable to only a few overquoted (and perhaps deliberately shocking) statements, is saturated with the Expressionistic language of its period.

Quite apart from these parallels with German Expressionism, the details and technicalities of Bell's argument betray an expressionist position time and again. Bell cannot accept, for example, that copies can possess significant form, on the grounds that 'the actual lines and colours and spaces in a work of art are caused by something in the mind of the artist which is not present in the mind of the imitator'.[57] His inability to sever the art-work from its creator is also shown in his need to calibrate individual artists: a rough sketch by Cézanne is *de facto* better than any of the work of Cézanne's disciples. By pages 277–8 of *Art*, Bell feels confident to tell his readers that 'For thousands of years men have expressed in art their ultra-human emotions, and have found in it that food by which the spirit lives'. The 'inhuman or superhuman' of page 25 has, by some mysterious sleight-of-hand, become 'ultra-human'. The commonly held belief that Bell's theory is an austerely formalistic one is, then, belied at every turn by his language of visions and spiritual insight.

Roger Fry, frequently classified with Bell as a rigid formalist, posits expressionistic theories even more openly than Bell: in our reaction to a work of art, 'there is the consciousness of purpose, the consciousness of a peculiar relation of sympathy with the man who made this thing in order to arouse precisely the sensations we experience'. He goes still further:

And when we come to the higher works of art, where sensations are so arranged that they arouse in us deep emotions, this feeling of a special tie with the man who expressed them becomes very strong. We feel that he has expressed something which was latent in us all the time, but which we never realised, that he has revealed us to ourselves in revealing himself. And this recognition of purpose is, I believe, an essential part of the aesthetic judgment proper.[58]

[55] *Concerning the Spiritual in Art*, 12.
[56] *Art*, 32, 33; *Concerning the Spiritual in Art*, 6, 3.   [57] *Art*, 60.
[58] 'An Essay in Aesthetics', in *Vision and Design*, 11–25 (p. 20).

Both Fry and Bell, moreover, though they had absorbed the ethos of Expressionism, rested uneasily with abstract art throughout their respective careers, a fact which in itself casts doubt on their emphasis on formal autonomy. In a review of 1913, written while he was meditating *Art*, Bell refers derisively to Kandinsky's 'patches of colour and scribble'.[59] Fry, on the other hand, found his initial hostility to Kandinsky softening on expressionistic grounds: 'I cannot any longer doubt the possibility of emotional expression by such abstract visual designs', he confessed in 1913.[60] It is ironic that the fullest surviving documentation of Lawrence's reaction to a specific instance of Bloomsbury art should relate to one of the very few abstract works ventured by Bloomsbury artists (Fry's own experiments with abstract art numbered no more than four or five), Duncan Grant's scroll which presented rectangular coloured shapes through an aperture (or so the plan was), to the accompaniment of Bach's music.[61]

'Reality' intrudes, then, into Bell's aesthetic time and again. Significant form is, as its historians have always recognized, opposed to *description*, but what it substitutes for this is *expression*, not an absolute formal autonomy. Bloomsbury aesthetics, in the final analysis, is neither rationalistic nor strictly formalistic (if formalism is seen to imply an exclusive concern for line and colour). Bell's theory of significant form is both intuitive and expressionistic in basis.

It is, then, entirely inaccurate to see Lawrence's reaction to Bloomsbury aesthetics in terms of a life–form distinction. Such a distinction cannot cope with the complexity of Bloomsbury aesthetics, nor with the fact that (as the next two chapters will try to demonstrate) Lawrence and the Bloomsbury art-critics concur on so many issues. For although Lawrence never subscribed to the Kantian legacy of Romanticism which survived in the theory of significant form, his aesthetics concurred with Bloomsbury's in practically every other respect. An indication of the extent to which Lawrence and Bloomsbury overlapped is the fact that, as I have already pointed out, Cézanne was, for both, the most significant figure in art-history, and for very similar reasons (Cézanne's importance is assessed in Chapter 6). The next chapter seeks to rearticulate the terms of the Lawrence–Bloomsbury debate and to place at its centre a new opposition between life or form (the two become curiously interchangeable) on the one hand, and 'text' on the other. Any supposed opposition between them then becomes less significant than their shared distrust of any art which premisses itself on a naïve–mimetic model of language. 'Life' is not the enemy, so much as logocentrism.

[59] 'The Allied Artists', *The Nation* (2 Aug. 1913), 676–7 (p. 677).
[60] 'Post-Impressionism Again', *The Nation* (29 Mar. 1913), 1060–1 (p. 1061).
[61] See *Letters*, ii. 262–4 (27 Jan. 1915).

5

LAWRENCE AND BLOOMSBURY II:
ART VERSUS TEXT

> We exist only in the Word, which is beaten out thin to cover, gild, and hide all things.
>
> ('Etruscan Places')

Lawrence and his Bloomsbury contemporaries shared many of the same concerns, and, in particular, they set out to dispel the myth of a naïvely mimetic art, seeing realism to be complicit with what would today be described as a logocentric model of language. It now seems, as I noted earlier, that this idea of a naïvely mimetic realism was something of a shibboleth, and that Lawrence and the Bloomsbury critics deliberately presented it in crude and reductive terms. It is unlikely that unproblematic, one-to-one correspondence between elements of language and world was ever really assumed by realist art, that art ever aspired to *be* the world, rendering itself curiously redundant, in the way that many modernist art theorists suggest. But this is what Lawrence and his Bloomsbury contemporaries tried to argue in order to further the cause of Post-Impressionism and other forms of modern art.

1. The Photographic Text

> He [Sir Lawrence Alma-Tadema] noticed that, in any proprietary article, it was of the first importance that the customer should be saved all the trouble. He wisely adopted the plan, since exploited by the Kodak Company, 'You press the button, and we do the rest'.
>
> (Roger Fry, 'The Case of the Late Sir Lawrence Alma-Tadema, O.M.', 1913)

> Through many ages, mankind has been striving to register the image on the retina *as it is*: no more glyphs and hieroglyphs. We'll have the real objective reality. And we have succeeded. As soon as we succeed, the kodak is invented, to prove our success. Could lies come out of a black box, into which nothing but light had entered? Impossible! It takes life to tell a lie.
>
> (D. H. Lawrence, 'Art and Morality', 1925)

The camera, as everyone knows, cannot lie. 'Well', the Victorian
painters may have said, 'so here is truth—scientific truth: let us see if
we cannot do as well, adding what the camera cannot give—sentiment. We will give photographic representation flavoured with sentiment. That is art.'

(Clive Bell, *Landmarks in Nineteenth Century Painting*, 1927)

The impact of the camera on late nineteenth- and early twentieth-century
aesthetic theory has added to the confusion and muddle surrounding the
life–form debate, whilst at the same time providing a clue to the unravelling
of the issues at stake; for the camera arrived at a time when art had, according to traditional art-historians, been moving closer and closer to an objective
registering of 'optical truth', having escaped the constraints of text (of text as
lesson) to which medieval art had been subject. The camera both guaranteed
the worth of the 'pseudo-photographic' paintings produced from the Renaissance onwards, with their quattrocento perspective, and, paradoxically,
rendered them redundant. The camera had, it seemed, erased all traces of
human error and interference: here at last was 'truth', 'life', 'reality', undistorted
by the limitations of human vision or painterly technique and, more importantly, uncontaminated by the language (and its concomitant morality)
with which human beings had sought to make sense of their alien, material
surroundings. But if the great achievement of the camera was that of
non-discursivity (a singularly 'modernist' achievement), why was it that
'modernists' like Bell, Fry, and Lawrence all objected so strongly to pseudo-
photographic art?

One answer to this question lies in the fact that, according to these critics
at least, the pseudo-photographic painters of the Victorian period had entered
into a conspiracy to conceal their own narrative strategies. By some mysterious sleight-of-hand, these painters, whilst being seen, by modernist critics
at least, to claim for their works a pristine photographic freedom from words,
had in fact steeped them in narrative. So convincingly did they persuade
viewers that they were *not* guilty of doing so, paradoxically using the camera
as witness to their innocence, that those reacting against their art, like Bell
and Fry, seemed to be reacting against 'life' itself. For photography is, of
course, the one language in which, in a curious sense, the signifier partakes,
in an essential way, of the signified; it is a kind of logocentrism turned literal.
Yet this fact is a highly misleading one; like all languages, photography is still
an interpretative strategy, part of a signifying practice. The same is true of
pseudo-photographic art.

Walter Benjamin's 'A Small History of Photography' (1931), sheds some
light on this subtle intermeshing of photograph and text. Benjamin detects

a crucial shift in photographic art, coinciding with its absorption into the world of industry and commerce. 'The first people to be reproduced', he explains, 'entered the visual space of photography with their innocence intact, uncompromised by captions.'[1] The camera, throwing up as it did details and textures and angles to which our conscious vision was unaccustomed, seemed, in its earliest phase, to have gained access to what Benjamin terms the 'optical unconscious':

For it is another nature that speaks to the camera than to the eye: other in the sense that a space informed by human consciousness gives way to a space informed by the unconscious. Whereas it is a commonplace that, for example, we have some idea what is involved in the act of walking, if only in general terms, we have no idea at all what happens during the fraction of a second when a person *steps out*. Photography, with its devices of slow motion and enlargement, reveals the secret. It is through photography that we first discover the existence of this optical unconscious, just as we discover the instinctual unconscious through psychoanalysis. (p. 243)

Benjamin's 'stepping out', which normally eludes our all-too-organized perceptions, seems to correspond to the 'inbetweenness' of which Lawrence speaks in 'Morality and the Novel' (1925). For Lawrence, art exists in what he terms 'the fourth dimension', 'in-between everything' (p. 171); rather than operating within the parameters of any given discipline, it challenges disciplinary boundaries. Oddly enough, however, Lawrence sees the photograph not in terms of *escape* from such boundaries, but as a reinforcement of them: 'The African fetish-statues have no movement, visually represented. Yet one little motionless wooden figure stirs more than all the Parthenon frieze. It sits in the place where no kodak can snap it.'[2] Here the photographic frame has become metaphor for any closed system or discipline, and the statue is seen to be art by virtue of the fact that it knows no containment or closure; it somehow overspills these disciplines and frameworks, residing in a kind of Derridian 'otherness'. For Lawrence does not refer here to the photograph in the first decade of its existence, preceding its industrialization; rather, he refers to the rise of the family photograph album, the Kodak snapshot, the picture postcard, in short to the permeation of photography by commerce of which Benjamin speaks in his essay. The increasing need for 'captions' seems to have marked the gradual assimilation of this new and strange phenomenon, the photograph, into the old epistemological structures. Where the camera might have revolutionized painting, through its access to

---

[1] Walter Benjamin, 'A Small History of Photography', in *One Way Street and Other Writings*, trans. Edmund Jephcott and Kingsley Shorter (London, 1978), 240–57 (p. 244). This essay was first published as 'Kleine Geschichte der Photographie', *Literarische Welt*, vii (1931).
[2] 'Art and Morality', in *Study of Thomas Hardy and Other Essays*, 168.

previously undetected areas of experience and perception, it allowed itself
instead, during the first half-century of its existence, to be absorbed back
into the discursive mode of the paintings which had sought to emulate it.
Those images which had at first seemed bewilderingly independent of their
beholders' assumptions and expectations, were slowly being converted into
sites of meaning.

Camera and 'text', then, are intimately linked. The connection is repeatedly made in Bell's *Art*, in Fry's art-criticism, and in Lawrence's writings on
art. All three critics wish to alert their readers to what they see to be the
dangerous complicity between, on the one hand, the camera's ability to
distort and misrepresent, and on the other the disproportionately high status
accorded to photography as a species of truth. See, for example, this famous
passage from 'Etruscan Places', where the camera is directly linked to the
constriction of paraphrase:

What, after all, is the horsiness of a horse? . . . What is it, that will never be put
into words? For a man who sees, sees not as a camera does when it takes a snapshot,
not even as a cinema-camera, taking its succession of instantaneous snaps; but
in a curious rolling flood of vision, in which the image itself seethes and rolls;
and only the mind *picks out* certain factors which *shall* represent the image seen.
(pp. 72–3)

The illusionist painters, as both Lawrence and the Bloomsbury art-critics are
at pains to show, were not even presenting the photographic 'realism' which
they were supposedly claiming as their prerogative.[3] This emerges very
clearly from Roger Fry's essay 'The Art of the Bushmen'. According to
Fry's analysis of an early Assyrian battle scene, 'the battle is schematic, all
the soldiers of one side are in profile to right, all the soldiers of the opposing
side are in profile to left. The whole scene is perfectly clear to the intelligence, it follows the mental image of what a battle ought to be, but is entirely
unlike what a battle ever is.' The art of the Bushmen, on the other hand,
concentrates on 'actual appearance' rather than 'lucidity of statement':
'Extremely complicated poses are rendered with the same ease as the more
frequent profile view, and . . . momentary actions are treated with photographic verisimilitude.' Photography can, if used as its earliest practitioners
used it, help the viewer to transcend his/her 'textual' prejudices:

[3] Much earlier, in 'Art and the Individual', written in 1908, Lawrence had been telling his
readers that, through visual art, 'they are purposely led to the edge of the great darkness,
where no word-lights twinkle'. But he makes it clear that it is a certain kind of 'transparent'
language which is rejected. The viewers 'had rather listen to a great din of a battle-piece and
exclaim "There, the trumpet sounds charge!, hark, you can tell it's horses galloping!".' He
calls this a 'tin-pan clash-of-swords imitation' ('Art and the Individual', in *Study of Thomas
Hardy and Other Essays*, 133–42 (p. 141)).

Most curious of all are the cases of which Fig. 4 is an example, of animals trotting, in which the gesture is seen by us to be true only because our slow and imperfect vision has been helped out by the instantaneous photograph. Fifty years ago we should have rejected such a rendering as absurd; we now know it to be a correct statement of one movement in the action of trotting.[4]

Unlike the camera in its earliest stages, illusionist art, according to Fry in his study of Cézanne, equates reality with those aspects of it seized upon by the everyday vision for the purposes of day-to-day living.[5] It presents objects in convenient profiles, people and animals in postures easily amenable to the human mind, and what pretends to be a momentary scene is in fact carefully arranged by the artist. In this sense, as Fry explains in 'An Essay in Aesthetics', illusionist art is essentially a visual presentation of 'labels': 'In actual life the normal person really only reads the labels as it were on the objects around him and troubles no further. Almost all the things which are useful in any way put on more or less this cap of invisibility' (p. 16). Such invisibility is for Fry the very antithesis of art. The same preoccupation informs Virginia Woolf's biography of a dog, *Flush* (1933), where the baby, each time he adds a new word to his vocabulary, is removed a stage further from Flush's world of pristine sensations, of light and colour and reflection uncontaminated by language; the child learns to 'read' appearances and thus to live life at one remove. It is as though vision itself becomes academized or institutionalized, just as the paintings of the Salon des Refusés in Paris eventually found their way into the official salon.

Lawrence's affinities with Cubism can be seen in the context of this reaction against pseudo-photographic painting. Picasso's *Demoiselles d'Avignon*, begun in 1906, heralded the Cubist movement in its synthesis of numerous impressions of an image seen from different angles; it was an attempt at the 'simultaneous' vision that the camera could never achieve. Picasso, like Lawrence and the Bloomsbury art-critics, was to find in African sculpture the inspiration for this subversion of the photographic vision. Of the works of his so-called primitivist phase, Picasso claimed that each figure could easily be realized in terms of free-standing sculpture.[6] Yet, like Cézanne's still-lifes (a second important influence on both Lawrence and Cubism), Picasso's *Demoiselles*, whilst on one level attempting a more comprehensive *representation* than pseudo-photographic art could achieve, none the less remained, on another level, pre-eminently 'painted' and profoundly anti-naturalistic; in this way, it could convey the utmost complexity without completing the picture. Illusionism, in deflecting attention away from the

---

[4] 'The Art of the Bushmen', in *Vision and Design*, 58–60.
[5] *Cézanne: A Study of His Development* (London, 1927), 58.
[6] *Picasso sculpteur: Cahiers d'art*, ed. Julio Gonzalez (Paris, 1943), 189.

painterly trace itself, was seen to cheat the viewer with a kind of false perspicuity, creating the illusion of a denotative simplicity, a one-to-one correspondence with objects in the 'outside' world; in this sense, it claimed an omniscience, a god-like view of things, which it did not in actuality possess. Lawrence expresses the same notion in 'Art and Morality' in terms of 'an isolated absolute, corresponding with a universe of isolated absolutes' (p. 165). This absolute picture is a falsehood, for as Lawrence himself reminds us, 'Realism is just one of the arbitrary views man takes of man'.[7]

In Chapter 3, we saw how Lawrence reproached Freud on the grounds that, whilst claiming to talk *about* the unconscious, he did not allow for the workings of the unconscious in his own ostensibly neutral discourse. For Lawrence, Freud's pseudo-scientific discourse shares the false perspicuity of pseudo-photographic art. Where mimetic language, according to modernists like Lawrence, makes claims concerning the art-work which assume equivalence, sameness, between work and world, art sets up an equivalence of a different kind, whereby the painted or written image both is and is not the 'thing' painted or written.[8] In Etruscan art, Lawrence argues, 'a lion could be at the same moment also a goat, and not a goat'.[9] In being neither 'something' in the usual sense nor 'nothing', art, for Lawrence, occupies a site in-between. This 'betweenness' is seen to be exemplified above all in Cézanne's work, an idea explored in Chapter 6.

2. *Discursive* versus *Painterly Art*

One way out of the art versus life deadlock in which critical understanding of Lawrence and Bloomsbury seems to have found itself is to adopt a semiotic approach to art. In this I am much indebted to Norman Bryson's *Word and Image: French Painting of the Ancien Régime*; in pointing away from the usual history of successive visual styles towards an alternative semantic

---

[7] 'Introduction to *Mastro-don Gesualdo* by Giovanni Verga', in *Phoenix II*, 279–88 (p. 281). This essay was first published in the Jonathan Cape *Traveller's Library* edition of Mastro-don Gesualdo (London, 1928).

[8] See Roman Jakobson, cited by Ben Brewster in 'From Shklovsky to Brecht: A Reply', *Screen*, 15/2 (1974), 87: 'Why need it be stressed that the sign is not confused with the object? Because alongside the immediate awareness of the identity of sign and object (A is A'), the immediate awareness of the absence of this awareness (A is not A') is necessary; this antinomy is inevitable, for without contradiction there is no play of signs, the relation between the concept and the sign becomes automatic, the course of events ceases and consciousness of reality dies.' This kind of equivalence is also central to a more Heideggerian aesthetic tradition. Merleau-Ponty, for example, argues that 'no grape was ever what it was in the most figurative painting and ... no painting, no matter how abstract, can get away from Being ... even Caravaggio's grape is the grape itself' (Maurice Merleau-Ponty, *The Primacy of Perception* (Chicago, 1968), 188).   [9] 'Etruscan Places', 68.

history, Bryson's study is invaluable, bringing as it does a whole vocabulary of semiotics to bear upon traditional art-historical language. Bryson explains how traditional art-historians see the spectrum of art to range from the discursive or textual at one end, to the 'real' at the other. In other words, received art-history places the hieroglyph at one end of the aesthetic spectrum, and, at the other, illusionistic still-life, epitomized in the legendary grapes of Zeuxis, the ancient Greek painter who painted a vine so lifelike that the birds flew down to peck at it. Bryson substitutes for the textual–real distinction a textual–painterly one. He retains the hieroglyph as the embodiment of the discursive or textual, but places at the opposite pole from this 'the irreducible life of the material signifier—the *painterly trace*, and as an exemplary case of that trace, the asemantic brushwork of abstract expressionism'.[10] He chooses Jackson Pollock's *Enchanted Garden* to illustrate this extreme of painterliness or 'figurality'. Western art-history can now be read, he argues, as a history of 'ceaseless conflict between the image as it seeks fullness and autonomy, and the renunciatory impulse which refuses the image that primal plenitude, and seeks its conversion from an end to a means, a means to meaning' (p. xvi).

Whilst finding Bryson's study an enlightening and enabling one, I would none the less wish to qualify his description of the Jackson Pollock in terms of 'the irreducible component of the image, that which can never belong to anything but the image itself: its paint' (p. 27). I would question the notion that the visual arts can somehow erase language completely from their domain. For if the notion of pure 'realism' (art as life), of a naïvely mimetic art, is a shibboleth used by Romantic or modernist art theorists against which to define their own enterprise, so the notion of pure art (uncontaminated by life or reference) is, in my view, a shibboleth. It seems to me that Jackson Pollock's work, whilst supremely painterly, none the less lays itself wide open, beneath the human gaze, to the incursion of discourse. Abstract art belies Bryson's notion of a struggle between the painterly and the discursive, in so far as its painterliness is not incompatible with, indeed seems logically bound up with, an extreme discursivity; for abstract art is a perfect example of the 'semantic vacuum' (Bryson's term) into which discourse can flood. In other words, the more pure painterliness attempts to assert itself in a work, the more the work lays itself open to the invasion of the text.

Painterliness, it seems, can never be completely liberated from discourse in the way that Bryson suggests when he speaks of the rare occasions in art when the image has been granted 'all the plenary autonomy enjoyed by the

---

[10] Norman Bryson, *Word and Image: French Painting of the Ancien Régime* (Cambridge, 1981), 27.

objects of the world' (p. xvi). To what does this plenary autonomy refer? Is this a Utopian dream of pure paint, pure signifier uncontaminated by meaning? If so, it is comparable to the dream of the pure signified (referred to in Bryson's preface), a dream very nearly fulfilled when the birds tried to peck at Zeuxis's lifelike grapes (p. xv). Numerous art-critics have been quick to point to a naïvety in the notion of realism, whereby the sign is assumed to be transparent, allowing uninhibited access to the referent.[11] Yet the concept of a pure formalism, of a pure signifier uncontaminated by reference, cannot be put into practice.

Where Bryson distinguishes between painterliness and discursivity, I would prefer to distinguish two different models of discourse. There must be some difference between the way in which an overtly painterly work like the Pollock is discursive and the way in which a non-painterly work (like the Zeuxis grapes) is discursive. To adopt Bryson's notion of the 'controlling grasp of the signified', I would suggest that the controlling grasp of a *fixed* signified, a one-to-one signifier–signified correspondence, *can* be eluded in painting, but that this is at the cost of admitting multiple signifieds, a rich plurality of meaning. This distinction serves to clarify Bryson's analysis of Vermeer's *Young Woman Seated at a Virginal*, in which he distinguishes between two kinds of brushwork:

> Whereas the representation of the lace in the girl's dress is based on a supposed one-to-one isomorphism between the 'original' and its 'copy', the representation of the gilding round the picture asserts considerable latitude of transcription: there is a gulf between the original and its representation . . . The signifier is visibly present on the canvas . . .[12]

The fact that the signifier is 'visibly present' on the canvas creates a rift between work and world into which multiple meanings can seep. The transparency of the Zeuxis grapes, on the other hand, is such that the painted grapes are supposedly a window on to some 'real' bunch of grapes outside art: the one simulates, aspires to *be*, the other. The grapes try to renounce their own painterliness altogether, to merge into, become, their signified. They attempt to conceal the conditions of their own production as image, and it is this which is the guarantee of the naïve-mimetic model of language I discussed in Chapter 2. Realist art can thus be rearticulated as the visual analogue of this naïve-mimetic model, whereby each of the images in a painting claims a one-to-one correspondence with an identical, isomorphic image in the outside world. This connection between the photograph or pseudo-photographic painting and mimetic discourse is a connection which Lawrence, Bell, and Fry all make.

---

[11] See e.g. Burgin, *The End of Art Theory*, 11.   [12] *Word and Image*, 24.

When paintings are openly figural or painterly (i.e. the more they draw attention to their own *production* as images), the more likely they are to be permeated by language of a second kind, by what I called in Chapter 2 differential language. They are no longer anchored to a precise signified through a close physical similarity to that signified, and this throws the viewer's attention back on to the rhetoric of the painting itself. Bryson's 'painterly' painting corresponds to Barthes's 'writerly' writing, which draws attention to its own linguistic textures. In *S/Z*, Barthes distinguishes between the *'lisible'* or 'readerly' classic text, which makes its readers into passive consumers, and the *'scriptible'* or 'writerly' text, which invites its readers to an active participation in the production of meanings which are infinite and inexhaustible.[13] Painterly or writerly art is not premissed on a one-to-one correspondence between the elements of art-work and world. It is premissed instead on a different model of textuality, the result in art of drawing attention to the materiality of the written or painted text (phones, pigment), which approaches the 'text' in Barthes's sense of music. Barthes contrasts this with the 'realism' which he sees to rest upon 'the supposed exteriority of the signified to the signifier'.[14] It remains true, of course, and Bryson is quick to point it out, that the conception of the 'real' changes with different cultures and periods, but this does not detract from the argument that 'realism' must involve adherence to the 'realistic' conventions of a given period, whereby the images are *seen* to simulate something exterior to themselves. This connection between realism and logocentrism is vital to an understanding both of Bloomsbury formalism and of Lawrence's own art-criticism.

3. Formalism-Realism

Michael Phillipson, in *Painting, Language and Modernity* (1985), gives a neat definition of formalism as 'that approach which begins with a separation between "form" and "content", subsequently privileges form over content, and finally subsumes content within form'. He goes on to argue that 'reductive in intent it seeks to establish the "essence" of painting in its formal features (the application of colour to a flat two-dimensional supported surface)' (p. 35). To apply this definition to the 'formalists' Clive Bell and Roger Fry would be to say that the pure signifier, pure pigment and canvas, was their concern (unlikely in view of the fact that both of them engaged very seriously with the whole question of literature and repeatedly attempted to incorporate literature into their aesthetics; unlikely, too, in view of the fact that both of

---

[13] *S/Z* (Seuil, 1970; trans. Richard Miller, London, 1975).
[14] Barthes, 'The Last Word on Robbe-Grillet', in *Critical Essays*, 198.

them were wary of abstract art.[15] Instead, Phillipson's definition of formalism could be turned inside out, to formulate *realism* as 'that approach which begins with a separation of "content" and "form", subsequently privileges content over form, and finally subsumes form within content'. This is certainly true of the Zeuxis grapes, where all formal concerns are channelled towards rendering as closely as possible a particular bunch of grapes 'outside' art. And indeed, in a curious way, this latter definition of realism would be more accurate than Phillipson's definition of formalism. For where realism, as Barthes argues, implicitly *splits* the sign into a signifier and an imagined signified, one inside the painting, one outside, formalism does not make this split. *This* is arguably the most crucial difference between the two. It is of course intellectually, and perhaps aesthetically, satisfying to have two schools of art-criticism, one which privileges form (as signifier) and one which privileges content (as signified), and many critics seem to fall into the trap of seeing this as a kind of logical necessity. But the incorporation of semiotics into literary and art criticism should by now have shown the way to an alternative formalist–realist distinction. 'Realism' can be rearticulated in terms of the mimetic model of language (in painting or writing) which attempts to *split* the sign and to deflect the viewer's attention away from the painting/writing on to the world itself (a piece of journalistic writing would be a good example of this kind of logocentrism). Formalism can then be seen as that art which draws attention back on to itself rather than away to specific signifieds, and which in this way opens itself up to semantic complexity, to what I have called the 'differential' model of language.

In Chapter 2, I argued that Lawrence's account of the organicist aesthetic, in refusing to split the sign into a signifier inside the painting and a signified implicitly outside the painting, initiates another kind of split within the sign, which problematizes the relationship between signifier and signified. But formalism also refuses to make the signifier–signified split, and this should immediately alert us to the fact that Lawrence may not have been as far away from Bloomsbury as he thought he was. It also points to an important link between modernist 'organicism' and structuralist models of art. In a letter of 1913, Fry puts forward the view that 'In proportion as poetry becomes more

---

[15] See Fry's review of *Art*, 'A New Theory of Art', *The Nation* (7 Mar. 1914), 937–9, where he expresses a wish that Bell would include literature in his theory and thereby 'open up the possibility of a true art of illustration'. See also Clive Bell, 'The Allied Artists', *The Nation* (2 Aug. 1913), 676–7 (p. 677), where he dismisses Kandinsky's 'patches of colour and scribble'. David Dowling, in *Bloomsbury Aesthetics and the Novels of Forster and Woolf* (London and Basingstoke, 1985), records in some detail the Bloomsbury art-critics' desire to include literature in their aesthetic theories, and their hasty recantations whenever they felt that they had taken the analogy with literature too far. This can be interpreted as a desire to include 'differential' language in their aesthetic, but not 'mimetic' language.

intense the content is entirely remade by the form and has no separate value at all. You see the sense of poetry is analogous to the things represented in painting.'[16] Elsewhere he explains that 'the purpose of literature is the creation of structures *which have for us the feeling of reality*, and that these structures are self-contained, self-sufficing, and not to be valued by their references to what lies outside' (my emphasis).[17] Though placed within a different critical lexicon, Fry is in fact putting forward a tentatively structuralist model of literature. Here he actually uses the term 'structure', where often he uses a phrase more typical of modernist aesthetics, 'organic whole'. It is of course the case that the expression 'organic whole' can carry all kinds of undesirable connotations of destiny and natural evolution which the term 'structure' does not generally carry. None the less, there is an important sense in which many of the arguments laid down by modernist aestheticians paralleled those being worked out by Continental linguisticians, though their terminology was often less rigorous and less systematic. Above all else, Fry seems to be positing a relational model of meaning, rather than attempting to banish signification as a whole from the art-work: 'There is, of course, the pleasure of rhythmic utterance, but this is already concerned with relations, and even this is, I believe, accessory to the emotion aroused by rhythmic changes of states of mind due to the meanings of the words.'[18]

4. Roger Fry: 'Imaginative' and 'Instinctive' Experiences

It seems necessary to look at Fry's so-called 'formalist' aesthetics again. It hinges on his careful distinction between what he terms 'instinctive' and 'imaginative' experiences. He illustrates his distinction in terms of two possible responses to an ordinary street-scene: 'If we look at the street itself', he explains, 'we are almost sure to adjust ourselves in some way to its actual existence. We recognise an acquaintance, and wonder why he looks so dejected . . .' If, on the other hand, we see the scene reflected in a mirror, it 'takes on the visionary quality, and we become true spectators, not selecting what we will see, but seeing everything equally, and thereby we come to notice a number of appearances and relations of appearances, which would have escaped our vision before'.[19] It is clear from this distinction that the devices of 'laying bare' and 'defamiliarization' (*ostranenie*), key devices for the Russian Formalists, are also central to Fry's own theory of art. Similarly,

[16] Letter to G. L. Dickinson (1913), cited in Virginia Woolf, *Roger Fry: A Biography* (London, 1940), 183.
[17] 'Some Questions in Esthetics', in *Transformations* (London, 1926), 1–43 (p. 8).
[18] Ibid. 5.   [19] 'An Essay in Aesthetics', in *Vision and Design*, 13.

Lawrence sees in free verse a way of dehabitualizing language: 'We can get rid of the stereotyped movements and the old hackneyed associations of sound or sense. We can break down those artificial conduits and canals through which we do so love to force our utterance. We can break the stiff neck of habit.'[20]

The distinction between a mimetic and a differential model of language can, I think, shed some light on Fry's imaginative–instinctive distinction. It is also the key to an understanding of Lawrence's distinction between 'art-speech' and ordinary discourse, Bell's distinction between 'significant form' and 'labels', and, ultimately, the distinction between a modernist aesthetics and Victorian illusionism. But where Lawrence sometimes tries to argue for a difference in *kind* between 'art-speech' and ordinary language, Fry seems to acknowledge that the difference must come, ultimately, from the way in which a work is *viewed* or *read*. He transfers the locus of the aesthetic from the symbols themselves to the viewers, to audience-response: it is possible, he argues, to view art and the world 'instinctively' (discursively or mimetically, in terms of 'labels') and 'imaginatively' (differentially, in terms of the complex patterns of signification which are set in motion as soon as one-to-one correspondence between signifier and signified is rejected). For Fry, the 'imaginative' vision is that which transforms *any* fragment of 'life' into a work of art. In linguistic terms, it promotes the shift from a mimetic to a differential reading. His argument is that viewers generally respond to illusionist paintings, like those of Sargent, as they would respond to a family snapshot or a street-scene. This argument is, I think, a highly questionable one, though most modernist aestheticians have recourse to it as a foil for their own theories. Having set up this illusionist–modernist distinction, however, Fry goes on, in various parts of his work, to deconstruct it by suggesting that any work of art, indeed anything at all, can be viewed 'imaginatively' rather than 'instinctively'. Even a street-scene, he argues, is *potentially* a rudimentary work of art; it is all a question of the viewer's framing, 'imaginative' vision, which takes what would otherwise be 'labels' out of their everyday, one-to-one context.[21] Compare Lawrence in the preface to *New Poems*:

---

[20] 'Preface to the American edition of *New Poems*', in *Phoenix*, 221.

[21] 'An Essay in Aesthetics', 13–14. The desire to escape the 'commonplace', which occurs in the aesthetics of both Fry and Lawrence, perpetuates, via Ruskin and others, the Wordsworthian notion of childhood visions which 'fade into the light of common day'; but Bloomsbury as a whole was also influenced by Bergson, who argued, 'We estimate the talent of a novelist by the power with which he lifts out of the common domain, to which language had thus brought them down, feelings and ideas to which he strives to restore, by adding detail to detail, their original and living individuality' (Henri Bergson, *Time and Free-Will: An Essay in the Immediate Data of Consciousness*, trans. F. L. Pogson (London, 1910), 164). This work was first published as *Essai sur les données immédiates de la conscience* (Paris, 1889).

Our birds sing on the horizons. They sing out of the blue, beyond us, or out of the quenched night. They sing at dawn and sunset. Only the poor, shrill, tame canaries whistle while we talk. The wild birds begin before we are awake, or as we drop into dimness, out of waking. Our poets sit by the gateways, some by the east, some by the west. As we arrive and as we go out our hearts surge with response. But whilst we are in the midst of life, we do not hear them.[22]

Here Lawrence's horizons are analogous to Fry's frame. The frame is the quickest and simplest way of foregrounding or defamiliarizing. But, as Fry recognizes, it also presupposes an audience or, in other words, an 'imaginative' respondent. In fact, one could argue that the audience or the frame (the two are synonymous) is the only real prerequisite for the shift from the mimetic or logocentric to the differential reading of art. If one subscribes, as I do, to this view, then one is forced to recognize that realist art could never have evoked the simplistic response which, according to Lawrence and all the Bloomsbury art-critics, including Woolf, it did. I am inclined to agree with Rita Felski, who subverts the traditional realist–modernist distinction by arguing that *realist* art, in practice, generates a greater variety of different readings than modern experimental texts which are, as she puts it, 'interpreted with monotonous regularity as metalinguistic propositions about the impossibility of representation'.[23] One possible way of negotiating this problem is to see the modernist reading (of texts or paintings as metalinguistic propositions) as no more than an initial step in the process whereby art *can* be opened up to an interesting variety of readings.

In Fry's case, then, to bracket off the 'instinctive' life is not to dissociate art from life altogether, as many critics have tried to assert. Rather, it is to increase and enrich the art-work's connections with life by making multiple 'readings' or responses possible. Fry is clear on the matter: 'What we desire in a work of art is the feeling of an inexhaustible wealth of significant relations which lie ready to hand for our investigation. We feel at once that a work of art has an idea that is intelligible, and that it is infinite in its possibilities.'[24] Alien pigment or even shape is not the issue. In the 'Essay in Aesthetics', Fry speaks of the aesthetic or imaginative in terms of a 'freer and fuller life':

For Bergson, the difficulties of doing this connect to the fact that language is necessarily linear; it can only operate through 'duration' (as opposed to 'real time'). Lawrence's preoccupation with the same problems may also have come from Bergson, or from William James's work on the stream-of-consciousness (see Chambers, *A Personal Record*, 112–13, and *Letters*, i. 544 [23 Apr. 1913]).

[22] 'Preface to the American edition of *New Poems*', 218.

[23] Rita Felski, *Beyond Feminist Aesthetics: Feminist Literature and Social Change* (London, 1989), 157.   [24] *The Arts of Painting and Sculpture* (London, 1932), 20–1.

It might even be that from this point of view we should rather justify actual life by its relation to the imaginative, justify nature by its likeness to art. I mean this, that since the imaginative life comes in the course of time to represent more or less what mankind feels to be the completest expression of its own nature, the freest use of its innate capacities, the actual life may be explained and justified in its approximation here and there, however partially and inadequately, to that freer and fuller life. (p. 15)

Here Fry's aesthetics suggests an enrichment of experience rather than a retreat from it. Lawrence himself makes a distinction between two types of apprehension which sounds strikingly similar to Fry's own: 'The plastic arts', he claims, 'are all imagery, and imagery is the body of our imaginative life'. He goes on: 'Our imaginative life is a great joy and fulfilment to us, for the imagination is a more powerful and more comprehensive flow of consciousness than our ordinary flow. In the flow of true imagination, we know in full, mentally and physically at once, in a greater, enkindled awareness.'[25] Neither critic, in distinguishing between two orders of experience, attempts to expunge the outside world from art altogether. In an important but often overlooked review of Clive Bell's *Art*, Fry shows how a formalist aesthetics can be made to assert a firm link between artistic microcosm and 'factual' macrocosm:

Why must the painter begin by abandoning himself to the love of God or Man or Nature, unless it is that in all art there is a fusion of something with form that makes the difference between the finest pattern-making and real design? . . . The common quality [in works of art] is significant form, that is to say, forms related to one another in a particular manner, which is always the outcome of their relation to x (where x is anything that is not itself form).[26]

And at a later stage in his career, Fry wishes to make it clear that he has never, even during his most rigidly 'formalistic' phase, abandoned representation: 'I may sometimes have used the word representation in opposition to design to denote more or less particularised representation, but I think in its context this use or misuse of the word is sufficiently clear.'[27]

To return to Bell's *Art*, we find that although, as the last chapter illustrated, it is an incoherent work, many of its inconsistencies can be accounted for if it is seen in context: like Fry's critical output, it is, primarily, a reaction against the naïve-mimetic model of art or what Bell calls 'scientific picture-making' (he also at times, confusingly, calls it 'literariness'); it is a reaction against what in a letter to the *Nation* Bell calls the 'official' view of art.[28]

---

[25] 'Introduction to These Paintings', 559.   [26] 'A New Theory of Art', 937, 938.
[27] 'Mr MacColl and Drawing', *Burlington Magazine*, xxxv (1919), 84–5.
[28] 'Mr Roger Fry's Criticism', *The Nation* (22 Feb. 1913), 853–4 (p. 854).

Terminology, here as elsewhere in aesthetics, can prove alarmingly am-
biguous. Taken at face value, Fry's rejection of the 'instinctive' life seems
anti-Lawrentian in the extreme; but, and this is the crux of the matter,
'instinctive', for Fry, denotes 'habitual' rather than 'bodily'. The issue is a
thorny one. Herbert Read picks on Fry's statement that 'art as created by the
artist is in violent revolt against the instinctive life, since it is an expression
of the reflective and fully conscious life', arguing that such a point of view is
'the antithesis of that expressed by Matisse and Picasso and the artists who
have come after them'.[29] But the fight with the cliché, as Lawrence understood, must be conscious; by surrendering our conscious mind we fall into
our old, too easy mental habits (he explains in 'Art and Morality' that
'instinct is largely habit', p. 163). And in the Foreword to *Women in Love*, as
we have already seen, Lawrence tells of the artist's 'passionate struggle into
conscious being' (p. 486).

It is, I think, misleading to oppose Fry's aesthetics, as Read does, to that
of a painter like Matisse. Both Fry and Matisse seem to be, as Lawrence is,
intensely preoccupied with problems of linguistic reification. Matisse argues
that the artist must 'return to the essential principles which made human
language', and that 'one must study an object a long time, to know what its
sign is. Yet in a composition the object becomes a new sign which helps
to maintain the force of the whole.' And he goes on: 'Each work of art is a
collection of signs invented during the picture's execution to suit the needs
of their position. Taken out of the composition for which they were created,
these signs have no further use.'[30] This is comparable with Lawrence's
pronouncement in 'Study of Thomas Hardy': 'Whenever art or any expression
becomes perfect, it becomes a lie. For it is only perfect by reason of abstraction from that context by which and in which it exists as truth' (p. 87).

The formal experimentation so central to modernism can be seen, then, to
represent an attempt to escape the constraints of language as coinage, of
language as a system of terms which have a fixed value independent of their
context. Leo Bersani encapsulates the paradox inherent in this experimentation when he describes the aesthetizing movement as both a 'coming-into-
form' and a 'subversion of forms'.[31] The subverting of the institutionalized
forms of the Royal Academy is a *self-renewing* battle with the cliché, a
perpetual transgression of newly established codes. Lawrence explains in
'Apocalypse' that 'What was a breath of inspiration becomes in the end a
fixed and evil *form*, which coils us round like mummy clothes' (p. 95); symbols
must not be allowed to diminish into 'a kind of glyph or label, like the gilt

[29] Read, *Icon and Idea* (London, 1955), 129.
[30] *Matisse on Art*, ed. J. D. Flam (London, 1978), 137.
[31] *The Freudian Body; Psychoanalysis and Art* (New York, 1986), 11.

pestle and mortar outside a chemist's shop' (p. 142). Form is only temporary resolution, acceptable on condition that it is prevented from reifying into semantic rigidity. It is worth noting, however, that creating 'a sign which refuses to signify' (Ad Reinhardt's expression) is far easier in the visual arts, where new *signifiers* are constantly available. Artists whose material is the written language are limited to a comparatively fixed body of signifiers, unless, of course, they take Joyce's approach in *Finnegans Wake*. As I tried to illustrate in Chapter 2, Lawrence's strategy is to use the same signifiers to express constantly shifting signifieds, so that meaning is always unstable and on the move.

5. Completeness–Incompleteness

For Lawrence, the language of art is both *complete* in the sense of self-sustaining, ultimately not subservient to other disciplines, and *incomplete* in the sense of not yielding any fixed or final reading. In 'Apocalypse', he explains that 'a book only lives while it has power to move us, and move us *differently*; so long as we find it *different* every time we read it' (p. 60). And again: 'No explanation of symbols is final'; this is because 'symbols are not intellectual quantities, they are not to be exhausted by the intellect.'[32] 'Complete' and 'final' (which are key Lawrentian terms) occur throughout Lawrence's fiction in two diametrically opposed senses. The first of these implies a dangerous and irresponsible solipsism. In *Women in Love*, for example, Gerald Crich responds to one of Hermione's guests at a studiedly cultured tea-party: 'He was finely and acutely aware of Mademoiselle's neat, brittle finality of form. She was like some elegant beetle with thin ankles . . .' (p. 239). A more explicit example of this usage occurs in a description of Gudrun: 'She finished life off so thoroughly, she made things so ugly and so final . . . This finality of Gudrun's, this dispatching of people and things in a sentence, it was all such a lie' (p. 263). There is a resonance here of 'sentence' in the sense of a judgemental sentence. And again Gudrun is seen surveying the scene at Breadalby: ' "Isn't it complete!" said Gudrun. "It is as final as an old aquatint" ' (p. 82). On the other hand, Birkin argues that the African carving in Halliday's flat of a woman in labour is art because 'It conveys a complete truth' (p. 79); it escapes the *partiality* of discursive structures, where partial suggests both 'incomplete' and 'biassed'.

The *autonomy* of the work of art becomes, in Lawrence's aesthetics, an autonomy of a very special kind. Art as language must inevitably be

---

[32] 'A Review of *The Book of Revelation* by Dr John Oman', in *Apocalypse and the Writings on Revelation*, 41.

intertextual, interacting infinitely with other languages, but its distinctiveness, for Lawrence, lies in the fact that, in the final analysis, it cannot be exhausted by these other discourses. For Lawrence, the art-work is valuable on account of its inability to shut out (a solipsistic self-referentiality would be anathema to him), but such openness is only possible after the art-work has ceased to attempt to relate to the outside in a 'closed' way. Language premissed on a mimetic model is characterized, for Lawrence, by a 'closed' openness, which means, in practice, appropriation. Logocentrism is synonymous with 'method' or 'discipline' (where 'discipline' has connotations of strictness, rigour, restriction). Precisely at those points where language thinks itself to be most empirical, it is, for Lawrence, most metaphoric; the language of mathematics, he argues, whilst granted most empirical or scientific validity, is, paradoxically, the most metaphoric of all.[33] For Lawrence art *does* interact with other domains of culture (where disciplines are self-enclosed), but it does not allow itself to be taken over by them. The 'readings' of art will of course be implicitly or explicitly political, but where different newspapers can appropriate the same quotation or the same photograph and use it for very different, even diametrically opposed, ideological ends, such photographs or statements *as art* resist this appropriation. This distinction can be found in the work of Jakobson: 'Art is part of the social edifice, a component correlating with others, a variable component, since the sphere of art and its relationship with other sectors of the social structure ceaselessly changes dialectically. *What we stress is not the separation of art, but the autonomy of the aesthetic function.*'[34]

Modernism is frequently criticized for *evasion*, as if appropriation or *invasion* were necessarily preferable. In 'Apocalypse', Lawrence argues that what he calls 'the language of isolation and exclusiveness' is the opposite of art. To return to Claudia Morrison's assertion, cited in the last chapter, that Lawrence equates the work of art with its 'didactic message', it seems that, on the contrary, Lawrence seeks to escape the discursive structures which make a rigid didacticism possible, which enable the moralist to assert a particular point and 'exclude or suppress all the rest'.[35] The artist, on the other hand, is found at the edge of these structures, like Cézanne who, in Lawrence's words, 'haunted the fringes of experience'.[36]

---

[33] 'Introduction to These Paintings', 574.
[34] Roman Jakobson, cited by Brewster in 'From Shklovsky to Brecht: A Reply', 86.
[35] 'Study of Thomas Hardy', 89.   [36] 'Introduction to These Paintings', 582.

6

LAWRENCE AND BLOOMSBURY III:
CÉZANNE'S APPLE

Taste the unsteady apples of Cézanne, and the nailed-down apples of
Fantin Latour are apples of Sodom. If the *status quo* were paradise, it
would indeed be a sin to taste the new apples. But since the *status quo*
is much more prison than paradise, we can go ahead.

('Art and Morality')

1. Lawrence, Fry, and Cézanne

In the last two chapters I have tried to argue that Lawrence and the
Bloomsbury art-critics had far more in common than the critical orthodoxy
on modernist aesthetics would suggest. The extent to which their interests
coincide is brought out, as I have already stressed, by the fact that they all
single out Cézanne's work as a kind of paradigm or benchmark for what they
think art should achieve. Bell's *Art*, though making universal claims about
art, was written very much as a defence of Cézanne's painting in particular,
whilst Roger Fry devoted an entire study to Cézanne. I have already noted
that Lawrence wrote his own longest essay in art-criticism, 'Introduction to
These Paintings' (a large part of which is devoted to Cézanne), shortly after
reading Bell's *Art*, in January 1929. In the same month, he also read Roger
Fry's *Cézanne: A Study of His Development* (1927), a work to which he makes
specific reference in his own essay. His comments on Fry's study are extremely
dismissive, and, taking them at face value, many critics have been content
to cite them as evidence of the radical Lawrence–Bloomsbury opposition
discussed above.[1] A close comparison of Fry's monograph with Lawrence's
'Introduction', however, reveals what barely falls short of substantial plagiarism,
on Lawrence's part, of Fry's argument, both on a general and on a more
detailed level.[2]

---

[1] See esp. 'Introduction to These Paintings', in *Phoenix*, 571–2, and Ch. 4 nn. 2 and 38
above.

[2] Before reading Fry's study, Lawrence had already written on Cézanne, most extensively
in the essay 'Art and Morality' (written in 1925). None the less, he goes on, in 'Introduction
to These Paintings', to expand his previous commentary in ways which correspond very

John Remsbury, in his article on Lawrence and Fry, argues that where Fry sees Cézanne's struggle in terms of a conflict between artist and medium, Lawrence sees it in terms of old and new ways of seeing.[3] Yet for Fry, too, Cézanne's quest is epistemological, a quest hindered by the self-renewing battle with the cliché. He evokes Cézanne's struggle against '*a priori* constructions', a struggle which he connects, as Lawrence does, with Cézanne's reluctance to depart from the style of the great Baroque painters he so admired. Fry praises *Maisons au bord de la Marne* for the fact that there is 'no hint of the imposition of a schematic idea', and goes on to explain that the 'geometrical scaffolding' in much of Cézanne's work is 'no *a priori* scheme imposed upon the appearances, but rather an interpretation gradually distilled from them by prolonged contemplation'.[4] Paralleling this, Lawrence, in the 'Introduction', describes Cézanne's landscapes in terms of 'acts of rebellion against the mental concept of landscape': because of the interference of such concepts, Cézanne only succeeded in 'knowing an apple, fully; and, not quite as fully, a jug or two'; his drawing was 'bad because it represented a smashed, mauled cliché, terribly knocked about' (pp. 569, 576). This is strikingly similar to Fry's observation in *Cézanne*:

It is in the still-life that we frequently catch the purest self-revelation of the artist. In any other subject humanity intervenes. It is almost impossible that other men should not influence the artist by their prejudices and partisanship. If the artist rebels against these, the act of rebellion is itself a deformation of his idea. If he disregards them and frees himself from all the commonplaces of sentiment, the effort still leaves its traces on his design. (p. 41)

For Fry, Cézanne 'could not . . . rid himself' of these 'obsessing images' and was therefore 'condemned to wrestle perpetually with the problem of giving them external expression. At times he even tried to revenge himself by satirical designs of a disconcerting kind' (p. 84). Fry cites *La Femme* as an

closely to Fry's argument. The only direct references he makes to Fry's study are extremely dismissive. See e.g. 571–2: 'It is a cant phrase with the critics to say "he couldn't draw". Mr Fry says: "With all his rare endowments, he happened to lack the comparatively common gift of illustration, the gift that any draughtsman for the illustrated papers learns in a school of commercial art". Now this sentence gives away at once the hollowness of modern criticism . . .' It is entirely of a piece with Lawrence's general reading habits that he should pick on an apparent weakness in Fry's argument, without acknowledging his numerous debts to Fry's study. He is swift to criticize Fry's reference to Cézanne's 'humility' before the object (p. 572), yet he uses the term 'arrogance' himself to describe the inverse process of controlling matter with the mind: Cézanne 'felt the tyranny of mind, the white, worn-out arrogance of . . . the mental consciousness' (p. 568). Lawrence and Fry are in fundamental agreement here, in that Fry's 'humility' consists precisely in freeing matter from subjectivity. This is just one example of the way in which a staged disagreement masks covert agreement.

³ John Remsbury, ' "Real Thinking": Lawrence and Cézanne', *Cambridge Quarterly*, ii (1966–7), 117–47 (p. 131).   ⁴ *Cézanne*, 35, 62, 70.

example. For Lawrence in the 'Introduction', Cézanne's 'rage with the cliché made him distort the cliché sometimes into parody, as we see in pictures like *The Pasha* and *La Femme*' (p. 576). 'Cézanne's apple hurts. It made people shout with pain', argues Lawrence, because, he implies, of its refusal to fit into people's clichéd preconceptions of what an apple should look like (p. 570). Fry puts forward the same argument in *Cézanne*:

The public expects a little more regard than this. It is shocked by such inconsiderate manners. Clever and contriving artists may indeed flout the public, but the very insults must be in essence only a more subtle kind of flattery. Before canvases which reveal so total an indifference to its expectations as these it is implacable, and one can see why Cézanne's works whenever they were exhibited achieved a derisive and humiliating failure. (p. 27)

Where illusionist art had, at least according to these critics, claimed to be a kind of Essential Copy or mirror on to the world, Cézanne's art, for both Lawrence and Fry, is rooted in the modernist acknowledgement that form, in graphic art as in any other language, fails to encompass reality in its entirety. Cézanne makes no claim to omniscience: 'I wished to copy nature . . . I could not', he explains. 'But I was satisfied when I had discovered that the sun, for instance, could not be reproduced, but that it must be represented by something else . . . by colour.'[5] Cézanne's symbol makes no pretensions to an exact copy of reality, and, by its confessed inadequacy, earns the right to stand for its immensely complex referent. The Royal Academicians, on the other hand, whilst all too happy to point to the gap between modern art and 'reality', fail, according to critics like Fry and Lawrence, to notice the gap between pseudo–photographic art and 'reality', a more pernicious gap for the very reason that we *are* the less likely to notice it.

We have seen that Lawrence's affinities with Cubism stem from his belief that the camera, with its static perspective, is too complete, and at the same time, paradoxically, too superficial. What Lawrence and Fry detect in Cézanne is the dual impulse which later proved to be characteristic of Cubism. There is, first of all, an attempt to be more *comprehensive* than all preceding artists, the attempt to achieve what Cézanne himself called '*réalisation*' (Lawrence explains: 'What Cézanne himself wanted was representation. He *wanted* true-to-life representation. Only he wanted it more true to life').[6] In the 'Introduction', Cézanne's apple becomes symbolic of what Lawrence terms 'for ever curving round to the other side, to the back of presented appearance'; the 'appleyness' in the portrait of Cézanne's wife 'carries with it also the feeling of knowing the other side as well, the side you don't see, the

[5] Maurice Denis, 'Cézanne, II', trans. Roger Fry, *Burlington Magazine*, xiv (1909–10), 275.
[6] 'Introduction to These Paintings', 577.

hidden side of the moon. For the intuitive apperception of the apple is so *tangibly* aware of the apple that it is aware of it *all round*, not only just of the front. The eye sees only fronts, and the mind, on the whole, is satisfied with fronts. But intuition needs all-aroundness, and instinct needs insideness' (p. 579).

Countering this, however, there is a *renunciatory* impulse, the need to forfeit any claim to completeness. In the 'Study of Thomas Hardy' Lawrence stresses the importance of imperfection and dynamism: 'Whenever art . . . becomes perfect', he warns, 'it becomes a lie' (p. 87). For Fry, as for Lawrence, the 'imperfection' of Cézanne's art is central to its achievement: Cézanne 'seems . . . hardly to arrive at the comprehension of his theme till the very end of the work; there is always something still lurking behind the expression, something he would grasp if he could. In short he is not perfect, and of many modern works one might predicate perfection.'[7] Bell had also pointed to the questing nature of Cézanne's work: 'His own pictures were for Cézanne nothing but rungs in a ladder', he had observed, 'at the top of which would be complete expression'.[8] The minute brushstrokes of modulated colours so often commented on by critics of Cézanne are in effect an endless process of deconstruction and reconstruction, a concrete embodiment of the process of *différance*. We saw in Chapter 2 that some kinds of language (Lacanian prose, for example) *seem* to manifest more textual stress or semantic instability than others. Paintings can also be seen to convey textual stress, and Cézanne's importance for both Lawrence and Fry can be read in these terms. In other words, if some illusionist paintings represent for both Lawrence and Fry the visual equivalent of the mimetic model of language, Cézanne's art is the painterly analogue of the 'differential' model.

Cézanne's reluctance to *complete* his picture entails an acknowledgement not only of the rift between the artefact and the external, phenomenal world, but also of the fact that the human consciousness is inescapably relative in its perceptions. It is this fact which leads Lawrence to distinguish, in 'Fantasia of the Unconscious', between two types of abstraction: the 'dynamic abstraction' (a concept which helps us to understand that a relative view is relative precisely *because* it is abstracting certain aspects) and the static 'adult abstraction' or generalization, which pretends to an absolute status (pp. 87–8). Cézanne's apple has no absolute value, but is seen as something different to everyone, a point Lawrence makes in 'Art and Morality': 'What an apple looks like to an urchin, to a thrush, to a browsing cow, to Sir Isaac Newton, to a caterpillar, to a hornet, to a mackerel who finds one bobbing on the sea, I leave you to conjecture. But the All-seeing must have mackerel's eyes, as

---

[7] *Cézanne*, 2.   [8] *Art*, 210.

well as man's' (p. 166). Once again, this is consonant with Fry's reading of Cézanne:

For him . . . the ultimate synthesis of a design was never revealed in a flash; rather, he approached it with infinite precautions, stalking it, as it were, now from one point of view, now from another – and always in fear lest a premature definition might deprive it of its total complexity. For him the synthesis was an asymptote towards which he was forever approaching without ever quite reaching it; it was a reality incapable of complete realisation.[9]

For Lawrence, art enacts in microcosm a cosmic relativity:

The universe is like Father Ocean, a stream of all things slowly moving . . . And since we move and move forever, in no discernible direction, there is no centre to the movement . . . There is nothing to do but to maintain a true relationship to the things we move with and amongst and against . . . And nothing is true, or good, or right, except in its own living relatedness to its own circumambient universe; to the things that are in the stream with it.[10]

Art, then, can only present endless perspectives on things, which emerge from the endless, ever-shifting relations between the artist and her/his world, between the elements of the art-work, between the art-work and the viewer. For Lawrence, 'Design, in art, is a recognition of the relation between various things, various elements in the creative flux', and for Fry, 'Our reaction to works of art is a reaction to a relation and not to sensations or objects or persons or events'. Fry argues his point by showing that there can be no art which employs the sense of smell: 'The evocations of smell are indeed so powerful that they would doubtless form the basis for an art similar to music in its deep emotional evocations, if only different perfumes could be perceived in relation to one another. It is this impossibility alone that deprives us of yet another art.'[11]

The human consciousness, then, unavoidably contributes to the object's 'reality', or, as Lawrence expresses it, 'The eye of man photographs the chimera of nature, as well as the so-called scientific vision.'[12] The relativity of human perception is such that the artist will never attain to the whole truth about an object, but none the less what he/she produces will be 'truer' than a pseudo-photographic representation. One of Cézanne's strengths, for these critics, is a painstaking loyalty to his own vision. As Fry expresses it, 'He never covers himself by a trick . . . Everything is frank to a fault, and

---

[9] *Cézanne*, 3.
[10] 'Art and Morality', in *Study of Thomas Hardy and Other Essays*, 167.
[11] Ibid.; Fry, 'Some Questions in Esthetics', in *Transformations*, 3, 4.
[12] 'Review of *A Second Contemporary Verse Anthology*', in *Phoenix*, 322–6 (p. 324).

audaciously honest'; and this in spite of 'his insatiable ambition to rival the masterpieces of the seventeenth century, to be grandiose and impressive'.[13] In Lawrence this becomes 'Grandeur impressed him terribly. Yet still stronger in him was the little flame of life where he *felt* things to be true. He didn't betray himself in order to get success.'[14]

The dual impulse to encompass and to renounce finds a physical correlative in the fact that Cézanne's paintings seem to be simultaneously dynamic and still. The camera and illusionist art freeze reality, conceiving of time and process as a series of detachable fragments, but only if painting is in some way dynamic can it give a sense of the dynamism or 'shiftiness', as Lawrence terms it, of the endlessly deferred reality it seeks to capture. Lawrence is emphatic that it was part of Cézanne's desire 'to make the human form, the *life* form, come to rest. Not static—on the contrary, mobile, but come to rest' (this process of 'coming to rest' seems to correspond closely to the 'framing' process achieved by Fry's imaginative vision). Lawrence goes on:

And at the same time he set the unmoving material world into motion. Walls twitch and slide, chairs bend or rear up a little, cloths curl like burning paper. Cézanne did this partly to satisfy his intuitive feeling that nothing is really *statically* at rest . . . and partly to fight the cliché, which says that the inanimate world is static, and that walls *are* still.[15]

This is reminiscent of Fry's comments on *Maisons au bord de la Marne*: 'Even the symmetry is never quite so exact as it seems at first sight—rather, the balance is always, as it were, menaced and redressed—it is a dynamic and not a static equilibrium.' And again: 'In spite of the austerity of the forms, all is vibration and movement. Nothing is less schematic than these works, even when, as here, the general forms have an almost geometrical appearance.'[16] Tony Pinkney makes a related observation: 'It is this "between" which is Cézanne's peculiar achievement, keeping both *langue* and *parole* tensely jostling one another, avoiding the one-sided extremes of pure subjectivity (as with Impressionism or Expressionism) or pure system (as with Mondrian or Malevich).'[17] A similar argument underlies Paul Klee's distinction between 'form' ('form is bad; form is the end, death . . .') and 'formation' ('formation is life'). The following statement of Klee's is reminiscent of Lawrence's description of Cézanne's work:

Our works . . . stay quietly in place, and yet they are all movement. Movement is inherent in all becoming, and before the work is, it must become, just as the world became before it was after the words 'In the beginning God created', and must go on becoming before it is (will be) in the future.[18]

---

[13] *Cézanne*, 27.   [14] 'Introduction to These Paintings', 571.
[15] Ibid. 580.   [16] *Cézanne*, 62, 51.   [17] *D. H. Lawrence*, 133.
[18] *On Modern Art* (London, 1954), 169, 355.

Where 'realism', for both Lawrence and Klee, is bound to already existing 'forms', Cézanne's art breaks free of these forms to engage with 'formation' itself.

For both Lawrence and Fry, a startling stillness emerges from these vibrations, from this restlessness made up of endless, tentative approaches towards the apple: the apple emerges in all its 'form and substance and *thereness*'.[19] Here, in the emphasis on the 'appleyness of the apple', there is an important link between Lawrence's art-criticism and Heidegger's aesthetics, to be explored in Chapters 8 and 9. Once again, Lawrence's interests locate him in a specifically German tradition. Another of his contemporaries to be preoccupied with the question of 'thingness' was Rilke, and it is possible that Rilke constitutes one more link in the complex chain which, in my view, joins Lawrence to Heidegger. The early Rilke was, like Lawrence, deeply under the influence of Nietzsche (Rilke and Nietzsche had a common friend in Lou Andreas-Salomé),[20] and, like Nietzsche's Zarathustra, Rilke was pre-occupied with 'die Dinge', describing himself as 'the disciple of things . . . with the disciple's humility'.[21] Heidegger is said to have remarked that his philosophy was simply the unfolding in thought of what Rilke had expressed poetically.[22] Rilke in his turn declared Cézanne to be the most important influence on his work after 1906, confessing that 'After the master's death, I followed his traces everywhere'.[23] Visiting a memorial exhibition of Cézanne's work at the Salon d'Automne in Paris in 1907, Rilke recorded his responses in a series of letters to his wife. 'Thingness', 'thereness', 'putting the apple to rest', all the central tenets of both Lawrence's (and Heidegger's) aesthetics are present in these letters. For Rilke, Cézanne's apples 'cease to be edible altogether, that's how thinglike and real they become, how simply indestructible in their stubborn thereness'; Cézanne's labour was one which 'no longer knew any preferences or biases or fastidious predilections'.[24] There is strong evidence to suggest that Lawrence was reading Rilke in 1924–5, and it is at about this time that Lawrence starts to comment on Cézanne in his own writings ('Art and Morality' was written in 1925), though he could not

---

[19] 'Introduction to These Paintings', 564.

[20] See e.g. Erich Heller's chapter on Rilke and Nietzsche in *The Disinherited Mind: Essays in Modern German Literature and Thought* (Cambridge, 1952), 97–140.

[21] Rilke, *Tagebücher aus der Frühzeit* (Leipzig, 1942), 89.

[22] J. F. Angelloz, *Rainer Maria Rilke* (Paris, 1936), 3. Heidegger quotes Rilke frequently in his later essays, where he becomes increasingly preoccupied with the notion of language as 'the house of Being' ('Letter on Humanism', in *Basic Writings*, ed. David Farrell Krell (New York, 1977), 193–242 (p. 193)). See esp. the essay 'What Are Poets For?' (*Poetry, Language, Thought*, 89–142). The 'Letter on Humanism' was first published as *Briefe über den Humanismus* in 1947.

[23] Cited in *Letters on Cézanne*, ed. Clara Rilke, trans. Joel Agee (London, 1988), p. vii.

[24] Ibid. 51, 32, 33, 65. These letters were first published as *Briefe über Cézanne* (Wiesbaden, 1952).

have had access to the letters just cited. Rilke in his turn read and admired Lawrence's work.[25]

The apple becomes symbolic, for both Lawrence and Fry, as for Rilke, of letting matter be itself. Fry observes that the artist 'increasingly resigned himself to accepting the thing seen as the nucleus of crystallization in place of poetical inspiration'. Eventually, Cézanne 'arrived at what was to be his most characteristic conception, namely, that the deepest emotions could only exude, like a perfume—it is his own image—from form considered in its pure essence and without reference to associated ideas'. He goes on to relate this directly to the 'appleyness' upon which Lawrence also focuses: 'He poses to himself as he wished his sitters to pose, "as an apple", and he looks at his own head with precisely the same regard that he turned on an apple on the kitchen table. But with this renunciation of all *parti pris* how much more eloquent and vital is the presence revealed to us.'[26] This appleyness is, for both Lawrence and Fry, directly opposed to illusionist art. And at this point I come to an important connection with Virginia Woolf, whose comments on painting constitute an important complement not only to those of her close friends Bell and Fry but also to those of Lawrence. For all these critics, illusionist art, championed as it was by the Royal Academy, was seen to be inherently reactionary, complicit with the *status quo*. But Woolf and Lawrence take this argument a step further: they draw a link between mimetic art and language on the one hand, and imperialism and violence on the other.

2. Woolf and the Royal Academicians

Virginia Woolf read Fry's study of Cézanne and called it 'a miracle', judging Fry 'the only great critic that ever lived'.[27] Woolf's arguments in fictional theory closely parallel those of Bell and Fry in visual art. Her ambivalent responses to her own 'forms', her language, which is full of 'the perils of glibness', parallels the objection to the copy-theory, and to the 'labelling'

---

[25] Lawrence's short essay 'On Being Religious' was published in 1924, and translated into German. Reading it in December of that year, Rilke wrote to Anton Kippenburg: 'I have read Lawrence's essay out loud again and again; it is strange, it contains sentences which I know exist almost word for word the same in my own papers.' The fragment 'Man is Essentially a Soul' (dating from 1925) is also thought to be a translation from Rilke. See Keith Sagar, *A D. H. Lawrence Handbook* (Manchester, 1982), 101. Rilke in his turn read Lawrence's *The Rainbow* when it was published in German in 1922, and said of it that it 'will mean a turning-point for me'. See Eudo C. Mason, *Rilke, Europe, and the English Speaking World* (Cambridge, 1961), 114–15.   [26] *Cézanne*, 10, 53, 56.

[27] Cited in David Dowling, *Bloomsbury Aesthetics and The Novels of Forster and Woolf* (London and Basingstoke, 1985), 97.

vision.[28] She repeatedly articulates the connection between certain kinds of language, and machinery or violence, a connection which Lawrence also makes. In her diary she describes a country walk with the Webbs: 'On a steely watery morning we swiftly tramped over a heathy common, talking, talking. In their efficiency and glibness one traces perfectly adjusted machinery' (this is reminiscent of the way in which, on the terrace of Breadalby in *Women in Love*, 'the talk went on like a rattle of small artillery', p. 84).[29] Woolf in one of her letters expresses a wish to avoid constructing 'a formal railway line of a sentence', while Bernard, the writer in *The Waves* (1931), frequently connects certain literary styles with militarism and empire-building: he abhors the 'biographic style' with its 'phrases laid like Roman roads across the tumult of our lives'.[30] But Woolf's most extensive examination of the connection between logocentrism on the one hand, and violence on the other, the more interesting here because it deals explicitly with painting, is to be found in her essay on a visit to the Royal Academy.

Woolf's essay 'The Fleeting Portrait' was first published soon after the close of the First World War, and it reverberates with ironic references to Empire and patriotism. The whole ethos of the Royal Academy, its very architecture ('the ceremonious steps leading up, the swing-doors admitting, and the flunkeys fawning'), seems calculated, argues Woolf, to whip up the most frenzied (and specious) emotions of nationalism, public-spiritedness, and devotion to the common weal: 'Once you are within the precincts, everything appears symbolic, and the state of mind in which you ascend the broad stairs to the picture galleries is both heated and romantic.'[31] Woolf goes on, interestingly, to present a series of logocentric or literalistic responses to the Academy paintings, the very responses ('the anecdotes of dogs and duchesses') which her mentor Roger Fry spent a lifetime of art-criticism trying to dispel (Woolf in her essay on Fry remarks that 'he detested the story-telling spirit which has clouded our painting and confused our criticism').[32] The responses are evoked by the numerous portraits of dukes and officers, of defenders of the realm and the English roses they defend, who all seem, on the spectator's approach, to come to life, like Madame Tussaud's

[28] *The Diary of Virginia Woolf*, ed. Anne Olivier Bell, 5 vols. (London, 1977–84), v. 335 (1 Nov. 1940). For an account of Woolf's connections with Fry, see Allen McLaurin, *Virginia Woolf: The Echoes Enslaved* (Cambridge, 1973), esp. chs. 2–8.

[29] *The Diary of Virginia Woolf*, iii. 126 (3 Feb. 1927).

[30] *The Letters of Virginia Woolf*, ed. Nigel Nicolson, 6 vols. (London, 1975–80), iii. 135 (3 Oct. 1924); *The Waves* (London, 1931), 284.

[31] 'The Fleeting Portrait', in *Collected Essays*, 4 vols. (London, 1966–7), iv. 204–11 (pp. 206–7).

[32] 'Roger Fry', in *Collected Essays*, iv. 88–92 (p. 90). An early review of *Mrs Dalloway*, Richard Hughes's 'A Day in London Life' (*Saturday Review of Literature*, (16 May 1925), 755), makes some striking connections between Woolf and Cézanne.

waxworks, warming to their beholder's gaze: a lady in full evening dress 'stands at the top of a staircase, one hand loosely closed round a sheaf of lilies, while the other is about to greet someone of distinction who advances towards her up the stairs' (p. 207). The narrator immediately endows the lady with the power of speech, (' "How nice of you to come!" '), and the characters she visits in turn are all made to voice the platitudes and clichés of an unthinking privileged class. Jingoistic, sexist, bloodthirsty attitudes are all condensed into a few worn clichés ('the flag of England', 'sweet chimes of home', 'a woman's honour', and so on).

A more 'homely' painting of an urchin in corduroys holding a fish sparks off a comparable set of commonplaces: 'the harvest of the sea, toilers of the deep, a fisherman's home, nature's bounty—such phrases formed themselves with alarming rapidity' (p. 208). But lurking amid this apparent idyll are the unmistakable signs of tragedy: the tear-glazed eyes of the woman, the uncanny resemblance of the little boy's breeches to those of his, as we now realize, dead, father. The painting reveals a narrative symbolism which Woolf quickly decodes, so that 'the story reels itself out like a line with a salmon on the end of it'. Woolf suddenly cuts short her verbal rendition of the painting, for 'the story when written out is painful, and rather obvious into the bargain' (p. 209).

Another painting, entitled 'Cocaine', may be more difficult to decode (and therefore, for Woolf, as she admits, a better painting), but still it invites a kind of literalistic moral exegesis:

People in the little group of gazers begin to boast that they have known sadder cases themselves. Friends of theirs took cocaine . . . Everyone wished to cap that story with a better, save for one lady who, from her expression, was acting the part of consoler, had got the poor thing to bed, undressed her, soothed her, and even spoken with considerable sharpness to that unworthy brute, unfit to be a husband, before she moved on in a pleasant glow of self-satisfaction. (pp. 209–10)

This is a parody of the logocentric reading, and that it is also a moralizing, judgemental response is no accident. The woman has responded in the way prescribed by the painting; she has shown herself amenable to what the Royal Academy catalogue describes loftily and self-applaudingly as 'the benignant influence of the canvas'. Suddenly and mysteriously, however, this 'benignant influence' becomes a violent attack on the onlookers, who find themselves being 'jabbed and stabbed, slashed and sliced' by these paintings, and in particular by the Sargent with which Woolf concludes the essay. It is no coincidence that the painting has a military subject:

A large picture by Mr Sargent called 'Gassed' at last pricked some nerve of protest, or perhaps of humanity. In order to emphasize his point that the soldiers wearing bandages round their eyes cannot see, and therefore claim our compassion, he makes one of them raise his leg to the level of his elbow in order to mount a step an inch or two above the ground. This little piece of over-emphasis was the final scratch of the surgeon's knife which is said to hurt more than the whole operation. After all, one had been jabbed and stabbed, slashed and sliced for close on two hours. The lady began it, the Duke continued it; little children had wrung tears; great men extorted veneration. From first to last each canvas had rubbed in some emotion, and what the paint failed to say the catalogue had enforced in words. But Mr Sargent was the last straw. Suddenly the great rooms rang like a parrot-house with the intolerable vociferations of gaudy and brainless birds. How they shrieked and gibbered! How they danced and sidled! Honour, patriotism, chastity, wealth, success, importance, position, patronage, power—their cries rang and echoed from all quarters. (p. 211)

The link between logocentrism and violence ('What the paint failed to say, the catalogue enforced in words') is clear.

The illusionism of the Academicians, according to which the immaculate features of the English landscape collude in a picture of a smoothly running prosperity, is linked by Woolf not only to a dangerous manipulation of attitudes (each feature of each painting 'has a symbolical meaning much to the credit of England'), but also to the colonizing spirit, to the exploitation of the world's resources which underpins the entire British empire: 'The geese are English geese, and even the polar bears, though they have not that advantage, seem, such is the persuasion of the atmosphere, *to be turning to carriage rugs* as we look at them.'[33]

As we saw in the last chapter, Norman Bryson expresses the problem of imperialism in art semiotically: Chardin's experimentation with space permits 'the absolute visibility of the signifier' and is 'part of a whole trend within French rococo, of liberating figurality from the controlling grasp of the signified'.[34] This neat distinction between signifier and signified is one Lawrence would have mistrusted, for it is essentially the form–content distinction in semiotic guise. But Bryson's point could be made in different terms as the liberation of art as a whole from logocentrism, from the tendency to read art-works in terms of fixed signifieds. It can be seen as a kind of political resistance on the part of art to the kinds of discourses which would coerce it into meaning exclusively this or exclusively that. Bryson cites LeBrun as an instance of the kind of painting which is unable to hold out against 'the authority of the text'. LeBrun's painting stresses the depth of the complicity between textuality and power in the *ancien régime* ('To question the supremacy of the discursive, before the double presence of LeBrun and Colbert, is both artistic heresy and political treason'); LeBrun, for Bryson, marks the *colonization* of the image by discourse.[35]

[33] 'The Fleeting Portrait', 210, my emphasis.
[34] *Word and Image*, 121.   [35] Ibid. 34.

Bryson goes on to analyse Diderot's *Salon* of 1765, and in particular the long digression at the centre of it which deals with the dream of Plato's cave.[36] Bryson's summary of Diderot's account is roughly as follows: Diderot dreams that he is in a dark cavern together with a crowd of people who are chained hand and foot, and whose bodies are gripped by wooden vices so that they cannot even turn their heads. Yet they are revelling, apparently oblivious to their captivity, for they are engrossed by the lifelike images being projected on to the wall of the cave by the kings, politicians, and priests, who, unbeknown to the prisoners, are standing behind them. Most of the prisoners take the images to be real, but a few are suspicious of the spectacle, and attempt to turn their heads round inside the vice. When they do so, the rulers shout out, ordering them to look back at the images. At this point in the narration, Diderot is interrupted by Grimm, who informs him that one of the images he is describing is in fact Fragonard's painting of *Corésus et Callirhoé*, and a dialogue ensues concerning the technical craft of the painting.

For Bryson, the whole digression represents a meditation on the *enslavement* of illusionism in painting: 'Instead of being humanised by exposure to the sign that seems to be alive (the sign that lacks the signifier), people are enslaved by its illusions. "Transparency" materialises as the actual slides the rulers use to distract and manipulate their subjects . . .' Bryson's analysis is influenced by Barthes, who similarly links transparency with ideological stridency.[37] It is this link between transparency and imperialism which seems to underpin Woolf's analysis of the Royal Academy paintings.

For Lawrence, as I have already stressed, realist art has its linguistic analogue in a naïve-mimetic or logocentric model of language. It is this model of language which is the prerequisite of scientific discourse and, by extension, technology, a technology which, for Lawrence, is inseparable from Western expansion and imperialism. Lawrence is the kind of thinker for whom nothing remains a localized issue. His critique of 'Logos' stretches far beyond questions of language to concern itself with cultural imperialism (the West's forcing of its own epistemologies on to the rest of the world), and with the *physical* threat to the planet posed by a capitalistic industrialism which is underpinned by those same epistemologies. The full symbolic burden borne by Cézanne's apple becomes clear. If, in Lawrence's mythology,

---

[36] Ibid. 195–6.

[37] Ibid. 196. Elizabeth Ermarth also connects realism in art with power; she argues that the realist consensus that makes such power available depends upon the management of distance: one must step back from particulars in order to grasp them (Elizabeth Deeds Ermarth, *Realism and Consensus in the English Novel* (Princeton, NJ, 1983), 35). For Heidegger, too, power is at the root of the representing gaze.

the consumption of the apple of the tree of knowledge initiated a 'fall' into Western metaphysics, Cézanne's apple calls for nothing less than the dismantling of a whole philosophical tradition. By the same token, it symbolizes the undoing of the environmental damage such a tradition has brought in its wake, and the restoration of some prelapsarian state: 'If the *status quo* were paradise, it would indeed be a sin to taste the new apples. But since the *status quo* is much more prison than paradise, we can go ahead.'[38]

[38] 'Art and Morality', 168.

7

ART AND TECHNOLOGY:
VICTORIAN PREDECESSORS

The sea they turned into a murderous alley and a soiled road of commerce, disputed like the dirty land of a city every inch of it. The air they claimed too, shared it up, parcelled it out to certain owners, they trespassed in the air to fight for it. Everything was gone, walled in, with spikes on top of the walls, and one must ignominiously creep between the spiky walls through a labyrinth of life.

(Women in Love)

Women in Love is both an intense scrutiny of the status of art and artists in modern society and a graphic and heartfelt evocation of the spread of the 'leprosy' of industrialism over the land. For Lawrence, the two issues, aesthetics and industrialism, are vitally connected, and the next three chapters will seek to establish the nature of this connection. This chapter starts by identifying the links between Lawrence's art-criticism and Victorian commentaries on industrialism (especially those of Carlyle and Ruskin, which Lawrence read early in his career), in order to go on to point to the ways in which Lawrence departed from the positions of his nineteenth-century predecessors.[1] Chapters 8 and 9 place him in a tradition of aesthetics of which one of the most influential exponents has been Martin Heidegger. The inclusion of Heidegger in an assessment of Lawrence's writings on art is not arbitrary, although, surprisingly, almost nothing has been published on the extensive links between these two thinkers.[2] In the Introduction, I stressed the fact that Lawrence and Heidegger shared important cultural and philosophical influences. Both found themselves caught up in the *völkisch* ideologies prevalent in Germany in the 1910s and 1920s. Nietzsche was probably the single most important philosopher behind these ideologies. It is on account of this shared cultural climate that the links between the aesthetic theories of Lawrence and Heidegger are so precise and so abundant.[3] Like

[1] Chambers records Lawrence's enthusiasm for Carlyle in 1906, and notes that by 1908 he had read much of Ruskin (*A Personal Record*, 101–2, 107).

[2] The section on Heidegger in Michael Bell's book on Leavis (see Introduction, n. 31) can, in view of Lawrence's influence on Leavis, be seen to articulate links between Lawrence and Heidegger.

[3] In the last chapter I noted that Rilke's emphasis on 'thingness' had constituted a possible link between the aesthetics of Lawrence and Heidegger. Heidegger pays particular attention to the 'anti-technology' themes of Rilke's poetry, and in 'What Are Poets For?', he comments

Lawrence, Heidegger was an energetic commentator on both art and the impact of capitalistic industrialism and technology on the environment. Heidegger's 'The Origin of the Work of Art', based on a lecture delivered in 1935, concerns itself with technology, just as 'The Question Concerning Technology' (1953) addresses the question of art; they are complementary texts, even though they are separated by nearly twenty years.[4] Heidegger's writings on art and technology constitute a valuable supplement to Lawrence's, in that they bring the issues forward into the age of information technology and cybernetics, testifying to the continuing relevance of Lawrence's concerns.

For both Lawrence and Heidegger, the violence that technology wreaks on the planet is the *indexical* trace of a violent, exploitative kind of thinking. This is not a question of parallels or analogies between a way of thinking and a way of treating the environment: rather, for both thinkers, one is the *direct physical consequence* of the other. Heidegger brings this out when he remarks in his essay 'The Thing' that 'Science's knowledge . . . already had annihilated things as things long before the atom bomb exploded'.[5] Similarly for Lawrence, the fact that the artists in *Women in Love* (Gudrun, Loerke) seem to have 'lost their way' is directly connected to the state of the mine-scarred earth.

1. Carlyle and the Mechanized Mind

Lawrence's readiness to intertwine the psychic and the technological into a single imagistic pattern must in the first instance have come from Carlyle and Ruskin, whom he had read widely by the age of 22. The merging of mentality and machinery finds its most concise formulation in Carlyle's well-known designation of the Victorian age as 'the Age of Machinery, in every inward and outward sense of that word'.[6] It is easy to see how Carlyle's unwearying attack on Benthamite utilitarianism and on the assumption that human beings are as straightforward and orderly as the machines they tend,

in detail on a passage from Rilke's *Book of Pilgrimage* (1901), in which the narrator deplores the transmutation of ancient gold into fixed coinage serving a mechanized capitalism. Heidegger finds in this a lament for the lost 'humanness of man' and 'thingness of things' which he sees to be dissolving into market values; the world, he argues, is becoming a vast market-place in which the traders 'trade in the nature of Being' (*Poetry, Language, Thought*, 114–15).

[4] See 'The Origin of the Work of Art', in *Poetry, Language, Thought*, 15–87 (a revised edition of the essay which appeared in *Holzwege* (Frankfurt, 1950) as 'Der Ursprung des Kunstwerkes'). The first version of the essay was a lecture given on 13 Nov. 1935, to the *Kunstwissenschaftliche Gesellschaft* at Freiburg. See also 'The Question Concerning Technology', in *The Question Concerning Technology and Other Essays*, 3–35. This essay first appeared as 'Die Frage nach der Technik' in *Vorträge und Aufsätze* (Pfullingen, 1954).

[5] 'The Thing', in *Poetry, Language, Thought*, 163–86 (p. 170).

[6] 'Signs of the Times', in *The Works of Thomas Carlyle*, xxvii. 56–82 (p. 59).

is rearticulated in Lawrence's emphasis on spontaneity and individuality. In the first chapter, I sketched the way in which, in both writers, this leads in political terms to a critique of democracy: Carlyle, whose later works become brutally authoritarian, has, like Lawrence, been accused of an incipient fascism.[7] He argues in *Chartism* (1839) that democracy is a self-defeating enterprise whereby individual endeavours somehow cancel each other out, giving 'a net result of *zero*'.[8] In Lawrence's case, however, there is a marked discrepancy between the anti-democratic political views expressed in works like *Aaron's Rod* (1922) and *The Plumed Serpent* (1926), and his writings on art: art is seen by Lawrence to subvert all attempts at authoritarianism (an idea explored at length in the final chapter).

Carlyle's linking of the machine and the psyche remains far more meta-phorical, or analogical, than Lawrence's. He criticizes the application of the *metaphor* of the machine to political and social life.[9] For Carlyle, the tech-nological progeny of the industrial revolution, the steam locomotives and stationary engines, are infiltrating the culture to such a degree that they are changing our perceptions of the way in which society, and the human psyche itself, might or should function ('Not the external and physical alone is now managed by machinery, but the internal and spiritual also . . . Men are grown mechanical in head and in heart, as well as in hand'). The machine has, he argues, 'struck its roots down into man's most intimate, primary sources of conviction; and is thence sending up, over his whole life and activity, in-numerable stems,—fruit-bearing and poison-bearing'.[10] For Lawrence, on the other hand, it is not a question of *modelling* society or human nature on the machine: the problem underlying our mechanized culture is far more deep-seated than that. Indeed, Lawrence turns the Carlylean situation up-side down, seeing the machines themselves as the poisonous and malformed fruit of a psyche which was already sick; the state of the external world is, for Lawrence, *physical symptom* of a chronic and deep-rooted psychic disorder. Hence in 'Education of the People', he describes the Great War as 'a ghastly and blasphemous translation of ideas into engines'.[11]

---

[7] See Shelston's introduction to *Thomas Carlyle: Selected Writings* (Harmondsworth, 1971), 22. See Carlyle's *Latter-Day Pamphlets* (*Works*, xx) and 'The Nigger Question' (*Works*, xxix. 348–83). Compare Lawrence's views on democracy in 'Democracy', *Reflections on the Death of a Porcupine and Other Essays*, 61–83. Compare also Heidegger: 'What threatens man in his very nature is the view that technological production puts the world in order, while in fact this ordering is precisely what levels every *ordo*, every rank, down to the uniformity of pro-duction, and thus from the outset destroys the realm from which any rank and recognition could possibly arise' ('What Are Poets For?', in *Poetry, Language, Thought*, 117).

[8] *Chartism, Works*, xxix. 118–204 (p. 158).   [9] *Works*, xxvii. 66.

[10] 'Signs of the Times', 60, 74.

[11] 'Education of the People', in *Reflections on the Death of a Porcupine and Other Essays*, 85–166 (p. 159). This essay was first published in *Phoenix*.

For Carlyle, the earth is a 'World-Steamengine' which holds its inhabitants 'imprisoned in its own iron belly'; on a literal level, iron has insinuated itself into the drab municipal architecture of nineteenth-century chapels and churches, but metaphorically it has worked its way into the ecclesiastical services themselves. 'Depend upon it, Birmingham can make machines to repeat liturgies and articles; to do whatsoever fact is mechanical. And what were all schoolmasters, nay all priests and churches, compared with this Birmingham Iron Church!'[12] This overwhelming sense of a de-aestheticized and de-spiritualized world (the two are inseparable for Carlyle), finds its way into Lawrence's work, as does the language of biblical prophesy which is so pervasive in Carlyle (an example would be Carlyle's lugubrious parody of Genesis, in which the fire-throated machines rise into day).[13] But in Lawrence the various threads are woven into a philosophical matrix which is ultimately very different from Carlyle's. Carlyle's repudiation of the mechanical springs from philosophical allegiances to Kant, Novalis, and other proponents of the German transcendentalism which Lawrence was to find so alien. People have, Carlyle argues in 'Signs of the Times', lost their belief in the Invisible (p. 71). Teufelsdröckh's impulse in *Sartor Resartus* (1836) is towards the ultimate truths lying behind the specious material world, a world strewn with 'old rags of Matter'; his 'Philosophy of Clothes' is a metaphor for his pseudo-Kantian philosophy, whereby the material world is a mere veil or vestment, a 'fresh or faded raiment' clothing a 'naked', transcendental reality which, like the Kantian noumenon, is not subject to the laws of time and space; behind the 'WHERE and WHEN' there is 'a universal HERE, an everlasting NOW'.[14] Carlyle's condemnation of the machine extends, in other words, into a condemnation of the material world itself. Teufelsdröckh is compelled 'to look through the Shows of things into Things themselves' (p. 164); works of art are for him, as they would later be for the German Expressionists, 'Eternity looking through Time' (p. 178).

Carlyle, then, seeks sanctuary from what he perceives to be a brute materialism in precisely that transcendentalist metaphysical tradition which for Lawrence is close to the source of the whole problem. Lawrence was to connect the instrumentalism and exploitation which is so often the subject of Carlyle's rich imagery ('We war with rude Nature; and, by our resistless engines, come off always victorious, and loaded with spoils'[15]) to the very transcendentalism which Carlyle saw as a refuge from that instrumentalism. Carlyle, in turning towards the metaphysical Idea, could not have been, in Lawrence's view, more misguided.

---

[12] *Chartism*, 146, 196.   [13] Ibid. 185.
[14] *Sartor Resartus, Works*, i. 165, 42–3.   [15] 'Signs of the Times', 14.

2. Ruskin, Iron, and Integration

Lawrence was of course as steeped in Ruskin as he was in Carlyle, and Ruskin himself declared more than once that he owed more to Carlyle than to any other living writer.[16] Ruskin goes further than Carlyle in articulating the links between human microcosm and industrial macrocosm, and his use of the imagery of iron is far more complex and elaborate than Carlyle's. In 'The Work of Iron, in Nature, Art, and Policy', Ruskin envisages a planet colonized by a horrifying steel-vegetation:

How would you like the world, if all your meadows instead of grass, grew nothing but iron wire—if all your arable ground, instead of being made of sand and clay, were suddenly turned into flat surfaces of steel—if the whole earth, instead of its green and glowing sphere, rich with forest and flower, showed nothing but the image of the vast furnace of a ghastly engine—a globe of black, lifeless, excoriated metal?[17]

It is an appalling image of a steel which will never decay to be assimilated organically back into the earth; of a stubborn, mute, unredeemed matter.[18] The starting-point of Ruskin's talk, which was addressed to a Tunbridge Wells audience in 1858, is the saffron stain on the marble basin of the health-springs there, a stain caused by rust, the interaction of iron from the soil with oxygen from the air. Invoking the 'breath of life' of Genesis, Ruskin shows how iron in combination with air *makes* the earth which feeds us, instead of making the often destructive implements of an instrumental culture; the 'hard, bright, cold, lifeless metal', is 'good enough for swords and scissors—but not for food'; only in union with oxygen can its 'merciless hardness' soften into 'fruitful and beneficent dust' (pp. 377–8). Ruskin notes, in a back-handed attack on capitalism, that the only metal which does *not* rust easily 'has caused Death rather than Life; it will not be put to its right use till it is made a pavement of, and so trodden under foot' (p. 377). Iron, Ruskin points out, is the vital pigmentation of the earth itself (and here pigmentation is deliberately resonant of both art and of physical well-being), essential aesthetically and biologically. Iron oxide veins and variegates the marbles of Sicily and Spain just as it veins and variegates the human body; crimson is both 'the noblest colour ever seen on this earth' (p. 384) and the sign of the iron which is in our very heart's blood. It becomes clear that the world *is* (or should be) a work of art for Ruskin, and that aesthetics is a matter of the

---

[16]   See e.g. *Works*, xii. 507.

[17]   Ruskin, 'The Work of Iron in Nature, Art, and Policy', *Works*, xvi. 375–411 (p. 378).

[18]   Compare Lawrence's description of an 'insentient iron world' in *Lady Chatterley's Lover*, 139–40.

health both of the planet and of the people who inhabit it. Ruskin's concern for the earth (his concern that 'iron roads are tearing up the surface of Europe'[19]) is, then, inextricably bound up with his concern for art. The work of art, far from closeting itself in the homes of a privileged élite, is the globe of the earth itself, for 'Nature paints for all the world, poor and rich together' (p. 383).

Following medieval typology, Ruskin sees in the union of iron and air the union of body and soul, the *integration* which was to be so central to Lawrence's philosophy. Just as, for Ruskin, the health of the environment depends upon this integration of iron and oxygen, so the health of the individual (inseparable from creativity in his/her work) is dependent upon an integration of body and soul, for 'without mingling of heart-passion with hand-power, no art is possible' (p. 385). If creativity is subordinated to mere *production*, *disintegration* results. In 'The Nature of Gothic', commenting on the 'division of labour' so crucial to factory production, Ruskin notes, 'It is not . . . the labour that is divided; but the men: Divided into mere segments of men— broken into small fragments and crumbs of life.'[20] Art in one's daily life is as necessary as bread; without it, the factory-workers 'feel their souls withering within them, unthanked' (p. 195). Ruskin prophesies a situation later realized through Gerald Crich in *Women in Love*, in which the workers have been robbed of their individuality, of their very humanity, and have become tools subserving higher powers; they are 'sent like fuel to feed the factory smoke' (p. 193). Precision, perfection, accuracy, all connote a dehumanization, a wrenching of the human body into alien geometric shapes and rigid lines.[21]

Ruskin protests against the spiked iron railings so dominant in the municipal architecture of his day on both aesthetic and political grounds: not only are they ugly, but they exert a 'costly tyranny', supposedly protecting the well-to-do from the 'rabble'.[22] He invokes the Book of Daniel (where we read that 'iron breaketh in pieces and subdueth all things') and Nebuchadnezzar's dream of a terrible apparition whose feet were partly iron and partly clay, symbolizing a kingdom partly strong, partly weak. Ruskin picks up the image to express the cruelty of industrialism, of a population grown callous and self-seeking: 'It seems', he argues, 'as if, in us, the *Heart* were part of iron, part of clay.'[23] In Lawrence, as we shall see shortly, the

---

[19] *Works*, iv. 128.

[20] 'The Nature of Gothic', in *The Stones of Venice, Works*, x. 180–269 (p. 196).

[21] Compare *Lady Chatterley's Lover*, 174–5: 'What have the leaders of men been doing to their fellow men? They have reduced them to less than humanness'; and p. 182: the colliers are 'distorted, one shoulder higher than the other . . . necks cringing from the pit roof, shoulders out of shape'. [22] 'The Work of Iron in Nature, Art, and Policy', 391.

[23] Ibid. 396. See Daniel 2: 40. *Lady Chatterley's Lover* was written late in life but in so many ways brings us back full circle to the youthful Lawrence's preoccupations and

tyranny of iron becomes the physical embodiment of the tyranny exerted by discursive modes of thought (premissed on a logocentric model of language) and by a metaphysical tradition which erodes the earth.

3. The Myth of the Fall

Many of Ruskin's doctrines were to be adopted wholeheartedly by William Morris, who late in life acknowledged a long debt to Ruskin's 'The Nature of Gothic' by printing it at the Kelmscott Press, and attaching an enthusiastic preface. It is probable that Lawrence read Morris at about the time he was reading Ruskin and Carlyle.[24] In his lecture series 'Hopes and Fears for Art', Morris reiterates the Ruskinian view that art is the cure for a sick society, as vital to human beings as the air they breathe, but what is perhaps more significant in terms of Lawrence's aesthetics is Morris's recourse to that same myth of a mind–body split to which so many late nineteenth- and early twentieth-century intellectuals subscribed (most famously, T. S. Eliot in his 'dissociation of sensibility' theory). As Eliot later would, Morris pinpointed the High Renaissance as a time in which self-consciousness blighted humanity's Edenic state.[25] He locates the nadir of this fall in the eighteenth century, and connects it with the disintegration that Ruskin had commented on, the severance of artist and labourer, which robs labourers of their autonomy and puts them at the mercy first of noble patron and later of industrial magnate. Further, for Morris as for Ruskin, aesthetics is not a matter for the few; it is a question affecting the entire landscape: 'One thing I know you will none of you like to plead guilty to; blindness to the natural beauty of the earth; and of that beauty art is the only possible guardian.'[26] If, for Morris and Ruskin, the way out of utilitarianism and materialism is through a kind of 'aestheticism', it is an aestheticism of a very different kind from that adopted by Gautier, Pater, and others, for whom the artist became the aloof, 'aristocratic' outsider. Like Lawrence, Ruskin and Morris use art

influences. See p. 158: 'The Wesleyan chapel . . . was of blackened brick and stood behind iron railings and blackened shrubs . . . the utter negation of natural beauty . . . the utter absence of the instinct for shapely beauty which every bird and beast has, the utter death of the human intuitive faculty was appalling.'

[24] See Richard Leslie Drain, 'Formative Influences on the Work of D. H. Lawrence' (unpublished Ph.D. dissertation, University of Cambridge, 1962), 156.

[25] Morris, 'Hopes and Fears for Art', in *The Collected Works of William Morris*, 24 vols. (London, 1910–15), xxii. 3–152 (pp. 56–7). Variants of Marxism also locate an 'original sin' in the division of mental from manual labour. See Adorno, *Negative Dialectics*, 177–8, and *Minima Moralia*, 63: 'The dissection of man into his faculties is a projection of the division of labour onto its pretended subjects, inseparable from the interest in deploying and manipulating them to greater advantage.'   [26] 'Hopes and Fears for Art', 33, 125.

as a touchstone for what the world itself should or could be. 'Aestheticization' of the world in this context does not imply a depoliticization of the world; it represents a politically charged move towards rescuing the world from a politics of capitalistic instrumentalism.[27]

Lawrence's ideas and the way in which they interrelate are often worked out and articulated imagistically, but when the implications of this imagery are unravelled, they reveal something which begins to look far more like Heidegger than like any of Lawrence's nineteenth-century predecessors. Ruskin, observing that the term for the spirit of God expressing itself in the world was *Logos*, argued that the unchallenged domination of the Word over the centuries had produced an enormous imbalance in our culture, but he did not make explicit the connections between this and his critique of industrialism.[28] It is left to Lawrence to voice these connections more explicitly.

Critics have pointed to the association, in Dickens, Ruskin, and other Victorian writers, between dirt and dragons.[29] Although the dragons and serpents in Dickens, Carlyle, and Ruskin imply a fallen world, Lawrence articulates the nature of that fallenness in a new way, transmuting the dragons and demons of industry into the dragons not just of dirt and smoke but of the Word itself. In 'Apocalypse', Lawrence characterizes the modern age as 'the day of the dirty-white dragon of the Logos and the steel-age': here 'dirty-white' fuses the notions of 'white consciousness' and industrial grime (p. 129). Further, the sense of imprisonment and claustrophobia which pervades Ruskin's descriptions of civic drabness and squalor, and of the Christian religion as practised in urban areas (he focuses on the undignified black iron railings of St Paul's Church, Covent Garden),[30] becomes in Lawrence a specific kind of psychic imprisonment. This is indicative of the way in which Lawrence's influences began to stretch far beyond the nineteenth-century British commentators on industrialism and to embrace the many Continental writers and philosophers he was able to read on leaving Nottingham; in particular, Nietzsche exerted a profound influence on him during the Croydon years.[31] Ultimately it is to this German tradition that one must turn in order to understand Lawrence's art-criticism, for if England is traditionally seen to be the home of empiricism and Germany of transcendentalism, if English culture is linked to particularity and German

---

[27] See below, pp. 188–9.   [28] See e.g. *Works*, iii. 87–92.

[29] See Nick Shrimpton, ' "Rust and Dust": Ruskin's Pivotal Work', in Robert Hewison (ed.), *New Approaches to Ruskin* (London, 1981), 51–67 (pp. 64–6).

[30] *Works*, vii. 382.

[31] Jessie Chambers recalls that Lawrence encountered Nietzsche's work in Croydon Library; she 'perceived that he had come upon something new and engrossing' (*A Personal Record*, 120).

culture to totality, there is also a strand within German philosophy which strives to turn against the transcendentalism that has so strongly influenced it: Marx, Nietzsche, and Heidegger all see themselves in their different ways to be abolishing transcendence and rewriting philosophy from the beginning, from the material here and now. This is Lawrence's project too.

Lawrence and Heidegger both construct in their different ways a myth of a prelapsarian Golden Age, located by Heidegger in ancient Greece and by Lawrence in different cultures at different points in his career, but most prominently in ancient Etruria. The imagery of 'Etruscan Places', of asphodel meadows and a land 'as mysterious and fresh as if it were still the morning of Time', is unmistakably Edenic (p. 27). At one level, Lawrence's entire life-work can be read as an allegory of the way in which the uncanny shapes of technology and urban sprawl, 'shapes not before known to man', have 'surprised' the earth.[32] Lawrence and Heidegger both try to argue that in ancient cultures like those of Greece and Etruria people were somehow able to respond to 'Being' spontaneously and openly, though in neither case is 'Being' identified with the transcendental idealist tradition (these ideas are investigated at length in the following chapters).[33] Both writers go on to develop this into a myth of a 'fall' into our present, technology-driven condition; they develop it via a similar route, taking as their starting-point what they perceive to be their wholesale rejection of the Western metaphysical tradition (Heidegger calls this his 'counter-metaphysic').[34] More generally, Platonic idealism, Cartesian subjectivity, and Kantian transcendence are all seen by both Lawrence and Heidegger to undermine the substantive, phenomenal world. Both writers, moreover, having absorbed so much Nietzsche, turn the tables on him: for both of them Nietzsche, who saw himself as overthrowing that tradition through his 'revaluation of all values', is seen, in his emphasis on the will-to-power, to mark the culmination rather than the overthrow of Western metaphysics.[35] All those bold repudiations which Nietzsche had called his own are now appropriated by Lawrence and Heidegger (rightly or wrongly) as theirs: the complete denial of a transcendental realm, of systems of philosophy or morality based on abstractions from the individual case.

For both Lawrence and Heidegger, the nature of art is crucial to an understanding of this whole question. For Lawrence this is brought out,

[32] *Lady Chatterley's Lover*, 176.

[33] See 'Reflections on the Death of a Porcupine', in *Reflections on the Death of a Porcupine and Other Essays*, 347–63 (p. 359): 'Being is not ideal, as Plato would have it.' This essay was first published in the collection of that name, Philadelphia, 1925.

[34] Cited by George Steiner in *Heidegger* (London, 1978), 72. See e.g. 'Introduction to *Memoirs of the Foreign Legion*', in *Phoenix II*, 303–61 (p. 358). This piece was first published as the introduction to *Memoirs of the Foreign Legion* by Maurice Magnus (London, 1924).

[35] See below, pp. 145–50.

as we saw in the last chapter, by his use of Cézanne's apple as a symbol: Cézanne's still-lifes represent the pinnacle of art's achievement, but they also represent a redemption, a retrieval of the apple of knowledge, the consumption of which precipitated the 'fall' into the Western philosophical tradition. If *Women in Love* is an inventory of the symptoms of a sickness, it is in Lawrence's writings on art that a hint can be found as to the cure. For Heidegger, too, art provides a route to a more 'authentic' mode of being. The next chapter looks in detail at the nature of this 'fallen' philosophical tradition, and Chapter 9 at the way in which both Lawrence and Heidegger turn increasingly in their work to the 'redemptive' powers of art.

8

LAWRENCE AND HEIDEGGER I:
THE WORLD AS OBJECT

1. Method and Violence

The opening of *Sons and Lovers* charts 'a sudden change' in the landscape, as the small mines or gin-pits which have been operating unobtrusively for centuries are 'elbowed aside by the large mines of the financiers'. The appearance of 'six mines like black studs on the countryside, linked by a loop of fine chain, the railway' (pp. 9–10), marks the beginning of what is a kind of *textualization* of the landscape, a process which is brought to consummation by Gerald Crich, the 'industrial magnate' of *Women in Love*; by *Lady Chatterley's Lover*, the village of Uthwaite has 'all the steel threads of the railways to Sheffield drawn through it' (p. 177). That the railway track and the discursive sentence could be in any way connected may seem hard to accept. Yet for Lawrence it is a very literal connection, and one which is examined with greater or lesser explicitness throughout his work.[1] Lawrence, as we have seen, saw his culture to be dominated by what he called 'the Logos', and directed much of his criticism against a mimetic or logocentric model of language premissed on a form/content split. It is this supposition of a form/content split in language which makes possible scientific discourse, and, by extension, scientific method, technology. Hence, in the essay 'Democracy', written in 1919, the excessive power wielded by the Logos in modern Western cultures ('Man's overweening mind uttered the Word, and the Word was God') has meant that the fabric of our civilization today is nothing but 'a flesh-and-blood-and-*iron* substantiation of this uttered Word'.[2]

The defacement of the earth's surface implemented by Crich's 'pure mechanical organisation' is overtly linked by Lawrence to the 'pure organic disintegration' (the mind–body split) which leads to a certain kind of conceptualization.[3] This complicity between the mind–body split and violence or coercion is traceable back to Lawrence's earliest writings. An early short story, 'The Old Adam', depicts the rather too self-conscious Lawrence-figure,

---

[1] Virginia Woolf also wishes to avoid writing 'a formal railway line of a sentence' (*Letters*, iii. 135).

[2] 'Democracy' in *Reflections on the Death of a Porcupine and Other Essays*, 69, my emphasis.

[3] See *Women in Love*, 231.

Severn, engaged in a brawl and 'wrapped on [his adversary] like steel, his
rare intelligence concentrated, not scattered'.[4] This anticipates the way in
which Gerald, in the final love-scenes of *Women in Love*, closes over Gudrun
'like steel': 'He felt strong as winter, his hands were living metal, invincible
and not to be turned aside' (p. 402). These scenes of internecine passion are
set against the 'vast abstraction of ice and snow' which, as we saw in Chapter
4, is the element of the overconscious Northern spirit, of Gerald's 'frost-
knowledge' (p. 254). This is not irrelevant when considering the psychical
state which could lead to the near-rape, and later the near-strangulation, of
Gudrun. The association of 'white consciousness' with violence is telescoped
into phrases like 'white-edged wrath' (p. 241) and 'white-cruel recognition'
(p. 242). Loerke imagines what it would be like if 'the world went cold, and
snow fell everywhere, and only white creatures, polar-bears, white foxes, and
men like awful white snow-birds, persisted in ice-cruelty' (p. 453). The snow
itself becomes both a whetstone on which Gudrun can sharpen her sadistic
psychic skills, and a keen-edged weapon in its own right: the snowflakes are
'sparks from a blade that is being sharpened' and the alpine wind is 'keen as
a rapier' (p. 420). Indeed, there is a whole 'metallic' vocabulary in *Women
in Love* which must be accounted for partly in terms of Lawrence's new
acquaintance with Futurism, but which, as we saw in the last chapter, also
suggests the imagery of Carlyle and Ruskin. It virtually always occurs in
contexts of 'disintegration'. In particular, blades and knives recur,[5] and in the
'Crème de Menthe' chapter, the knife metaphor is literalized when the
Pussum suddenly turns on a stranger in the Café Royale in an act of unex-
pected viciousness, 'jab[bing] a knife across his thick, pale hand' (p. 70).

The connection between logocentrism and violence is drawn out more
fully in *Studies in Classic American Literature* (1923). Here, what Lawrence
sees as the Americans' tendency towards an *intellectual* violation of Nature
(described as their obsession with 'this Nature-sweet-and-pure business',
p. 25) is closely bound up with their *physical* rape of Nature, through mechanization and industrialization.

Lawrence sees an appropriative violence lurking in the very 'framing' of
reality into method which must take place before we can embark upon the
scientific endeavours which, in his view, always lead to the domination of
nature. Method, according to Lawrence, subjugates phenomena and presses
them into its own service, and it does so by establishing its own parameters

---

[4] 'The Old Adam', in *Love Among the Haystacks and Other Stories*, 71–86 (p. 82). This
story first appeared in the collection entitled *A Modern Lover* (London, 1934), 45–72.
[5] We watch the Pussum 'becoming hard and cold [towards Halliday] like a flint knife'
(p. 80); 'Gerald looked at him with eyes blue as the blue-fibred steel of a weapon' (p. 204);
also, in *Sons and Lovers*, Paul examines Miriam 'with an intellect like a knife' (p. 230).

in advance, setting up its own object of enquiry, and proceeding to record how nature reports itself when set up *in this particular way*. In this sense method projects the *already known* on to phenomena; it can never really encounter the unknown. This is what Birkin suggests: ' "You can only have knowledge, strictly . . . of things concluded, in the past" ' (p. 86). For Lawrence, the machine, which is exploitative method turned literal, epitomizes this re-hearsing of the already known: 'The modern virtue is machine-principle, meaning the endless repetition of certain sanctioned motions. The old *virtus* meant just the opposite, the very impulse itself, the creative gesture, drifting out incalculable from human hands.'[6] Hence Gerald Crich is able to co-ordinate the activities of the mine into 'one pure, complex, infinitely repeated motion, like the spinning of a wheel'.[7]

Such images of circularity recur with marked frequency in *Women in Love* (most notably in Loerke's frieze, discussed more fully in the next chapter, where peasants are seen 'whirling ridiculously in roundabouts', p. 423). Gudrun and Gerald watch Winifred Crich's rabbit, an unwilling captive, run 'round and round the court . . . as if shot from a gun, round and round like a furry meteorite, in a tense hard circle that seemed to bind their brains' (p. 243). The people gathering at Breadalby are like chess-figures, 'the same figures moving round in one of the innumerable permutations that make up the game. But the game is known . . .' (p. 99). And, as we saw in Chapter 4, Birkin declares a hatred of 'ecstasy' (the ecstasy which Lawrence connects with the mind–body split) on the grounds that 'It's like going round in a squirrel cage' (p. 251).[8]

Here Lawrence's critique of method leads straight to the heart of Heidegger's philosophy: for Heidegger, too, method involves a rehearsing of its own procedures rather than an encounter with the unknown, and is there-fore inherently circular or repetitious. Heidegger provides a concise illustra-tion of this problem: 'If we come upon three apples on the table, we recognise that there are three of them. But the number three, threeness, we already know.'[9] In a lecture on the origin of art delivered in Athens in 1967, Heidegger argues that the basic feature of the entire cybernetic projection of the world

---

[6] *The Symbolic Meaning*, 43.   [7] *Women in Love*, 228.

[8] In the essay 'Him With His Tail in His Mouth', Lawrence links Platonic idealism, the Logos, and an imprisoning circularity: 'Plato was prepared. He popped the Logos into the mouth of the dragon, and the serpent of eternity was rounded off. The old dragon, ugly and venomous, wore yet the precious jewel of the Platonic idea in his head' (*Reflections on the Death of a Porcupine*, 309). Similarly, in *The Rainbow*, Winifred links the 'idea' to 'serpents trying to swallow themselves because they are hungry' (p. 318).

[9] 'The Age of the World Picture', in *The Question Concerning Technology and Other Essays*, 115–54 (pp. 118–19). See also 'The Thing', in *Poetry, Language, Thought*, 170: 'Science al-ways encounters only what its kind of representation has admitted beforehand as an object possible for science.'

is the *Regelkreis*, the circular process by which information flows out from its source in society and back again via a feedback mechanism. Heidegger extends this to all relations of human beings to their world in the modern technological age, and sees it (as the term *Regelkreis* implies) as a kind of enslavement. He sees its most ironic instance to be that of futurology, which, far from uncovering any 'future', can only extend the present indefinitely.[10] In so far as method projects the already *known*, it is devoid of innocence; it is testament, for Heidegger, as for Lawrence, to a fallen world.

The mind–body split is on several occasions connected by Lawrence to the Cartesian self-consciousness whereby each individual finds the hub of reality in him/herself, in his/her own ego. It is as a result of this that post-Renaissance Western philosophy is for Lawrence the story of 'the will of man rising frenzied against the mystery of life itself, and struggling insanely to *dominate*'.[11] This rather idiosyncratic interpretation of the history of Western philosophy has much in common with Heidegger's. Heidegger, seeking to account for a current state of affairs in which method holds sway, finds a focal point in the radical change, in the seventeenth century, in the meaning of the term 'subject'.[12] To illustrate the change, he invokes the ancient Greek culture and what he sees to be one of its key terms (one of those terms which for Heidegger could evoke the sensibility of an epoch): *hypokeimenon* ('subject', literally 'that-which-lies-before'). For the ancient Greeks, Heidegger suggests, this term referred to the reality that 'presenced' itself before human beings. He goes on to argue that with Descartes, *hypokeimenon* came to find its locus in the self-consciousness, in the unity of thinking and being, posited in the *ego cogito [ergo] sum*, so that humanity could now *represent* reality to itself, as an *object* of thought.[13] Heidegger sees all subsequent thinkers in the Western metaphysical tradition to be trapped in this notion of 'objectness'. The Kantian 'phenomenon', for example, is 'the object of a representing that runs its course in the self-consciousness of the human ego', which is why the Kantian noumenon, or 'thing-in-itself', is inaccessible to us: the 'thing-in-itself', argues Heidegger, is simply the object 'without reference to the human act of representing it'; if it is not being represented to the human ego, it cannot be known at all. For Heidegger, on the other hand, 'thingness' is inseparable from *presencing*.[14]

For Heidegger, the paradox inherent in the concept of absolute *objectivity* (and this can be extended to the concept of realist art investigated in earlier

[10] 'Die Herkunft der Kunst und die Bestimmung des Denkens', in *Distanz und Nähe: Reflexionen und Analysen zur Kunst der Gegenwart*, ed. P. Jaeger and R. Lüthe (Würzburg, 1983), 11–22.   [11] *The Symbolic Meaning*, 26.
[12] 'The Origin of the Work of Art', in *Poetry, Language, Thought*, 23.
[13] 'The Age of the World Picture', 131–2.   [14] 'The Thing', 177, 174.

chapters) is that it is no less than a supreme manifestation of *subjectivity*.[15] Expressed in different terms, positivism and idealism amount to the same thing. Further, in a characteristic piece of etymological unravelling, Heidegger shows how the German *Gegenstand* ('object', 'that which stands against') can be seen to articulate the fact that humanity's relationship with the world has become one of confrontation.[16] We are, he suggests, suddenly alienated from the things around us and this alienation means that we can begin to control them externally, to transform them into things-to-be-used-and-consumed. The 'objectness' of objects amounts, for Heidegger, to their *availability* or readiness-for-use; he calls this supply of the available the 'standing-reserve'.[17]

Heidegger then goes on to relate these concepts to the 'Being' which is so central to his epistemology. That humanity should feel called upon to treat the things of the world as standing-reserve is, he argues, the result of a 'challenging claim' issued by Being, a claim which Heidegger calls Enframing (*das Gestell*).[18] And although for Heidegger this claim or summons issues from Being itself, it is also, paradoxically, a challenging summons in which Being seems to withdraw. He sees the Enframing structure as something which, as it were, *wrenches* things into conformity (conformity to humanity's needs), and prevents them from appearing as they intrinsically are in themselves: the Being of phenomena slips beneath or is subsumed by their readiness-for-use and orderability.[19] It is because of this that, for Heidegger, the Enframing domain is a dangerous one, in which our very humanity is under threat; for it is a domain in which, he argues, language may become a mere instrument of information, and human beings themselves may be sucked up into the standing-reserve, becoming nothing more than instruments themselves, at the disposal of others. Heidegger expresses this in terms of objects disappearing into the 'objectlessness' of standing-reserve, and finds an extreme example of it in something like information technology

---

[15] 'The Age of the World Picture', 133.   [16] 'The Thing', 167.

[17] 'The Question Concerning Technology', 17. Compare Adorno, who traces the 'administered world' back to a similar separation of mind from the material world: 'Once radically parted from the object, the subject reduces it to its own measure; the subject swallows the object, forgetting how much it is an object itself' ('Subject-Object', in *The Essential Frankfurt School Reader*, ed. Andrew Arato and Eike Gebhardt (New York, 1987), 499). For Heidegger, it is the 'objectification' of the world which leads to a culture of 'exchanges' ('What Are Poets For?', in *Poetry, Language, Thought*, 135).

[18] 'The Question Concerning Technology', 19.

[19] Compare Kant's *Interesse* (see below, pp. 162–4); compare also Schopenhauer's Principle of Sufficient Reason, the 'enframing' [Heidegger's term] of phenomena as *Vorstellungen* ('representations') in the subjective categories of time, space, and causality (for Schopenhauer, causality is nothing but time and space taken together anyway). For Schopenhauer, perception is determined by interest and ultimately the will-to-live: 'Perception is based on the will-to-live' (i.e. perception according to the Principle of Sufficient Reason). (See *The World as Will and Representation*, i. 95–165.)

which 'processes' everything as 'data'. Turning to Nietzsche's *The Gay Science* (1882) and the madman's proclamation that God is dead, Heidegger argues that we have indeed killed God, and done away with, destroyed, the earth, because the 'I-ness' of the *ego cogito* has meant nothing less than 'the act of doing away with the suprasensory world that *is* in itself'.[20]

Interestingly, from the point of view of the Lawrence reader, Heidegger uses the example of coal-mining to illustrate this instrumentalism. He explains how the earth becomes standing-reserve when it is 'challenged into the putting out of coal and ore'; the earth is no longer earth but has become a 'mineral deposit'. By contrast, the work of the peasant does not challenge the soil of the field. But even farming, argues Heidegger, has in this technological age come under the grip of Enframing: agriculture has become the mechanized food industry. Nothing is simply 'present' as itself; everything is directed towards the furthering of *something else* (i.e. towards maximum yield at minimum expense). Most ironically of all, he argues, the river Rhine remains a river, a river set against a beautiful landscape, 'In no other way than as an object on call for inspection by a tour group ordered there by the vacation industry'. In all this Heidegger traces the same link that Lawrence had traced between mentality and machinery, between *vorstellen* (to represent) and *herstellen* (to produce/manufacture).[21]

2. *Gerald Crich as* Übermensch *and 'Technological Man'*

For Heidegger, the self-consciousness of the subject established by Descartes finds its fullest expression in the Nietzschean concept of the will-to-power. For Nietzsche himself, the Judaeo-Christian era marked the birth of subjectivity, in that it marked the end of a barbaric era of compulsion and the beginning of a period of hegemony, of the introjection of the law implicit in the notion of 'virtue'. For Nietzsche, this is to give way in its turn to a new era in which we can overcome our subjectivity (this is the capacity of the *Übermensch*) and give the law unto ourselves, become the artists of ourselves.[22] But this kind of mastery is not perceived by Heidegger as freedom;

---

[20] 'The Word of Nietzsche: "God is Dead" ', in *The Question Concerning Technology and Other Essays*, 53–112 (p.107). Compare Lawrence in the 'Introduction to *The Dragon of the Apocalypse* by Frederick Carter', where he speaks of 'losing' the sun, by replacing it with 'thought-forms' (*Apocalypse and the Writings on Revelation*, 52); also 'Apocalypse', 76: 'Landscape and the sky, these are to us the delicious background of our personal life, and no more. Even the universe of the scientist is little more than an extension of our personality, to us.'

[21] 'The Question Concerning Technology', 14–16. The Schopenhauerian *Vorstellung* is already warped by will and its tool, the Principle of Sufficient Reason.

[22] See e.g. 'The Birth of Tragedy', sect. 5 (pp. 36–42), and sect. 24 (pp. 140–4).

on the contrary, for Heidegger, when the whole world is ingested by the *Übermensch*, freedom no longer exists because there is nothing outside the subject to guarantee that freedom: 'otherness' has been eliminated. For Heidegger, the will-to-power, in finding every aspect of reality to be at the service of the preservation-enhancement of the subject's will, and in its 'epistemophilia' or lust for knowledge, is the final expression of the subjectness of the subject. Erich Heller has shown how the *Übermensch*, as the 'transfigurer' of existence ('*der Verklärer der Daseins*'), is a transfigurer at the cost of impoverishing the world: 'With every new gain in poetic creativity the world as it is, the world as created without the poet's intervention, becomes poorer.'[23] For Lawrence and Heidegger, humanity's task is to enrich the present world by conceding to it *as it is*. They see in Nietzsche's stance a solipsistic aloofness, a withdrawal, implicit in his claim that 'We possess *art* lest we *perish of the Truth*', and in his description of 'The Birth of Tragedy', sixteen years after it was written, in these terms: 'Throughout the book I attributed a purely esthetic meaning—whether implied or overt—to all process: a kind of divinity if you like, God as the supreme artist, amoral, recklessly creating and destroying, realizing himself indifferently in whatever he does or undoes . . .'[24] Here the difference between the Nietzschean and the Heideggerian aesthetic is decisive. Nietzsche's emphasis on sovereignty is for Heidegger the most extreme manifestation of nihilism in Western philosophy. Indeed, for Heidegger, the Nietzschean superman and his own version of technological man become one and the same. And since Lawrence has made precisely the same connection as Heidegger between Nietzschean metaphysics and a machine-driven, consumer society, it can come as no surprise that Gerald Crich seems to offer a supreme example of both Heidegger's 'technological man' and of the will-to-power.

Affinities between Lawrence and Nietzsche have been traced by many critics, perhaps most fully in Colin Milton's 1987 study, yet there are several occasions on which Lawrence directly criticizes Nietzsche's notion of the will-to-power. In 'Study of Thomas Hardy', Lawrence states that '[Being part of life] is different from the sense of power, of dominating life. The Wille zur Macht is a spurious feeling' (p. 104). And the Nietzschean references scattered throughout *Women in Love*, where they occur most overtly, are pejorative. Gudrun is 'exalted' by the Alpine snowscape into feeling 'übermenschlich—more than human' (p. 394), and Ursula, after witnessing the well-known episode in which Gerald forces his Arab mare to stand,

[23] Heller, *The Disinherited Mind*, 135.
[24] *The Will to Power*, trans. Walter Kaufmann and R. J. Hollingdale, ed. Walter Kaufmann (New York, 1968), sect. 822, p. 435; 'A Critical Backward Glance', 'The Birth of Tragedy', 3–15 (p. 9).

terror-struck, at the railway-crossing while a train passes, comments, 'It is just like Gerald with his horse—a lust for bullying—a real Wille zur Macht—so base, so petty' (p. 150). Here Lawrence is guilty of distorting the meaning of 'will-to-power'; he comes dangerously close to using the phrase to mean something like 'willpower', which is as far as could be from Nietzsche's definition. In fact, Lawrence's use of the term 'will', in his treatment of Gerald as in many other places in his work, has much in common with the usage of another of the *völkisch* ideologues mentioned in the opening chapter, Ferdinand Tönnies, author of *Gemeinschaft und Gesellschaft* (1887). Tönnies distinguished between two kinds of will, which he called *Wesenwille* and *Kürwille*. While *das Wesen* denotes 'being', 'nature', or 'essence', the verb *küren* means 'to choose'. The notion of a 'natural will' is thus opposed to the notion of an arbitrarily imposed will. Tönnies associated *Kürwille* with what Max Weber later termed *zweckrational* behaviour (*Zweck* denotes 'purpose'), meaning an act calculated with a view to a specific end.[25] Gerald Crich's will clearly corresponds to Tönnies' *Kürwille*. Yet the will-to-power for Nietzsche is more like Tönnies' *Wesenwille*. It is not to do with calculated acts, but is made up of the whole shifting network of (biological) forces out of which the substance of the world is spun, forces which cannot be pinned down by any essentialist project. This shifting bodily subtext of all our conscious life is also something in which Lawrence is passionately interested, and there would be a strong case for arguing that he in fact approves of the notion of a natural will, based on spontaneity rather than force, and that the true Nietzschean of *Women in Love* is not Gerald with his 'lust for bullying', but Birkin. As we saw earlier with Roger Fry, Lawrence often stages overt disagreements with philosophers and critics only to agree with them at a more covert level. When attacking Nietzsche, both Lawrence and Heidegger seem to construe the will-to-power as something corresponding to Tönnies' *Kürwille* rather than to Nietzsche's own concept.

In the chapter 'The Industrial Magnate', having had 'a vision of power' (p. 222), Gerald 'vibrate[s] with zest before the challenge' issued by the coal-industry (p. 224), fully intent on bleeding the mine for all it is worth (p. 223):

There was plenty of coal. The old workings could not get at it, that was all. Then break the neck of the old workings. The coal lay there in its seams, even though the seams were thin. There it lay, inert matter . . . subject to the will of man. The will of man was the determining factor. Man was the arch-god of the earth . . . And it was his will to subjugate Matter to his own ends.

Suddenly he had conceived the pure instrumentality of mankind . . . As a man as

---

[25] See Ringer, *The Decline of the German Mandarins*, 164.

of a knife: does it cut well? Nothing else mattered . . . Everything in the world has its function, and is good or not good in so far as it fulfils this function more or less perfectly. Was a miner a good miner? Then he was complete. Was a manager a good manager? That was enough.[26]

And just as Heidegger warns that it is precisely in the midst of this objectlessness, where man is under threat of becoming standing-reserve himself, that he 'exalts himself to the posture of lord of the earth', so Gerald imagines himself to be 'the arch-god of the earth' and 'the God of the machine'.[27] He is a perfect example of the Heideggerian dictum that 'Self-assertive man, whether or not he knows and wills it as an individual, is the functionary of technology'.[28] Robbed of his own being and reduced to his own role as director of the mine, Gerald has nihilistic visions in which he is no more than 'a purely meaningless babble lapping round a darkness'; pondering his face in the mirror, he is no longer sure that he exists at all: 'He dared not touch it for fear it should prove to be only a composition mask. His eyes were blue and keen as ever, and as firm in their sockets. Yet he was not sure that they were not blue false bubbles that would burst in a moment and leave clear annihilation' (p. 232). Just as the colliers in Lawrence's fiction have taken on the characteristics of the minerals they mine, becoming 'fauna of the elements, carbon, iron, silicon: elementals', so Gerald has become so much a part of the mine-workings that the electricity that powers them seems to have insinuated itself into his own veins: it flows 'turgid and voluptuously rich, in his limbs'.[29] Gudrun, who is Gerald's match in these terms, suffers the same symptoms: pondering Gerald she finds that 'his instrumentality appealed so strongly to her, she wished she were God, to use him as a tool' (p. 418); her face, too, is 'mask-like' (p. 9). Technology, which for Lawrence, as for Heidegger, is ultimately a form of idealism, eventually dominates the masters themselves; in this it parallels the capitalism that Marx had also seen to be inherently idealist:

Lastly, it is essential that in this competition landed property, in the form of capital, manifest its dominion over both the working class and the proprietors themselves who are either being ruined or raised by the laws governing the movement of capital. The medieval proverb *nulle terre sans seigneur* [there is no land without its lord] is thereby replaced by that other proverb, *l'argent n'a pas de maître* [money knows

---

[26] Compare Clifford Chatterley (*Lady Chatterley's Lover*, 22), who sees the miners as 'objects rather than men, parts of the pit rather than parts of life, crude raw phenomena rather than human beings along with him'.

[27] 'The Question Concerning Technology', 27; *Women in Love*, 223. Compare Clifford Chatterley (*Lady Chatterley's Lover*, 126): 'Power! He felt a new sense of power flowing through him . . . He was finding out: and he was getting things into his grip.'

[28] 'What Are Poets For?', 116.   [29] *Lady Chatterley's Lover*, 182; *Women in Love*, 65.

no master], wherein is expressed the complete domination of dead matter over mankind.

Gerald is ultimately, in fact, one of Marx's alienated workers; he experiences 'the relation to the sensuous external world, to the objects of nature, as an alien world inimically opposed to him'.[30]

At the end of the 'Industrial Magnate' chapter, we are told that Gerald 'liked to read books about the primitive man, books of anthropology' (p. 232). The irony inherent in this is that anthropology itself, as a study of the world *in terms of man*, is, for Lawrence and Heidegger, just another symptom of the subjectness of the subject. This is something Heidegger investigates in 'The Age of the World Picture':

> The more extensively and the more effectually the world stands at man's disposal as conquered, and the more objectively the object appears, all the more subjectively, i.e. the more importunately, does the *subiectum* rise up, and all the more impetuously, too, do observation of and teaching about the world change into a doctrine of man, into anthropology. (p. 133)

Where anthropology had traditionally been seen as the study of more 'primitive' cultures by the 'civilized' world, Lawrence and Heidegger invert the hierarchy to make the anthropological project itself another way in which the rampaging ego lays hold of its environment. At the time of writing *The Rainbow* (1915), Lawrence himself had been reading several anthropological works. One of them, as we have already seen, was Leo Frobenius's *The Voice of Africa* (1913). In the preface to his study, Frobenius tells his readers with some irony that, according to 'a great light of the church', the Africans 'had no souls and were the burnt-out husks of men'.[31] Lawrence picks up the metaphor to invert it, in connection with the miners who have been not en*light*ened but dehumanized by the soulless, mechanistic culture of modern 'civilized' man. In *Women in Love*, Gerald's response to the 'savages' he has encountered on his travels is telling: ' "On the whole they're harmless – they're not born yet, you can't really feel afraid of them. *You know you can manage them*." '[32] The 'reign of brute-force' which, as Frobenius reports, nineteenth-century anthropologists saw presiding over Africa now holds sway over the Western world.[33] That côterie of artists in *Women in Love* who perceive themselves to be at the highest pitch of culture are obliquely linked to the reptiles and creeping animals of a primeval swamp: Loerke's hands are

---

[30] *Economic and Philosophical Manuscripts of 1844*, 102, 111.

[31] Frobenius, *The Voice of Africa*, i, p. xiii. See also the descriptions of the miners in *Lady Chatterley's Lover*: they are 'haggard, shapeless, and dreary as the countryside' (p. 20); 'weird, distorted, smallish beings like men' (p. 174); 'weird fauna of the coalseams' (p. 182).

[32] *Women in Love*, 66, my emphasis.   [33] *The Voice of Africa*, p. xiii.

'prehensile' (p. 423); he is 'a mud-child' (p. 427); he 'lives like a rat, in the river of corruption' (p. 428). In *The Rainbow*, Winifred Inger, associated with the modern technology through her alliance with Ursula's Uncle Tom, is seen by Ursula in terms of 'clayey, inert, unquickened flesh, that reminded her of the great prehistoric lizards' (p. 325).

For both Lawrence and Heidegger, then, the light of reason becomes that of an intellectual barbarism; the *malpais* of prehistory and the *buenpais* of posthistory are curiously reversed. Nietzsche had argued that Socratic reason was a 'counter-tyrant' even stronger than the tyrant instincts, but, for Heidegger and Lawrence, Nietzsche himself, far from being a prophet of a 'great noon', 'the time of the brightest brightness' as Heidegger mockingly calls it, is shrouded in nihilistic darkness.[34] In 'What Are Poets For?', Heidegger follows Rilke in equating 'objectness' with opacity and a benighted world (p. 108), and in the same essay he proclaims apocalyptically that 'The essence of technology comes to the light of day only slowly. This day is the world's night, rearranged into merely technological day. This day is the shortest day. It threatens a single endless winter' (p. 117). This same play of light and dark pervades Lawrence's work: in 'Apocalypse', he explains that 'Socrates and Aristotle were the first to *perceive* the dawn' (p. 91), the implication being that as soon as dawn is *perceived*, dusk is inevitable; and a similar irony pervades the passage in *The Rainbow* where 'the trains rushed and the factories ground out their machine-produce and the plants and animals worked by the light of science and knowledge' (p. 437).[35] In the 'Study of Thomas Hardy', Lawrence connects light with what he calls 'absolving the concrete reality':

Since the Renaissance there has been the striving for the Light, and the escape from the Flesh, from the Body, the Object . . . In painting, the Spirit, the Word, the Love, all that was represented by John, has appeared as light. Light is the constant symbol of Christ in the New Testament. It is light, actual sunlight or the luminous quality of day which has infused more and more into the defined body, fusing away the outline, absolving the concrete reality. (p. 82)

He finds in Impressionism the equivalent in art of this emphasis on light (the light of reason) at the expense of the body.

[34] 'The Word of Nietzsche', 102.
[35] Carlyle also uses this play of light and dark: the cause-and-effect philosophers are not 'dwelling in the daylight of truth' as they claim to be, but 'in the rush-light of "closet-logic" ', suggesting solipsism ('Signs of the Times', *Works*, xxvii. 75). The opening paragraph of *Sartor Resartus* plays on the metaphor of the 'Torch of Science', from which 'innumerable Rush-lights and Sulphur-matches, kindled thereat, are also glancing in every direction, so that not the smallest cranny or doghole in Nature or Art can remain unilluminated' (*Works*, i). Compare *Lady Chatterley's Lover*, 23: 'The field of life is largely an artificially lighted stage today.'

3. Rootlessness

> Man has made such a mighty struggle to feel at home on the face of
> the earth, without even yet succeeding.
>
> ('Study of Thomas Hardy')

> The higher its consciousness, the more the conscious being is ex-
> cluded from the world.
>
> (Heidegger, 'What Are Poets For?')

It is easy to see how the birth of subjectivity can be made, by both Lawrence
and Heidegger, to account for the 'rootlessness' of modern existence. If
phenomena are made into objective entities, separate and distinct from the
perceiving subject, then human beings are as it were severed from the
environment, uprooted, and consigned to curiosity and a self-perpetuating
need for diversion. Gudrun has 'an insatiable curiosity to see and to know
everything'; at Laura Crich's wedding, she watches the wedding-guests with
'objective curiosity' as though they were marionettes in a theatre.[36] In
Heidegger, the 'forgetting' of the mystery of Being leads to a very similar
state which he calls 'errancy', one of the symptoms of which is also *Neugier*
(curiosity, lust for novelty): man 'wanders from one being to another in a
state of confusion, driven about hither and thither, looking for a satisfaction
that no being can give, searching for a repose that no being, torn from the
roots of ultimate meaning in mystery, can offer'.[37] Restlessness is the mood
of many of the over-conscious characters scattered throughout Lawrence's
fiction. As early as *The White Peacock*, a lark's nest inhabited by two fledgelings
leads Cyril to reflect on his own 'unhoused' condition: 'It seems as if I were
always wandering, looking for something which they had found even before
the light broke into their shell.'[38] In *Women in Love*, Gudrun's nature is
'profoundly restless' (p. 211); unable to have more than a casual relationship
with Gerald, she decides that 'Perhaps it was not in her to marry. She was
one of life's outcasts, one of the drifting lives that have no root'; comparing
herself with Ursula, she finds that she is 'jealous, unsatisfied' (p. 376). It
would be impracticable to recount here the countless times that words like
'casual', 'mocking', 'playful', and 'ironic' are reiterated in the novel, with
their implications of disengagement.[39] Gudrun and Gerald epitomize the

---

[36] *Women in Love*, 234, 14. See also pp. 64, 410.

[37] 'On the Essence of Truth', in *Basic Writings*, 117–141 (pp. 135–6).

[38] *The White Peacock*, ed. Andrew Robertson (Cambridge, 1983), 220. Towards the beginning of *Lady Chatterley's Lover*, Connie realizes that 'a restlessness was taking possession of
her like a madness' (p. 28).

[39] 'Casual' occurs on pp. 37, 40, 76, 89, 431, etc.; 'playful', p. 37; 'mocking', 'ironic',
pp. 37, 433.

ruthless, restless, errant humanity that peoples the novel as a whole. Just as, for Lawrence, this restless curiosity is symptom of a hypertrophied reason ('white consciousness'), so Heidegger warns that 'Thirst for knowledge and greed for explanations never lead to a thinking inquiry. Curiosity is always the concealed arrogance of a self-consciousness that banks on a self-invented *ratio* and its rationality.'[40]

It was noted in the first chapter that this impulse to *root* (the rootlessness of Lawrence's itinerant life was, after all, an expression of this impulse) and the opposition, in both Lawrence and Heidegger, to the metropolitan and the vagrant, to anonymous mass existence, comes from Spengler and others like Tönnies who drew the distinction between *Gemeinschaft* (community) and the *Gesellschaft* (society) that has supplanted it. As we saw in that chapter, this distinction was to have disastrous consequences when exploited by Nazism. Werner Sombart, for example, used it to stir up the anti-Americanism that was so much part of the *völkisch* ethos.[41] But the same distinction also fed into left-wing attacks on a capitalistic, postmodern culture. Lawrence describes a culture in which the tendency to 'objectify', and thus to experience everything at one remove, is so endemic that human beings are turning away from actual reality in favour of a pseudo-reality simulated by machines: 'We don't *want* to look at flesh and blood people—we want to watch their shadows on a screen. We don't *want* to hear their actual voices: only transmitted through a machine.'[42] Our world has, according to Lawrence, become a world in which nothing is itself, everything is simulacrum. Gazing at the mine-torn countryside, Gudrun perceives that 'Everything is a ghoulish replica of the real world', and Birkin sees around him 'myriad simulacra of people'.[43] In Heideggerian terms, it is a 'destitute' world, which 'can no longer discern the default of God as a default'.[44]

For Lawrence, these are all symptoms of the same alienation of humankind from nature initiated by Western metaphysics. Lawrence criticism is

---

[40] 'A Dialogue on Language', in *On the Way to Language*, 1–54 (p. 13).

[41] Both Lawrence and Heidegger shared their anti-Americanism with Rilke. In 'What Are Poets For?' (p. 113), Heidegger cites one of Rilke's letters, written in 1925, in which he complains of the intrusion, from America, of 'empty indifferent things, sham things, *dummies of life . . .*'; they are all examples of 'the substitute—*Ersatz*' (p. 130). He also cites a much earlier letter (1 Mar. 1912), in which Rilke complains of things 'shifting their existence more and more over into the vibrations of money, and developing there for themselves a kind of spirituality . . .' (p. 113). In an essay published in 1911, Sombart, exploring the relationship between technology and culture, argued against popular music: he saw a shallow and internationalized 'mechanically' made street music to have replaced 'organically' developed folksong. See 'Technik und Kultur', *Archiv*, 33 (1911), 305–47 (esp. pp. 342–7).

[42] 'Men Must Work and Women as Well', in *Phoenix II*, 582–91 (p. 590). This essay first appeared as 'Men and Women' in *Star Review*, 2 (Nov. 1929), 614–26.

[43] *Women in Love*, 11, 127. See also *Lady Chatterley's Lover*, 25, where Connie experiences 'the simulacrum of reality'.   [44] 'What Are Poets For?', 91.

scattered with chapter headings like 'The Failure of the Flight' which testify to Lawrence's inability, in his own life, to find the pristine culture in which 'integrated' being might be possible.[45] The new world heralded by *The Rainbow* conspicuously fails to materialize in the novel's sequel, *Women in Love*. Oswald Spengler's sinister solution to the rootlessness of modern existence is to resign himself to a Destiny which he firmly believes to be ineluctable. He exhorts his readers in this expansive, technological age, 'to devote themselves to technics instead of lyrics, the sea instead of the paintbrush, and politics instead of epistemology'; this is what Adorno calls Spengler's 'complicity with the world'.[46] Against the same background, Lawrence takes a different approach: like Heidegger, he begins increasingly, in his writing, to appeal to art itself as a redemption, as a means of 'stepping out' of an instrumental culture.

[45] 'The Failure of the Flight', in Billy T. Tracy, Jr., *D. H. Lawrence and the Literature of Travel* (Epping, 1981), 73–90.

[46] *Decline of the West*, 41; Adorno, 'Spengler After the Decline', in *Prisms*, 65.

9

LAWRENCE AND HEIDEGGER II:
THE WORLD AS WORK OF ART

In *Women in Love*, the sealed world of snow in which Gerald and Gudrun enact the last death throes of their murderous relationship is contrasted by Ursula with a relinquished Eden:

Below her lay the dark fruitful earth . . . towards the south there were stretches of land dark with orange trees and cypress, grey with olives . . . ilex trees lifted wonderful plumy tufts in shadow against a blue sky . . . She wanted at this instant to have done with the snow-world, the terrible static, ice-built mountain tops. She wanted to see the dark earth, to smell its earthy fecundity, to see the patient wintry vegetation, to feel the sunshine touch a response in the buds. (p. 434)

In the last chapter of *Kangaroo* (1925), 'plumes' recur in a rare, paradisal vision of the Australian bush:

By the stream the mimosa was all gold, great golden bushes full of spring fire rising over your head, and the scent of the Australian spring, and the most ethereal of all golden bloom, the plumy, many-balled wattle . . . the most delicate feathery yellow of plumes and plumes and plumes and trees and bushes of wattle, as if angels had flown right down from heaven to settle here, in the Australian bush.[1]

But the 'plumes' of Lawrence's fiction are also the plumes of smoke issuing from the funnels of steam-engines or mine-workings: in *Lady Chatterley's Lover*, the colliery towns send forth 'a whole array of smoke plumes and steam' (p. 177).[2] The world as work of art, which, in Lawrence's mythology, the ancient Etruscans were privileged to enjoy, is gradually being eroded.[3] It is under threat, Lawrence argues, from the instrumental, 'objectifying' vision which can only see things as commodities, or, to use Heidegger's phrase, as 'standing-reserve'.

1. Futurism and Solipsism

For Lawrence and Heidegger, it is the light of reason which, in shedding its rays, appropriates and thereby abolishes things; art, for both of them, comes into being in a more crepuscular world in which this obliterating

---

[1] *Kangaroo* (London, 1955), 362–3.   [2] See e.g. *Sons and Lovers*, 89.
[3] For Lawrence on the Etruscans, see below, pp. 181, 184–6.

movement of consciousness is somehow arrested. For art, in their view, is not under the sway of method; through an assertion of its own materiality, it exceeds method, and thus imposes a limit on human presumption. In a culture founded upon method, and consequently upon violence and the will-to-power, art, in its absolute otherness to the laws of instrumental reason, is seen by them to commit itself to weakness and non-violence, in a kind of aggressive humility. But it can only do this if it is responded to as art. For both Lawrence and Heidegger, whatever form method may take in its approach to art, it will fail to make contact with art itself; for method starts out from a site external to art, and seeks to contain it. Instead, art invites what Heidegger calls 'the poverty of reflection' which is 'the promise of a wealth whose treasures glow in the resplendence of that uselessness which can never be included in any reckoning'.[4] For many critics, this kind of language is impossibly mystical and obfuscating. What possible grounds can there be for placing art beyond the reach of scientific method? In spite of their strictures on aesthetics, both Lawrence and Heidegger can be seen as the ultimate aesthetes. Yet to believe that scientific method is all-embracing and all-knowing is, for these two thinkers, the ultimate humanistic presumption.

In linking art with powerlessness, Lawrence and Heidegger are directly opposed to Nietzsche, for whom beauty is a *stimulant* to the will-to-power. If for Nietzsche the feeling of artistic rapture (*Rausch*) is a feeling of attunement so strong that nothing is foreign to it,[5] for Lawrence this is the acme of the subject's refusal to acknowledge the 'otherness' of phenomena, to recognize that they have a separate existence outside and beyond human subjectivity. Art produced under the sway of the will-to-power is, for Lawrence, a contradiction in terms, and this accounts for his hostile reaction to the Futurists. The first Futurist manifesto, which appeared in 1909, reads like a programme for a wholesale assault on the earth's resources. Marinetti promises to sing of 'greedy railway stations that devour smoke-plumed serpents', 'deep-chested locomotives whose wheels paw the tracks like the hooves of enormous steel horses, bridled by tubing', and so on, declaring that 'no work without an aggressive character can be a masterpiece. Poetry must be conceived as a violent attack on unknown forces, to reduce and prostrate them before man'.[6] In a letter of 1914, Lawrence records his reaction to Futurism:

[4] 'Science and Reflection', in *The Question Concerning Technology and Other Essays*, 155–82 (p. 181).
[5] See 'Twilight of the Idols', 110; see also Heidegger's critique of Nietzsche, 'The Word of Nietzsche: "God is Dead" ', in *The Question Concerning Technology and Other Essays*, 74–112.
[6] F. T. Marinetti, *Manifesto of Futurism*, first published in Italian in Milan, 1909; reprinted in French in *Le Figaro*, 20 Feb. 1909; reprinted in *Marinetti: Selected Writings*, trans. R. W. Flint and Arthur A. Coppotelli, ed. R. W. Flint (New York, 1972), 41–4 (pp. 41–2).

The one thing about their art is that it *isn't* art, but ultra scientific attempts to make diagrams of certain physical or mental states. It is ultra-ultra intellectual . . . It's the most self-conscious, intentional, pseudo-scientific stuff on the face of the earth. Marinetti begins: 'Italy is like a great dreadnought surrounded by her torpedo boats'. That is it exactly—a great mechanism. Italy has got to go through the most mechanical and dead stage of all—everything is appraised according to its mechanical value—everything is subject to the laws of physics.[7]

Where Marinetti himself, in the 'Technical Manifesto of Futurist Literature' (1912), finds it essential to 'destroy the *I* in literature' and substitute the 'lyric obsession with matter',[8] Lawrence sees in Futurism the boldest example of the assertion of *I* in our culture. Futurism reappears in the guise of Duncan Forbes's art in *Lady Chatterley's Lover*, 'all tubes and valves and spirals and strange colours, ultra modern', and the link with barbarism is reasserted, for this is an art which 'murders all the bowels of compassion in a man' (p. 307). The Ajanta frescoes had evoked a different reaction. Lawrence had commented in 1915 that 'That which we call passion is a very one-sided thing, based chiefly on hatred and Wille zur Macht. There is no Will to Power here—it is so lovely—in these [Ajanta frescoes].'[9]

For Lawrence, the subjectivity of both artist and viewer/reader should not be allowed to dominate to the extent that the art-work becomes dangerously solipsistic, unconnected with anything outside the artist's, or viewer's, controlling consciousness.[10] Loerke in *Women in Love* is both 'creature' and 'final craftsman', a god incapable of real creation, able only to *re*create himself: 'Loerke, in his innermost soul, was detached from everything, for him there was neither heaven nor earth nor hell. He admitted no allegiance, he gave no adherence anywhere' (p. 452). He produces an equally solipsistic work, 'a picture of nothing . . . It has nothing to do with anything but itself' (p. 430). This assertion of the ego in art is the equivalent of Gerald Crich's technological megalomania which leads only to *production*, not creation. The connection between the two is made explicit in Loerke's assertion that 'machinery and the acts of labour are extremely, maddeningly beautiful' (p. 424).

For Lawrence, then, art resists the desire for interpretative control or mastery. Such mastery is trapped in a hermeneutic circle (Heidegger's *Regelkreis*), where the interpreter reads back from the text or painting only what s/he has put into it in the first place (we saw in the previous chapter

---

[7] *Letters*, ii. 181 (2 June 1914).

[8] 'Technical Manifesto of Futurist Literature', in *Marinetti: Selected Writings*, 84–9 (p. 87).   [9] *Letters*, ii. 489 (27 Dec. 1915).

[10] See Birkin's comment on the catkins in Ursula's drawing class: 'It's the fact you want to emphasise, not a subjective impression to record' (*Women in Love*, 36).

how such circularity is, for both Lawrence and Heidegger, a feature of scientific method). Loerke's industrial frieze (dominated itself by images of circularity) is based on Mark Gertler's *Merry-Go-Round* (1916), an extraordinarily violent painting with its strident, metallic colours and a design which for one critic suggests a military helmet or even a medieval hellmouth.[11] The riders, in military garb and posture, are held in by the grip of a powerful centrifugal force, and indeed it is an almost suffocating *inwardness* which characterizes the overall structure. What would seem to be the fairground lights in the night-sky are pressing inwards and downwards towards the merry-go-round, apparently sealing it in from the surrounding darkness. It is easy to see how Lawrence would read the painting in terms of the 'enclosure of the ego', of the people whom, in 'Introduction to These Paintings', he describes as 'hermetically sealed and insulated from all experience' (p. 584).[12] This is reminiscent of *Women in Love* and Ursula's observation that 'no flowers grow upon busy machinery, there is no sky to a routine, there is no space to a rotary motion' (p. 193); the ego's effacement of otherness is obliquely linked to a literal effacement of the earth. The same claustrophobia permeates the Café de Pompadour in the opening of the *Crème de Menthe* chapter:

... the faces and heads of the drinkers showed dimly through the haze of smoke, reflected more dimly, and repeated ad infinitum in the great mirrors on the walls, so that one seemed to enter a vague, dim world of shadowy drinkers humming within an atmosphere of blue tobacco smoke. There was, however, the red plush of the seats to give substance within the bubble of pleasure. (p. 62)

The 'bubble of pleasure' is like the sealed world of snow towards the end of the novel, which exists 'as if there were no beyond' (p. 434), as a kind of experiential vacuum.

2. *Art and Instrumentalism*

In Cézanne's still-lifes, Lawrence finds an example of an art which seems curiously independent of the consciousness that created it. Cézanne's apples

[11] Paul Delany, *D. H. Lawrence's Nightmare* (New York, 1978), 260.
[12] The description of the night-sky above the Tevershall mines in *Lady Chatterley's Lover* is, on an impressionistic level, highly suggestive of Gertler's painting: 'On the low dark ceiling of cloud at night red blotches burned and quavered, dappling and swelling and contracting, like burns that give pain' (p. 20). This whole passage is informed by the imagery of Hell: 'the house was full of the stench of this sulphurous combustion of the earth's excrement . . . on the Christmas roses the smuts settled . . . like black manna from the skies of doom' (pp. 19–20); Clifford's life is described as taking place 'in a vacuum' (p. 23); and later we find another Gertlerian scenario: 'Round the near horizon went the haze, opalescent with frost and smoke, and on the top lay the small blue sky. So that it was like being inside an enclosure, always inside. Life always a dream or a frenzy, inside an enclosure' (p. 51).

are '*casually* related to man. But to those apples, man is by no means the absolute.'[13] In the 'Introduction to These Paintings', Lawrence contrasts this with Van Gogh's expressionism:

Van Gogh's earth was still subjective earth, himself projected into the earth. But Cézanne's apples are a real attempt to let the apple exist in its own separate entity, without transfusing it with personal emotion. Cézanne's great effort was as it were to shove the apple away from him, and let it live of itself. It seems a small thing to do: yet it is the first real sign that man has made for several years that he is willing to admit that matter *actually* exists. (pp. 567–8)

In Chapter 6, I discussed Lawrence's emphasis on 'appleyness' and suggested that the work of Rilke (more specifically, Rilke's emphasis on 'thingness') may provide one of the 'empirical' links between Lawrence and Heidegger. For Heidegger in 'The Origin of the Work of Art', art lets the thing itself rest 'in its own thing-being' (p. 31), where representation does not. By 'letting be' Heidegger does not mean, any more than Lawrence, leaving alone or ignoring; on the contrary, he wants to encourage the kind of 'caring' consciousness that will let things shine forth as what they are. Heidegger calls this the 'preservation' (*die Bewahrung*) of the work, remembering the sense of *die Wahre* (attention, care, heed, protection) (p. 66). Heidegger, like Lawrence, is wary of the way in which metaphors of light can suggest on the one hand the light of reason, and on the other some kind of window or transparency on to the noumenal. His 'shining forth' is meant to imply the inverse of such metaphors, and to suggest the way in which matter itself comes to the fore.

We have seen how, for Heidegger, the way in which we order things as 'standing-reserve', as pieces of equipment ready for use, causes their materiality (their 'thingness') to disappear into their usefulness and serviceability. The more suitable the material (the sharper the stone blade of the axe— Heidegger uses more or less the same example as Gerald Crich),[14] the more easily it disappears into the equipment-being of the piece of equipment.[15] Heidegger argues that the piece of equipment lacks the independence and self-sufficiency of the art-work, for in the art-work the material, far from vanishing, somehow comes into its own, 'shines forth', as Heidegger expresses it, as itself. As soon as colours, materials, sounds, are measured or 'explained' in terms of wavelength, weight, chemical make-up, and so on, they disappear. The 'redness' of red has nothing to do with its wavelength; yet somehow this 'redness' finds what Heidegger calls 'sanctuary' in the art-

---

[13] 'Art and Morality', in *Study of Thomas Hardy and Other Writings*, 168.
[14] See above, pp. 147–8.
[15] 'The Origin of the Work of Art', in *Poetry, Language, Thought*, 46.

work. He applies the same principle to literature as to painting: the poet may use the same words as an ordinary speaker, Heidegger explains, but where the ordinary speaker 'uses up' the words, the poet uses them 'in such a way that the word only now becomes and remains truly a word'.[16] Compare Lawrence's analysis of Van Gogh in 'Morality and the Novel':

The vision on the canvas is a third thing, utterly intangible and inexplicable, the offspring of the sunflower itself and Van Gogh himself. The vision on the canvas is forever incommensurable with the canvas, or the paint, or Van Gogh as a human organism or the sunflower as a botanical organism. You cannot weigh nor measure nor even describe the vision on the canvas . . . It is in-between everything, in the fourth dimension. (p. 171)

The instrumental culture in which we live may of course attempt to 'use up' art by appropriating and absorbing art-works, transforming them into propaganda, institutionalizing and evaluating them through art-dealing and museums. In 'Introduction to These Paintings', Lawrence deplores the gradual transformation of artefact into commodity: 'As for Gainsborough, all one can say is: What a lovely dress and hat! What really expensive Italian silk! The painting of garments continued in vogue, till pictures like Sargent's seem to be nothing but yards and yards of satin from the most expensive shops' (p. 560).

Lawrence's objections to the commodification of art link him, of course, not only with Heidegger but also (again) with Bloomsbury.[17] The Bloomsbury art-critics were vehemently opposed to art turned commercial. Sargent's yards of satin are, one suspects, sold in the same shop as the highly scented soap of Fry's article on Alma-Tadema, the soap of which, according to Fry's sardonic reading of Alma-Tadema's work, the Romans, 'their furniture, their clothes, even their splendid marble divans', were made. Fry goes on:

The artist arrived at this conclusion not as a result of his profound archaeological researches, but . . . by reference to commercial customs. He noticed that, however ill-constructed a saleable article might be, it had one peculiar and saving grace— that of 'shop-finish' . . . It requires great ingenuity and inventive skill . . . to remove completely the marks made upon a vessel by the potter's hand. But I believe that no piece of pottery is worthy to be presented to the general public until this has been done, and the surface reduced to dead mechanical evenness.

[16] Ibid. 48.
[17] This objection to art as commodity is a feature both of 'High Modernism', occurring, for example, in Greenberg's criticism of ersatz culture or kitsch, and of certain strands of Marxist thinking, especially the art-criticism of the Frankfurt School (see esp. Horkheimer and Adorno, *Dialectic of Enlightenment*, and Adorno, *Negative Dialectics* and *Aesthetic Theory*).

Fry coins the term 'opificer' to describe the artist who panders to the general public, to the consumers who like to be given ' "in another line" precisely the kind of article which they are accustomed to buy and sell'. To do this entails, on the part of the artist, 'an extreme of mental and imaginative laziness'; it is merely mechanical repetition, crushing human spontaneity.[18] We can see here that, however much Fry dissociates himself from Ruskin (for whom art is a morally edifying experience), he has inherited Ruskin's discourse concerning a deadening mechanical labour (Marx's 'alienated labour'). Like Fry and Lawrence, Ruskin is opposed to imitation, to copying, to exact finishes. His language is uncompromising: a woman who buys glass beads is 'engaged in the slave-trade'; if she wears cut jewels purely for their value she is a 'slave-driver'.[19] The old Venice glass, muddy, whimsical, and clumsily cut, is for Ruskin infinitely preferable to its clear, precisely cut, modern equivalent. The gargoyles and idiosyncrasies of Gothic are for Ruskin, in his somewhat idealized picture of the medieval past, 'signs of the life and liberty of every workman who struck the stone' (pp. 193–4); they militate against a situation in which human beings are degraded into ciphers. Fry perpetuates all these principles, and that several Lawrence critics should have so neatly equated Loerke in *Women in Love* with Roger Fry is puzzling in view of Fry's anti-mechanistic stance.[20]

In Lawrence's *The Lost Girl* (1920), Dr Mitchell's home is cluttered with what Fry would call 'opifacts', objects appealing primarily to a sense of proprietorship (pp. 260, 263). And in *Women in Love*, Birkin is tired of 'Art—music—London Bohemia—the most pettifogging calculating Bohemia that ever reckoned its pennies' (p. 60). For both Lawrence and Heidegger the whole paraphernalia of a *Kulturbetrieb* or art-industry is concerned only with the art-work as object.[21] Hermione Roddice in *Women in Love*, is, like so many of the characters in that novel, only a *Kulturträger* (p. 16): 'And all the while the pensive, tortured woman piled up her own defences of aesthetic knowledge, and culture, and world-visions, and disinterestedness. Yet she could never stop up the terrible gap of insufficiency' (p. 17). In Lawrence's view, art resists, ultimately, such attempts to subsume it.

---

[18] Roger Fry, 'The Case of the Late Sir Lawrence Alma-Tadema, O.M.', *The Nation* (18 Jan. 1913), 666–7.

[19] 'The Nature of Gothic', *The Stones of Venice, Works*, x. 197–8.

[20] Kim A. Herzinger, in *D. H. Lawrence in His Time* (Lewisburg, Pa., and London, 1982), places Lawrence in the 'cultural matrix' of his time, tracing links between Lawrence's preoccupation with the machine and Georgianism, but does not mention Bloomsbury.

[21] See 'The Origin of the Work of Art', 40–1.

3. World and Earth

In 'The Origin of the Work of Art', Heidegger evolves a terminology of 'world' and 'earth' to articulate art's capacity to elude method (pp. 40–50). The 'earth' (materials/colours/sounds/words) out of which the 'world' of the art-work towers forth is, he explains, that which both comes to the fore and shelters. It shelters in that it 'shatters every attempt to penetrate into it' (p. 47). The earth (the redness of red) only appears as itself when it is preserved as that which by its very nature cannot be disclosed/explained.[22] When we seek to articulate the earth, argues Heidegger, it is always as though we were reaching into the void. If we consciously *seek* the meaning of a work of art, we will never find it, and consequently it is only by becoming 'innocent' that we can respond to art in its own art-being. This is not unconnected with Heidegger's belief that the mystery of being is inseparable from the being of each individual life-process/art-work/phenomenon, and cannot be demystified by any *essentialist* project. If art, for Heidegger, 'opens up . . . the Being of beings' (p. 39), he makes it clear at various points in his work that we should not interpret Being in terms of any kind of essence. Lawrence, in his discussion of 'the horsiness of the horse' in 'Etruscan Places', makes the same point (p. 72), and in the essay 'Democracy' we find the assertion that 'Every living creature is single in itself, a *ne plus ultra* of creative reality, *fons et origo* of creative manifestation' (p. 73). Here, in their preoccupation with origins, we have Lawrence and Heidegger at their most mystical, and, for many critics, their most suspect.

Because the meaning of the work of art is not present in an open and articulated form, and because the more impossible it is for the viewer to externalize the meaning, the more the 'thereness' of the art-work shines forth in its own being, Heidegger sees art in terms of a dialectical reciprocity between hiddenness and radiance (*'In der Unverborgenheit waltet die Verbergung'*); it is the 'strife' between the two which enables each to come into its own. We find the same emphasis on strife in Lawrence, particularly in the essay 'The Crown', and Lawrence derives this notion, as Heidegger does, from Heraclitus.[23] Hence for Heidegger (as for Lawrence)

---

[22] Compare Adorno: 'Culture is the condition that excludes the attempt to measure it' ('These zur Kunstsoziologie', in *Kölner Zeitschrift für Soziologie und Sozialpsychologie*, 19/1 (Mar. 1967), 91, trans. Jay in *Adorno*, 118).

[23] Lawrence probably encountered Heraclitus through John Burnet's *Early Greek Philosophy* (London, 1892), which he read in 1915. See *Letters*, ii. 364 (14? July 1915), 652 (5 Sept. 1916). Burnet cites Heraclitus: 'Homer was wrong in saying: "Would that strife might perish from among gods and men!" He did not see that he was praying for the destruction of the universe; for, if his prayer were heard, all things would pass away . . .' (*Early Greek*

the form–content distinction becomes meaningless. It is only in aesthetic theories which offer a discursive interpretation of the art-work, constantly referring the work to something else, that the form–content distinction arises; it is a distinction which, as Heidegger expresses it, 'is an encroachment upon the thing-being of the thing'.[24]

We saw in the analysis of Bloomsbury 'formalism' how confusing the form–content distinction could be. In 'The Origin of the Work of Art', Heidegger launches a full-scale attack on the value of the distinction in aesthetics:

The distinction of matter and form is *the conceptual schema which is used, in the greatest variety of ways, quite generally for all art theory and aesthetics.* This incontestable fact, however, proves neither that the distinction of matter and form is adequately founded, nor that it belongs originally to the domain of art and the art work. Moreover, the range of application of this pair of concepts has long extended far beyond the field of aesthetics. Form and content are the most hackneyed concepts under which anything and everything may be subsumed. And if form is correlated with the rational and matter with the irrational; if the rational is taken to be the logical and the irrational the alogical; if in addition the subject-object relation is coupled with the conceptual pair form-matter; then representation has at its command a conceptual machinery that nothing is capable of withstanding. (p. 27)

Heidegger then goes on to show how the distinction is always linked to *instrumentality*. For it is in the production of *equipment* that the form–content distinction has value: the making of equipment requires both the formative act and the choice of material (p. 28).

4. Disinterestedness

In Kant's *Critique of Judgement*, we find a well-known meditation on the 'disinterestedness' of aesthetic judgements. For Kant, judgements concerning the 'good' (whether 'good' is taken to mean 'useful', or to refer to the morally 'good' in itself) are always bound up with interest. Judgements of the beautiful, on the other hand, are always contemplative or disinterested; they are indifferent to whether the object of their contemplation actually exists or not (p. 43). Heidegger draws attention to what he sees to be an important misunderstanding surrounding Kant's use of the term

---

Philosophy, 136, cited by Kalnins in the explanatory notes to *Apocalypse and the Writings on Revelation* (p. 228)). See Lawrence's poem 'Strife', in *Complete Poems*, 714. This poem first appeared in *Last Poems*, ed. Richard Aldington and Giuseppe Orioli (Florence, 1932).

[24] 'The Origin of the Work of Art', 30.

'disinterested' in aesthetics, and his argument sheds light on the misreading of Bloomsbury formalism discussed in Chapters 4–5.[25] Heidegger argues that many art theorists have misunderstood Kant's third critique, and that Schopenhauer in particular is guilty of an influential misreading of the term 'disinterested'. Schopenhauer reads into this term that the aesthetic state is one in which the will, all striving, is temporarily arrested. Nietzsche, following Schopenhauer's reading of Kant, dismissively asserts that 'Since Kant, all talk about art, beauty, knowledge, and wisdom has been smudged and besmirched by the concept "devoid of interest" '.[26]

According to Heidegger, both Schopenhauer and Nietzsche miss the point that for Kant 'interest' concerns strictly that which is important *in the light of something else*; the 'beautiful' for Kant is that which cannot be considered in the terms of something else. Far from putting the will out of action, the beautiful demands a supreme effort of will towards that which has worth *in itself*. The Schopenhauerian reading of 'interest' wrongly suggests, argues Heidegger, that with the exclusion of interest all relations to the art-object are suppressed. For Kant the opposite is true: by suppressing all interests which place the art-work in the light of something else, the essential relation to the art-object itself is highlighted. According to the Heideggerian reading of Kant, *schön* ('beautiful') is closely related to *scheinen* ('to shine'): the beautiful is the coming forth into radiance of the object as itself.[27]

It is important that this emphasis on the 'autonomy' of the art-work should not be misconstrued. When Heidegger states that the viewer should refrain from the usual evaluating and assessing, he means that art should be removed from the realm of instrumentalism. In Section 5 of the *Critique*, Kant argues that delight in the beautiful is the only free delight, for 'All interest presupposes a want, or calls one forth; and, being a ground determining approval, deprives the judgement on the object of its freedom' (p. 49). We can see the importance that this statement had for Heidegger in his assessment of a society *enslaved* to instrumentalism; the aesthetic judgement for Kant allows 'the free play of our powers of cognition' (p. 83). Heidegger, along with Adorno and Horkheimer, recognized the importance of Kant's 'purposiveness without purpose'; for Adorno, the inverse of this is 'the scheme of things to which bourgeois art conforms socially: purposelessness for the purposes declared by the market'.[28]

[25] For the following account of Heidegger's position with regard to Kant's disinterestedness, I am indebted to Joseph J. Kockelmans, *Heidegger on Art and Art Works* (Dordrecht, 1985), 31–2.

[26] Heidegger, *Nietzsche, I (The Will to Power as Art)*, trans. David Farrell Krell (New York, 1979), 107–8.   [27] Ibid. 110.

[28] Horkheimer and Adorno, *Dialectic of Enlightenment*, 158.

Through his notion of aesthetic autonomy, then, Heidegger is anxious to rescue art from instrumentalism. He does not mean, by aesthetic autonomy, that 'life' as a whole should be expunged from aesthetics (whatever that would entail); on the contrary, the autonomy of art gives rise to the semantic complexity brought out in Heidegger's analysis of the 'shoeness' in Van Gogh's painting of a pair of peasant shoes:

There is nothing surrounding this pair of peasant shoes in or to which they might belong—only an undefined space. There are not even clods of soil from the field or the field-path sticking to them, which would at least hint at their use. A pair of peasant shoes and nothing more. And yet—

From the dark opening of the worn insides of the shoes the toilsome tread of the worker stares forth. In the stiffly rugged heaviness of the shoes there is the accumulated tenacity of her slow trudge through the far-spreading and ever-uniform furrows of the field swept by a raw wind. On the leather lie the dampness and richness of the soil. Under the soles slides the loneliness of the field-path as evening falls. In the shoes vibrates the silent call of the earth, its quiet gift of the ripening grain and its unexplained self-refusal in the fallow desolation of the wintry field. This equipment is pervaded by uncomplaining anxiety as to the certainty of bread, the wordless joy of having once more withstood want, the trembling before the impending childbed and shivering at the surrounding menace of death.[29]

It is, suggests Heidegger, only in the picture that we notice all this about the shoes: the peasant woman simply wears them. It is this difference between wearing and responding which is crucial, for although Heidegger takes into account the instrumentality of the shoes as one of their features, his reading of them is not, he claims, an instrumental reading: it allows the shoes a plenitude of connotation and suggestion which they could never have as objects of instrumentalism. It would be easy to take issue with Heidegger at this point and to argue that his analysis of the shoes *is* an instrumental one, in that it uses the shoes to further a Spenglerian organicist vision with highly suspect political overtones. Heidegger would presumably retort that his reading by no means exhausts what the painting can be made to yield. This semantic plenitude is all-important: Heidegger, having given the above evocation of the Van Gogh shoes, comments warily that 'If anything is questionable here, it is rather that we experienced too little in the neighborhood of the work and that we expressed the experience too crudely and too literally'.[30] Here thingness or materiality (the shoeness of the shoe) is directly connected, as it is in Lawrence's aesthetics, to polysemy.

---

[29] 'The Origin of the Work of Art', 33–4.   [30] Ibid. 36.

5. *Presence*

The question of presence, in both Lawrence and Heidegger, is problematic. In direct opposition to Kantian ontology, they both see thingness to be inseparable from *presencing*.[31] Derrida has exposed the double fiction of, on the one hand, the perfect empiricism of a universal language of painting that would achieve pure representation, capturing 'things-in-themselves', and, on the other, that of the perfect phonetic writing that would be a pure representation of speech. This kind of pure presence, the absolute erasure of the signifier by the signified, is impossible.[32] This argument is by now a familiar one in aesthetics. Victor Burgin, for example, criticizes modernism's emphasis on the 'presence' of the art-object as logocentric, and argues that the rise of photography has served to confirm the modernist notion that the art-object, the painting or sculpture, has a *presence* which it, photography, seems by comparison to lack: photography bears no trace of 'the founding presence of a human subject'.[33]

It is not, however, this kind of presence with which either Lawrence or Heidegger is concerned. On the contrary, they both anticipate Derrida in their deconstruction of the linguistic structures which seek to lay hold of presence. In their writings on art they are concerned rather with the presence of word *as word* or painting *as painting*, not with the presence of a *signified*, nor with 'the founding presence of a human subject'. For where the discursive mode (what I have called the naïve-mimetic model of language) logocentrically focuses on a supposed signified, assumes the presence of a signified, the differential mode emphasizes the painting as painting or the poem as poem. The apparently tautological nature of this is something which does not disturb Heidegger, as he makes clear in an essay entitled, simply, 'Language':

Language itself is language. The understanding that is schooled in logic, thinking of everything in terms of calculation and hence usually overbearing, calls this proposition an empty tautology. Merely to say the identical thing twice—language is language—how is that supposed to get us anywhere? But we do not want to get anywhere. We would like only, for once, to get just where we are already.[34]

Heidegger's incantatory claim throughout this essay that 'language speaks' is defiantly devoid of teleology. In practice, recognizing language as language or a painting as painting does not mean reducing the art-work to paintstrokes or phonemes, but rather recognizing its power of resonance *as*

---

[31] See e.g. 'The Thing', in *Poetry, Language, Thought*, 174.
[32] See e.g. *Writing and Difference*, and the essay 'Différance', in *Margins of Philosophy*, 1–27.   [33] *The End of Art Theory*, 34.
[34] 'Language', in *Poetry, Language, Thought*, 187–210 (p. 190).

sign, and allowing this resonance its full capacity (we saw this in Heidegger's analysis of the Van Gogh), avoiding logocentrism.

The 'presence' of art, for both these thinkers, depends on a specific kind of response on the viewer/reader's part, a response which has nothing to do with the 'grasping', exploitative response of the Cartesian subject. Lawrence believes that new worlds can be created every day, in a quotidian miracle, provided we open ourselves up to Being in what he calls 'an act of attention' ('An act of pure attention, if you are capable of it, will bring its own answer').[35] In a review of Crosby's *Chariot of the Sun,* he speaks of 'the essential act of attention, the essential poetic and vital act', which ' "discovers" a new world within the known world'.[36]

For Heidegger in 'The Origin of the Work of Art', it is through art that the viewer enters the region of what he calls 'the open', the clearing in which beings can presence as what they really are. Again he invokes ancient Greece as a kind of aestheticized environment, an open region in itself: the Greeks, he tells us, called this open region *ta alethea,* the region of the unconcealed (p. 36). For Heidegger, art is *not* a (logocentric) attempt at the making present of something which exists or has existed elsewhere: rather, art enacts *the way in which such beings come to presence,* the 'happening of truth at work' (p. 36). But the fact that truth achieves realization in the art-work does *not* make beauty incompatible with the notion of form (and here we look back again to the revised view of the 'formalism' of Bloomsbury in Chapters 4–6). For Heidegger remembers that *forma* was once the 'isness' of what is (p. 81). He dispenses with the Platonic hierarchy of creators whereby the artist occupies the lowest place, as the copier (*mimetes*) of the objects produced (in bronze, wood) by the *demiourgos klines* who in their turn are below the god who creates the *eidos* (the pure outward appearance). The artist becomes not the copier but the creator, and the Platonic *eidos* is dismissed as inadequate to deal with the *thingness* of the thing (p. 81). For although in a Van Gogh painting a pair of peasant's shoes has a *presentness* and a *thereness* which is *in excess* of sensory data (which cannot be reduced to canvas, brushstrokes, pigment), it is none the less a 'thereness' which is *inseparable from* these sensory data.

6. *Art as Creation*

Art, then, for both Lawrence and Heidegger, is a bringing to presence of a whole new thing, a coming-to-presence out of the not-present; it does not

---

[35] 'Etruscan Places', 55.
[36] 'Review of *Chariot of the Sun* by Harry Crosby', in *Phoenix,* 261, 255.

present us with anything which exists or has existed elsewhere (to attempt to do this would be, as we have seen, a logocentric enterprise).[37] Art for these two thinkers is a creation of a very originary kind, a re-enactment of Genesis. Heidegger links the creation of the art-work to the breaking forth of blossom from the bud, unfolding its own being for the first time. He distinguishes between this kind of creation (which the Greeks called *phusis*) and the bringing into being of an art-work by the artist (which the Greeks called *techne*).[38] For Heidegger, both *phusis* and *techne* are kinds of *poiesis*, a bringing into being. Lawrence writes of creativity in a similar vein. Clifford Chatterley is an example of a writer whose work, bound in by method and intentionality, can only be derivative, not genuinely creative: his words 'were not the leafy words of an effective life, young with energy and belonging to the tree. They were the hosts of fallen leaves of a life that is ineffectual.'[39] Heidegger speaks of an 'original leap' (*Ursprung*) of truth into the art-work, a leap out of that which cannot be mediated. Like Lawrence, he dispenses with intentionality. The miracle of the art-work, he argues, has little to do with the artist who made it:

It is not the 'N.N. fecit' that is to be made known. Rather, the simple 'factum est' is to be held forth into the Open by the work: namely this, that unconcealedness of what is is happened here, and that as this happening it happens here for the first time; or, that such a work *is* at all rather than is not.[40]

This kind of freshness is conspicuously absent in the world of *Women in Love*, a world in which nothing seems to be able to blossom. Gudrun asks jadedly of her sister, 'Don't you find yourself getting bored? . . . Don't you find, that things fail to materialise? *Nothing materialises!* Everything withers in the bud' (p. 8). It is a world doomed to a stale sameness and repetition, in which Ursula is 'sick of the beloved past' (p. 356), in which no one 'transcended the given terms' (p. 305). Of Breadalby, the meeting place of a cultural élite, the narrator comments, 'There seemed a magic circle drawn about the place, shutting out the present, enclosing the delightful, precious past' (p. 84).

For Lawrence, as for Heidegger, art *creates* reality rather than being against or apart from reality, and consequently we see again, as we have seen in previous chapters, that the art–reality distinction is meaningless for him.

---

[37] Spengler notes that the distinction between 'being' and 'becoming' is unhelpful, and following Goethe he distinguishes instead between 'the becoming' and 'the become' ('the become' he connects with 'the hard-set' and 'death' (*Decline of the West*, 53–4)). The physicist, the logician, the evolutionist are grouped together as being concerned with *the become*; only the artist or the 'real' historian 'sees the becoming of a thing' (*schaut, wie etwas wird*), and can re-enact this becoming.   [38] 'The Origin of the Work of Art', 59.

[39] *Lady Chatterley's Lover*, 61.   [40] 'The Origin of the Work of Art', 78, 65.

He is in a tradition of art-criticism whose more recent exponents include, for example, David Jones, for whom in art ' "Something" not "nothing", moreover a new "something", has come into existence'. For Jones, a painting does not *represent* a mountain; rather 'it *is* mountain, under the form of paint'.[41] Throughout Lawrence's work there is an emphasis on 'building up a new world, a whole new world with a new open sky above us', an emphasis on spring, rebirth, and resurrection, and if the new world prophesied at the end of *The Rainbow* fails to materialize, art offers compensation. For if we extinguish all 'self-insistence and self-will', Lawrence argues, we will 'see a new world unfolding round us', and it is precisely in art, as the other of method, that this 'self-insistence' is suppressed.[42]

7. *Art* versus *Aesthetics*

For Heidegger, the formation of a discipline of aesthetics by Baumgarten in 1735 meant the death of art as such. Art became the object of *aesthesis*, of sensuous apprehension.[43] Aesthetics threatened to solve the enigma of art, to dissolve the 'thingness' of the art-thing away. In Heidegger's 'A Dialogue on Language', the Inquirer (a Heidegger figure) discusses this issue with a Japanese philosopher. He questions the value of aesthetics in considering the nature of Japanese art, on the grounds that aesthetics grows out of *European* thinking and philosophy.[44] Throughout the dialogue, reference is made to what the Japanese call *Iki*, and the nearest we ever come to a definition of *Iki* is that it is that which endows Japanese art and poetry with their nature, makes them what they are (p. 13). Throughout the discussion, the Japanese philosopher fears that 'every explication of *Iki* will fall into the clutches of aesthetic ideation' (p. 43).

The period of great art, for Heidegger, was before artists claimed for themselves a special vocation apart from that of craftsmen, before works were restored and exhibited, before plays and musical compositions were reproduced time and again in purpose-built auditoriums. For Lawrence, too, the beauty of Etruscan art was that it was integrated unselfconsciously into the Etruscans' lives as a whole; it was 'not a theory or a thesis'. Greek beauty, on the other hand, was 'too much cooked in the artistic consciousness'.[45]

---

[41] David Blamires, *David Jones* (Manchester, 1978), 30.

[42] 'The Reality of Peace', in *Reflections on the Death of a Porcupine and Other Essays*, 25–52 (pp. 33, 29). This essay first appeared in *English Review*, xxiv and xxv (May–Aug. 1917), 415–22, 516–23, 24–9, 125–32.   [43] 'The Origin of the Work of Art', 79.

[44] 'A Dialogue on Language', in *On the Way to Language*, 1–54 (p. 2).

[45] 'Etruscan Places', 114, 107. Compare Adorno and Horkheimer: 'To speak of culture was always contrary to culture. Culture as a common denominator already contains in embryo that schematization and process of cataloguing and classification which brings culture within the sphere of administration' (*Dialectic of Enlightenment*, 131).

Far from making the art-work into an 'object' of aesthetic connoisseurship or degrading it into the stimulator of aesthetic *experiences*, argues Heidegger, we should make our home in the work.[46] 'Experience' is a term which is used and reused throughout *Women in Love*, and, in Lawrence's characteristic way, it is used now positively, now negatively. The conversation between Ursula and Gudrun on the opening page points to a crucial ambiguity in the term:

'You don't think one needs the *experience* of having been married?' she asked. 'Do you think it need *be* an experience?' replied Ursula. 'Bound to be, in some way or other,' said Gudrun, coolly. 'Possibly undesirable, but bound to be an experience of some sort'. 'Not really,' said Ursula. 'More likely to be the end of experience'.

Gudrun's obsession with 'experience' (Gerald also sees his life in terms of 'getting experiences', p. 57, and the Pussum, in her turn, is 'determined to have her experience' with Gerald, p. 74)[47] is comparable to that of the sensation-seeking debauchees of, say, Huxley's *Point Counter Point* (1928), a novel upon which Lawrence left his mark (and in which he appears, in the character of Rampion). It approximates to the self-enclosed obsession with aesthetic 'thrill' to which Lawrence objects in 'Introduction to These Paintings'. For Ursula, experience is the opposite of this, an openness of response, not simply a recycling of the already given.[48]

In a society which has 'unhoused' us, art is seen by Lawrence to be a dwelling-place, a refuge.[49] 'Dwelling in' or 'being with' the art-work means that the relationship between art-work and respondent is one of *contiguity*. Ideally, for Lawrence, this would also be the relationship between human beings and the natural world. He praises R. H. Dana's *Two Years Before the Mast* on this basis, and he also finds examples of a 'contiguous' relationship with the environment in the Hopi and Pueblo Indians, whose rituals were experienced as a share in cosmic events, not an attempt at mastery over the

---

[46] 'The Origin of the Work of Art', 79.

[47] See also *Lady Chatterley's Lover*, 12: 'Both sisters had their love experience by the time the war came.' Throughout this passage, the repetition of the term 'thrill' indicates the same inauthenticity of emotion.

[48] Walter Benjamin was to distinguish between *Erfahrung* (the integration of events into meaningful traditions) and *Erlebnis* (isolated experience, robbed of any meaningful context). He argued that Heidegger and others had been privileging *Erlebnis* over *Erfahrung*, mistaking for spontaneity and freedom from intellectual tyranny what was in fact just another reflection of the uprootedness of late capitalist society (see *Charles Baudelaire: A Lyric Poet in the Era of High Capitalism*, trans. Harry Zohn (London, 1973)). But here we see Heidegger regretting a culture in which art has been demoted to the level of 'aesthetic experiences'.

[49] Compare Heidegger, who argues that, instead of *dwelling in* the world, we have been *building on* it ('Building Dwelling Thinking', in *Poetry, Language, Thought*, 149).

elements.[50] Again, Lawrence describes art in terms of 'the living conjunction or communion between the self and its context'.[51]

Ent-sprechen ('correspondence') is the Heideggerian term for the appropriate relationship to the art-work. Art provides the clearing (*die Lichtung*) in which truth can dwell, and which has nothing to do with the light of reason by which truth is *perceived*. And so, in what Heidegger calls 'The Age of the World Picture', where the world itself has separated from us and become an *object* of contemplation (here the relationship between *Bildung*, as intellectual cultivation, and *Bild/Vorbild*, 'picture', is crucial),[52] we can in the 'pictures' of art enact an utterly different relationship. It is the Heideggerian distinction between 'fantasizing' (when man as representing subject 'pictures' form—the sexual connotations are also present in Lawrence's objection to a self-enclosed (= masturbatory) sensationalism in our culture today) and *fantasia*, a coming-into-presence of something for the benefit of man who also presences towards that which appears.[53]

For Lawrence, then, art is a form of 'meaning-at-oneness, the state of being at one with the object', where 'object' does *not* have the connotations of Heidegger's 'object', but rather of 'thingness'.[54] The sense of a separate *thing* is as important for Lawrence as the sense of fusion: Van Gogh's sunflowers are 'the offspring of the sunflower itself and Van Gogh himself'; the sunflower has its own entity and does not come into being merely as a result of the perceiving subject.[55]

For both Lawrence and Heidegger, although we live in a world in which things are at hand, easily available, instantaneous, we are none the less oblivious, in our forgetting of Being, and in our constant search for arcane meanings, to the 'nearness' of things. If we *are* able to respond or 'correspond' to the nearness of things, we will (for both Lawrence and Heidegger) be aware of the 'wonder' inherent in them. There are scenes throughout Lawrence's fiction in which characters suddenly become susceptible to the 'wonder' of their environment; in 'Hymns in a Man's Life', Lawrence argues that this 'wonder' is 'the most precious element in life'.[56] And, in *Etruscan Places*, Lawrence regrets that whereas 'the ancients saw, consciously, as children now see unconsciously, the everlasting *wonder* in things' (p. 69), to us, 'the peoples of the Idea', paradise has become 'an inadequate fiction' (p. 76).

[50] See *Studies in Classic American Literature*, 105–23, and 'Mornings in Mexico', 65.
[51] *The Symbolic Meaning*, 117.   [52] 'Science and Reflection', 180.
[53] 'The Age of the World Picture', in *The Question Concerning Technology*, 147.
[54] 'Making Pictures', in *Phoenix II*, 605.   [55] 'Morality and the Novel', 171.
[56] 'Hymns in a Man's Life', in *Phoenix II*, 597–601 (p. 598). This essay first appeared in *Evening News*, 13 Oct. 1928.

10

AN 'ANTI-IMPERIALIST' AESTHETICS

Despite all conquest of distances, the nearness of things remains absent.

(Heidegger, 'The Thing')

It is a strange thing, but when science extends space *ad infinitum*, and we get the terrible sense of limitlessness, we have at the same time a secret sense of imprisonment. Three-dimensional space is homogeneous, and no matter *how* big it is, it is a kind of prison.

(Lawrence, 'Introduction to *The Dragon of the Apocalypse* by Frederick Carter')

1. A 'Green' Aesthetics

The *völkisch* ideologies that were such a formative influence on both Lawrence and Heidegger went on to be used, within Heidegger's lifetime but after Lawrence's premature death, in the services of a *Blut und Boden* fascism. When used somewhat differently, they also persisted in green politics, and it is no accident that it is currently Germany where green politics has the strongest foothold.[1] It is one of the strangest paradoxes that these *völkisch* ideologies could be used by Nazism on the one hand, and on the other by certain strands of radical feminism, particularly eco-feminism. If Lawrence has been linked with fascism, his aesthetics also brings him close to some contemporary 'eco-feminist' writers. Like them, and like Adorno, he connects chronological time with oppression and the domination of nature.[2] Like them, too, he was influenced by the anthropologist Jane Harrison (whom Virginia Woolf also greatly admired). Harrison posited the concept of the 'holophrase', which, she argued, verbalized experience 'without separating emotion and reason, feeling and thought'.[3] Eco-feminists follow Harrison in

---

[1] See Anna Bramwell, *Blood and Soil: Richard Walther Darré and Hitler's Green Party* (Bourne End, 1985).

[2] Adorno agreed with Benjamin that chronological time must be ruptured through *Jetztzeit* ('Now-time'). See Benjamin, 'Theses on Philosophy of History', in *Illuminations*, ed. Hannah Arendt, trans. Harry Zohn (London, 1973), 255–66 (p. 263).

[3] Harrison, cited in Andrée Collard, with Joyce Contrucci, *Rape of the Wild* (London, 1988), p. x.

associating the mind–body split and the privileging of mind over matter with a patriarchal language which degrades the earth. They argue that in societies using holophrastic language, the destruction of the earth and the mutilation of the creatures who inhabit it, through experimentation or inhumane farming, is not a possibility.[4]

The damage wreaked by technology in the West has also been linked by some theologians and sociologists to the Hebrew, monotheistic tradition which displaces the worship of 'mother earth' on to that of an external God.[5] This displacement is, for eco-feminists as for Lawrence, just another manifestation of the transcendentalist mind–matter split. Harrison explains the way in which the shedding of plant and animal forms by patriarchal gods put an end to all kinds of totemistic thinking and feeling. Around 1913, when Lawrence was reading Harrison, he became increasingly anxious to subvert an anthropocentric, 'ridiculously mindful' culture and to emphasize humanity's kinship with the rest of the earth.[6] In the 'Study of Thomas Hardy', written at this time, Lawrence praises Hardy's *Return of the Native* for its powerful evocation of the surging life of Egdon Heath itself, vast and uncharted. Art is seen by Lawrence to reach beyond human ken, admitting the unknown and untrodden; it reserves a place for what he calls 'sentient non-knowledge' (p. 35).

The idea of the totem, as Jane Harrison stresses, rests on that of (literal) kinship between human beings and other species. Bruce Chatwin's *The Songlines* is a moving evocation of the fight for survival of the totemic culture of the Australian Aboriginals. It is of particular interest here in that its philosophical inspiration comes largely from Heidegger and Rilke, from the same German tradition in which I have attempted to locate Lawrence. The creation myths of the Australian Aboriginals tell of the 'Ancestors', the totemic beings who issued from their long slumber beneath the crust of the earth and began to wander the surface of the Australian continent, naming in song, and thus bringing into being, every feature of the landscape, every plant and animal.[7] The landscape and its inhabitants were imbued with, and preserved through, the spirit of song; they were 'sacred ikons', ruling out, as sacrilege, the possibility of an Alice to Darwin railway, 'three hundred miles of steel, slicing through innumerable songs' (p. 17). Chatwin cites Rilke on the subject of singing things into existence, and explains that 'In aboriginal

---

[4] See ibid., pp. x–xi.

[5] See also Carolyn Merchant's study of the mutation, across the centuries, of attitudes towards 'Nature': *The Death of Nature: Women, Ecology, and the Scientific Revolution* (London, 1982). Merchant shows how, until well into the eighteenth century, the concept of 'Mother Earth' as a living, nurturing entity actually functioned as an ethical constraint on mining activities (pp. 29–41).   [6] See *Letters*, i. 503 (17 Jan. 1913); ii. 183 (5 June 1914).

[7] Bruce Chatwin, *The Songlines* (London, 1987), 2.

belief, an unsung land is a dead land: since, if the songs are forgotten, the land itself will die'.[8] Song is the sustenance and guardianship of the land, and this is made literally true in Australia when the white man's ignorance of the songlines scars the landscape beyond recognition, through mining and railways and urban settlements. The message Chatwin preaches in the novel is 'renunciation': 'The world, if it has a future, has an ascetic future' (p. 148). A moving evocation of what such renunciation would imply comes towards the end of the novel, where Titus, a Duburunga Aboriginal, reacts to the proposal of new mining developments in the area:

'We've got a lot of important Dreamings in the area. We've got Native Cat. We've got Emu, Black Cockatoo, Budgerigar, two kinds of Lizard; and we've got an 'eternal home' for Big Kangaroo. At a guess I'd say he was your oilfield or whatever. But he's been sleeping there since the Dreamtime and, if I have a say in the matter, he's going to go on sleeping for ever'. (p. 321)

Chatwin cites not only Rilke, but Heidegger, for whom technology is related to the fact that our day-to-day language, which originated as poetry, is now 'a forgotten and therefore used-up poem, from which there hardly resounds a call any longer'.[9]

We saw in the last two chapters that scientific method, for both Lawrence and Heidegger, precludes genuine newness or discovery, preventing what Heidegger calls the 'original leap' of art.[10] Hence 'progress', which has method as its vehicle, is, as Lawrence observes, always 'along the given lines'.[11] Much nineteenth-century writing had used the railway as an emblem of progress; Lawrence uses it to deconstruct the whole concept of progress, transforming the image of teleology into that of a blind, relentlessly self-perpetuating instrumentality which takes no account of the havoc it wreaks on its way. There is a strong anti-teleological strain in Lawrence's writings on art, and it is directly linked to his emphasis on the 'presence' of the substantive world.

'Progress', of course, has resonances of the 'progress of the species' and popularized Darwinian theory. Carlyle had linked the two ideas of progress (the industrial and the genealogical) in *Chartism*: 'The Saxon kindred burst forth into cotton-spinning, cloth-cropping, iron-forging, steam-engineing, railwaying, commercing and careering towards all the winds of Heaven, in this inexplicable noisy manner; the noise of which, in Power-mills, in progress-of-the-species Magazines, still deafens us somewhat' (p. 184). We know

---

[8] Heidegger refers to the same Rilke poem as Chatwin, namely the third Sonnet to Orpheus, and the line 'Song is existence' ('What Are Poets For?', in *Poetry, Language, Thought*, 138).   [9] Chatwin is citing 'Language', in *Poetry, Language, Thought*, 208.
[10] 'The Origin of the Work of Art', in *Poetry, Language, Thought*, 78.
[11] 'Men Must Work and Women as Well', in *Phoenix II*, 582.

Lawrence to have read Darwin very early in his career, and to have been familiar with the works of other evolutionary theorists such as T. H. Huxley, Herbert Spencer, and Auguste Comte.[12] The Darwinian evocation, in *The Origin of Species* (1859), of plenitude, dynamism, and struggle in the natural world would not have been anathema to Lawrence, nor would Darwin's anti-humanist stance, his emphasis on the 'interdependence of beauty and beast' which, as Gillian Beer tells us in *Darwin's Plots*, made so many Victorians shudder.[13] But Darwin's depiction of a host of incessantly renewable life-forms was not something upon which Lawrence seemed to focus. Instead, he focused on what he saw to be the deterministic aspects of Darwinism, which, throughout his life, he found unsettling: 'I don't believe in evolution, like a long string hooked onto a First Cause, and being slowly twisted in unbroken continuity through the ages. I prefer to believe in what the Aztecs call suns: that is, worlds successively created and destroyed.'[14]

By the time Lawrence was writing, Darwinian theory had been absorbed into the culture in a rather oversimplified and distorted form; it was frequently conflated with a teleology which was in fact quite alien to it. Gillian Beer portrays Darwin struggling against the odds to purge his language of intentionality; terms like 'natural selection' suggest an organizing force at work.[15] Darwin proved unable to prevent teleology from infiltrating popular conceptions of his theories, perhaps because the nineteenth century was witnessing such a proliferation of examples of technological 'progress'. We find Spengler, for example, arguing that teleology is 'the deepest and most characteristic tendency both of Darwinism—the megalopolitan-intellectual product of the most abstract of all Civilisations—and of the materialist conception of history which springs from the same root as Darwinism and, like it, kills all that is organic and fateful'.[16] H. G. Wells's *Outline of History* (1920), with which Lawrence was familiar, traces an evolutionary progress through the history of humanity, a progress culminating in the capitalist entrepreneur, someone like the eponymous hero of Wells's *The World of William Clissold* (1926), which Lawrence reviewed and disliked: 'Cave-men, nomads, patriarchs, tribal Old Men, out they all come again', Lawrence complains, 'in the long march of human progress. Mr Clissold, who holds forth against "systems", cannot help systematizing us all into a gradual and systematic uplift from the ape.'[17]

[12] See Chambers, *A Personal Record*, 84, 112; Nehls, *A Composite Biography*, iii. 609.

[13] Gillian Beer, *Darwin's Plots: Evolutionary Narrative in Darwin, George Eliot and Nineteenth-Century Fiction* (London, 1983), 9.

[14] 'Mornings in Mexico', in *Mornings in Mexico and Etruscan Places*, 4.

[15] *Darwin's Plots*, 49–76.   [16] *Decline of the West*, 120–1.

[17] 'The World of William Clissold, by H. G. Wells', in *Phoenix*, 346–50 (p. 348). This review first appeared in *Calendar*, 3 (Oct. 1926), 254–7.

Teleology and narrative are a central preoccupation in modernist works of this period, and perhaps *the* central preoccupation in Dorothy Richardson's *Pilgrimage*, of which the first volume appeared in 1915. Miriam, the central figure, remembers a key period in her life as 'that blazing alley of flowers without beginning or end'.[18] Darwinian theory is an undercurrent in the volume *The Tunnel* (1919), in which Miriam meets Hypo Wilson (a portrait of H. G. Wells); in the first discussion of Wilson/Wells's work, evolutionary ideas are intertwined with the notion of scientific and technological 'advancement':

There was nothing but man; man, coming from the ape, some men a little cleverer than others, men had discovered science, science was the only enlightenment, science would put everything right; scientific imagination, scientific invention. Man. Women were there, cleverly devised by nature to ensnare man for a moment and produce more men to bring scientific order out of primeval chaos; chaos was decreasing, order increasing; there was nothing worth considering before the coming of science; the business of the writer was imagination, not romantic imagination, but realism, fine realism, the truth about 'the savage', about all the past and present . . .[19]

Both notions of scientific progress and of progress of the species are seen by Richardson to uphold a patriarchal culture which her own aesthetics (both quintessentially modernist and, in some ways, quintessentially 'feminine') subverts. Richardson's syntax, in the more experimental volumes of *Pilgrimage*, attempts to rid language of teleology and closure, as does that of Virginia Woolf, another writer to link linearity with patriarchy. Woolf takes a stand against the methodology of someone like Mr Ramsay in *To the Lighthouse* (1927), who perceives his own academic researches in terms of a march through the alphabet. She craves a device that would transcend the discipline of a teleological sequence, a discipline which, at the most basic level, syntax itself seems to impose. 'Why should there be an end of stages?', Bernard asks in *The Waves* (1931), 'And where do they lead?'[20] The implicit plotting of discursive language, its pretensions to causality, are bound up, for Richardson and Woolf, with a larger 'plot' against, on one level, the natural world which is subdued in the name of human progress, and on another level the female sex. Hypo Wilson's language in *Pilgrimage* is ridden with such plots: he 'ask[s] questions by saying them—statements', and the aggression implicit in this (Miriam senses a 'strange direct attack' from him) cannot be dissociated from his eventual seduction of Miriam.[21]

Lawrence's work is closely bound up with this modernist attempt to

---

[18] *The Tunnel* (1919), in *Pilgrimage*, 4 vols. (1967; London, 1979), ii. 213.

[19] Ibid. 122.   [20] *To the Lighthouse* (London, 1927), 56–9; *The Waves*, 133.

[21] *The Tunnel*, in *Pilgrimage*, ii. 110, 112.

subvert linearity. Like Woolf and Richardson, he draws a parallel between linguistic 'plots' and physical aggression. He plays on the word 'point': points can be the points of weapons, the points (full-stops) of sentences, and the points (purposes) of teleologies; but life, argues Lawrence, has no full-stops and no points.[22] Clifford Chatterley is in many ways another Hypo Wilson; he unconsciously betrays the patriarchal structure of linear progress through his preoccupation with the Chatterley genealogy (linearity as lineage) and the perpetuation of tradition: ' "That's why having a son helps; one is only a link in a chain" '; Connie's telling response is that she is 'not keen on chains'.[23]

It is easy to see how an aesthetics of organic wholeness could be reinforced, or even motivated in the first place, by this desire to escape linearity: a single, self-contained, 'complete' unit implicitly subverted the conception of time that underpins Darwinism, and that Lawrence finds so oppressive: 'Our idea of time as a continuity in an eternal straight line has crippled our consciousness cruelly. The pagan conception of time as moving in cycles is much freer, it allows movement upwards and downwards, and allows for a complete change of the state of mind, at any moment. One cycle finished, we can drop or rise to another level, and be in a new world at once.'[24] Gudrun in *Women in Love* seems to be fettered to her past:

It was as if she drew a glittering rope of knowledge out of the sea of darkness, drew and drew and drew it out of the fathomless depths of the past, and still it did not come to an end, there was no end to it, she must haul and haul at the rope of glittering conscious, pull it out phosphorescent from the endless depths of the unconsciousness, till she was weary, aching, exhausted, and fit to break, and yet she had not done. (p. 346)

There is an abhorrence of chains of any kind in *Women in Love*, metaphoric chains of cause and effect, or literal chains.[25] In the scene in which Gerald forces the Arab mare to stand, frantic with fear, at the railway-crossing, the passing of the train is evoked in the following way:

Meanwhile the eternal trucks were rumbling on, very slowly, threading one after the other, one after the other, like a disgusting dream that has no end. The connecting chains were grinding and squeaking as the tension varied, the mare pawed and struck away mechanically now, her terror fulfilled in her, for now the man encompassed her . . . (pp. 111–12)

---

[22] 'Do Women Change?', in *Phoenix II*, 539–42. This essay first appeared in *Sunday Dispatch*, 28 Apr. 1929, as 'Women Don't Change'.
[23] *Lady Chatterley's Lover*, 54.
[24] 'Apocalypse', in *Apocalypse and the Writings on Revelation*, 97.
[25] See ibid. 93–4, for another diatribe against teleology and chains.

Similarly, the expanding Midlands towns of Lawrence's fiction, oppressive and dehumanizing, are nearly always characterized by an insidious linearity. Tevershall in *Lady Chatterley's Lover* is a 'raw straggle' or a 'long squalid straggle' of a village which 'trailed in utter hopeless ugliness for a long and gruesome mile'; its houses are seen 'crawling like some serpent up the hill'.[26] And in an earlier version of that novel, *John Thomas and Lady Jane*, we witness an extraordinary reversal of Darwinian evolution as the rows of houses climb the hill 'like the scales of some long, sharp-ridged reptile'.[27]

For Lawrence, the linear version of time upon which Darwinian theory rests can never capture 'presence', since it is based on the method in which presence is continually *deferred*. It posits itself (as, for Lawrence, Christianity does too) on absence rather than presence. Towards the beginning of *Darwin's Plots*, Gillian Beer points to an important ambiguity at the heart of Darwinian theory:

The 'ascent' or the 'descent' of man may follow the same route but the terms suggest very different evaluations of the experience. The optimistic 'progressive' reading of development can never expunge that other insistence that extinction is more probable than progress, that the individual life-span is never a sufficient register for change or for the accomplishment of desire . . . (p. 9)

For Lawrence, both readings, optimistic and pessimistic, amount to the same thing: a subordination of the present, of individual lives at any given time, to narrative. When Beer goes on to point to the ways in which Darwinian theory has been misappropriated politically, and in particular to the eugenic argument of Nazism, its acting out of 'artificial selection' (p. 17), she gives us a clue to what it was Lawrence found so disturbing. In the Introduction, we saw him locating a point in our culture at which a change in consciousness marked 'the death of the body' in the name of method.[28] Just as Darwinian theory subordinates individual lives, whole species indeed, to a larger narrative, so the eugenics of Nazism quite literally sacrifices human lives, whole races, for the sake of a narrative of Aryan 'progress'. A repression of the concrete present for some projected, intangible future can have literally murderous consequences. This is the weight of meaning behind Lawrence's blunt statement that 'All goals become graves'.[29]

It is noticeable in this regard that Clifford Chatterley's emphasis on a (patriarchal) lineage is inseparable from his transcendentalism: he regards the body as an 'encumbrance', and when Connie affirms her faith in the body,

---

[26] *Lady Chatterley's Lover*, 19, 173, 199.
[27] *John Thomas and Lady Jane* (London, 1927), 205.
[28] 'Apocalypsis II', in *Apocalypse and the Writings on Revelation*, 196.
[29] 'Him With His Tail in His Mouth', in *Reflections on the Death of a Porcupine*, 311.

his reply is simply that 'a woman doesn't take a supreme pleasure in the life of the mind'. He unwittingly makes the connection between 'spiritual ascent' and 'physical wasting'.[30] His own life effort is represented by the mines and the physical devastation they leave in their wake; he has impoverished the earth in the name of advancement. It is an advancement, moreover, towards a future state which can never be realized in the present, in that progress forges relentlessly on.

Lawrence's linking of evolutionary narrative with a devaluing of the body had found some extraordinarily literal manifestations in the work of late nineteenth-century evolutionary theorists. One, by the name of Joseph Le Conte, actually proposed, in his *Evolution: Its Nature, Its Evidences, and Its Relation to Religious Thought* (1888–91), that if evolutionary progression took its course unhindered, men might be able to transcend this material realm altogether, moving from an 'outer lower life' to an 'inner higher life', the life force distilling itself into a kind of embodied spirit.[31] This transformation of man into immortal mind could, he said, take place at any moment. But in order to facilitate it, man would have to divorce himself from nature: 'Spirit must break away from physical and material connection with the forces of Nature', he said, just as 'the embryo must break away from physical umbilical connection with the mother'. The imagery Le Conte uses in describing this transcendence is strikingly genderized. The transcendence of man into the realm of the ideal would be his liberation from the world of the earth-mother into the higher plane of the masculine spirit. He writes: 'In man spirit emerges above the surface into a higher world, looks down on Nature beneath him, around on other emerged spirits about him, and upward to the Father of all spirits above him. Emerged, but not wholly free—head above, but not yet foot-loose.'[32] The state of man is presented, then, as a struggle between mother/earth and father/mind. Nature is no longer perceived as a benevolent, nurturing force, but as a primitive stage of experience which it is man's duty to overcome and 'civilize' in the name of evolutionary progress.

It is interesting to look at the contexts in which Lawrence makes Darwinian theory his specific target; they almost always relate to art and creativity. In 'Study of Thomas Hardy', the evolutionary theory of Darwin, Spencer, and T. H. Huxley is linked to the paintings of Turner (and to Christianity) on the grounds that it sacrifices the body to what Lawrence calls the 'Male

---

[30] *Lady Chatterley's Lover*, 250. For further elaborations on Clifford's transcendentalism, see p. 285, where he describes human beings as 'submarine fauna' whose souls only occasionally penetrate to the ether above, 'bursting out from the surface of Old Ocean into real light'.

[31] Joseph Le Conte, *Evolution: Its Nature, Its Evidences, and Its Relation to Religious Thought* (1888–91; 2nd edn. New York, 1897). For this account of Le Conte, I am indebted to Bram Dijkstra, *Idols of Perversity* (Oxford, 1986), 216–17.

[32] Le Conte, *Evolution*, 321, cited in Dijkstra, *Idols of Perversity*, 217.

Principle' of abstraction (pp. 97–8). And it is in 'Introduction to These Paintings' that we find the confession that 'I can't, with the best will in the world, believe that the species have "evolved" from one common life-form' (p. 575). These contexts suggest that through art, or through that kind of (bodily) art, like Cézanne's, in which 'matter *actually* exists', Lawrence sought a means of subverting the evolutionary 'chain'. On many occasions he links art to the present, most insistently in the preface to the American edition of *New Poems* where he celebrates free verse as the 'poetry of the sheer present', and consoles himself that 'one realm we have never conquered: the pure present. One great mystery of time is terra incognita to us: the instant.'[33]

Lawrence's dislike of realist art can be explained in terms of this emphasis on presence. He links realism to the exploitation or erosion of the physical world. How it is that the two could be linked is brought out very clearly in Elizabeth Ermarth's study of realism. Ermarth shows how the linear conception of time is central to realism in art, in that the forms of realism are sequence-bound, incomplete at any given moment in time. She argues that it is only when time and space are seen to be homogeneous that 'it becomes possible to chart both the differences and similarities in nature which give rise to the generalisations in science and art known as laws'.[34] Ermarth cites Raphael's *School of Athens* as an example of this sequence-bound realism, pointing out that its viewers do not explicitly see that the blocks in the parquet floor are square; but even though the form of the blocks presented is trapezoid, the viewers clearly apprehend the squareness: the squareness is grasped as an *abstraction* from their immediate experience (p. 18). The realist project (objected to so strongly by Fry, Bell, and Lawrence as a rationalistic/scientific project) can be seen, then, to imply an erosion of presentness. Ermarth shows how the idea of depth, the quattrocento perspective to which Bell was so hostile, dematerializes the surfaces of things; the real becomes hidden rather than openly present (p. 20). Invisibility has an important role to play in both the snapshot and the realist painting. The way in which both are viewed is series-dependent, not simply in the broad sense of 'This was taken/painted just before or just after such and such happened . . .', but in the sense that to view 'realistically' is to say that an object can be grasped in any one instance only partially or in aspect, and a more complete apprehension can only be inferred, rationalistically, from a series of comparisons (p. 34). In viewing the realist painting, we assume the presence of aspects which simply cannot be seen; all the figures in the realist painting are signs pointing beyond themselves.

---

[33] 'Preface to the American edition of *New Poems*', in *Phoenix*, 220, 222.
[34] Ermarth, *Realism and Consensus in the English Novel*, 17.

Ermarth distinguishes between the typological structure of medieval historiography, in which the valid references are vertical, and the linear, chronological thinking to which this gives way. Correspondingly, medieval painting emphasizes discrete, discontinuous forms, rather than partial expressions of hidden wholes.[35] The same distinction is present in Lawrence's analysis of the Book of Revelation, which he sees to exemplify 'not the modern process of progressive thought, but the old pagan process of rotary image-thought. Every image fulfils its own little cycle of action and meaning, then is superseded by another image . . . Every image is a picture-graph, and the connection between the images will be made more or less differently by every reader.'[36] He goes on:

To appreciate the pagan manner of thought we have to drop our own manner of on-and-on-and-on, from a start to a finish, and allow the mind to move in cycles, or to flit here and there over a cluster of images. Our idea of time as a continuity in an eternal straight line has crippled our consciousness cruelly. The pagan conception of time as moving in cycles is much freer, it allows movement upwards and downwards, and allows for a complete change of the state of mind, at any moment. One cycle finished, we can drop or rise to another level, and be in a new world at once. But by our time-continuum method, we have to trail wearily on over another ridge.[37]

Realist perspective abstracts, then, from the concrete, individual case, depriving objects of completeness. Abstraction involves suppression of certain sense data in favour of others. Hence it is that the (metaphorical) erosion of presence in realist art can translate into the (literal) erosion of the world through technology.

In Lawrence's aesthetics, time is not conceived as a linearity that can be measured, charted, in the abstract. Paradoxically, it is through a more mobile, dynamic conception of time and change, not bound up with instrumental method, that presence is captured. In *The Symbolic Meaning*, Lawrence opposes 'plenum' and 'plenary presence' to the 'will', 'volition', 'voluntary control': 'We have our being in the central creative mystery, which is the pure present, and the pure Presence, of the soul—present beyond all knowing or willing. Knowing and willing are external, they are as it were the reflex or *afterwards* of being' (p. 37). Repeatedly this 'presentness' is linked by Lawrence to creativity: he speaks of 'the Presence from which issues the first fine-shaken impulse and prompting of new being, eternal creation which is always Now. All time is central within this ever-present creative Now.'[38]

The repudiation of the concept of the 'progress' of mankind was by no

---

[35] Ibid. 6–16.   [36] 'Apocalypse', 95.   [37] Ibid. 96–7.
[38] *The Symbolic Meaning*, 39.

means unique to Lawrence at this period; it was in fact germane to the 'conservative revolution' described in the first chapter, and to Spengler's *Decline of the West* (the link with Spengler should immediately alert us to the double-edged nature of this rejection of progress).[39] What is particularly striking about Spengler, from the point of view of the Lawrence reader, is that (following Goethe) he connects the classical Greek consciousness with the 'Pure Present' so valuable to Lawrence, and with the absence of a suffocating sense of chronology. That the Athenian people in the last years of Pericles made astronomical theorists liable to impeachment was, for Spengler, 'expressive of the determination of the Classical soul to banish distance, in every aspect, from its world-consciousness'.[40] Other symptoms of this, for Spengler, are the Hellenic wooden architecture (showing a lack of concern for the future, and, by the same token, for the past), and the lack of an alphabet. By contrast, the ancient Egyptian culture expressed a 'care' for past and future through the choice of granite and basalt as building materials, through the denial of death implicit in the Egyptian mummy, and through the creation and perpetuation of an alphabet. In art, the Egyptians favoured portraiture, in literature biography, thus perpetuating the lives of their great ones through time.

Lawrence's 'Etruscan Places' contrasts Etruscan and Roman cultures in exactly the same way. Though the Etruscan language, as Lawrence points out, was once the predominant language of central Italy, there can be no doubt that part of its charm for him comes from its ephemerality, from its now complete indecipherability, and from the fact that the tomb-inscriptions themselves look as though 'someone had just chalked them up yesterday without a thought' (p. 11). Etruscan 'carelessness' is contrasted with Roman 'care'. The architectural details tie in with Spengler's argument. The Greek and Etruscan temples are made of wood, 'small, dainty, fragile, and evanescent as flowers'; and Lawrence comments that 'it is better to keep life fluid and changing than to try to hold it fast down in heavy monuments' (p. 25). With the Etruscan decline and the Romanization of Etruria, spontaneous works of art give way to commercially oriented memorial stones (p. 30), bearing the portrait of the deceased.

The link with Spengler shows, however, that we are on dangerous territory. Cyclical theories of time, traditionally associated with the organic, with Nature, and with women, none the less have, as I tried to show in the first chapter, a sinister capacity for violence. Cyclical time can have the effect of absolving people of all ethical responsibility and ethical choice; it is in *linear* time that actions have consequences. As happened with Nazism, the cyclical

---

[39] See esp. *Decline of the West*, i. 16.   [40] Ibid. 9.

version of history gives rise to the idea of destiny: history takes its course as 'naturally' and inevitably as the seasons of the year.

2. Art and Imperialism

'Etruscan Places' sets up an antithesis between art on the one hand and imperialism on the other. This antithesis is implicit, too, in Birkin's remark in *Women in Love*: 'You have to be like Rodin, Michael Angelo, and leave a piece of raw rock unfinished to your figure. You must leave your surroundings sketchy, unfinished, so that you are never contained, never confined, never dominated from outside' (pp. 356–7). The raw rock, like the paintedness of Cézanne's still-lifes in oil, their thick impasted coats of pigment defiantly separating artistic microcosm from the world at large, becomes a stand against manipulation, against imperialism. *Women in Love*, we remember, is set against a backdrop of cultural and political ferment; political manifestos and new theories of art are burgeoning side by side. Hermione's friends are at the cutting edge of these developments: ' "Barnes is starting his school of aesthetics, and Olandese is going to give a set of discourses on the Italian national policy" ' (p. 298). In Italian Futurism, a specific aesthetic theory and a specific nationalistic policy are inseparably bound together. In allowing itself to be appropriated politically, Italian Futurism is, for Lawrence, aesthetically redundant. None the less, art-as-propaganda has its uses: 'If by writing tract-novels you can move governments to improve matters, then write tract-novels by all means. If the government, however, plays up, and does its bit, then the tract-novel has served its purpose and descends from the stage like a political orator who has made his point.'[41] Lawrence does not wish to separate art from politics completely; rather, he defines art in terms of surplus or excess: it always contains something over and above any straightforward political message. In 'Apocalypse', as we have already seen, he explains that 'a book only lives while it has power to move us, and move us *differently*; so long as we find it *different* every time we read it' (p. 60).

In 'The Genealogy of Morals' (1987), Nietzsche proclaims that the artist is the imperialist who stamps the whole world with his image: born rulers are, he argues, 'the most spontaneous, the most unconscious artists that exist'; their work is 'an instinctive imposing of forms'; both artist and conqueror are spurred on by a 'terrible egotism'. He even goes so far as to speak of the natural 'cruelty' of the artist (pp. 220–1). The same notions of

---

[41] '*Max Havelaar*, by E. D. Dekker (Multatuli, pseud.)', in *Phoenix*, 236–9 (p. 236). This was first published as the preface to E. D. Dekker (Multatuli, pseud.), *Max Havelaar*, trans. W. Siebenhaar (New York, 1927).

stridency and power are central to the Nietzschean model of language: language is seen to originate in 'the lordly right of bestowing names', thereby taking possession of things (p. 160). For Nietzsche, in other words, the aesthetic and the ascetic are polar opposites. Heidegger reverses the Nietzschean position, complaining that 'Man acts as though *he* were the shaper and master of language, while in fact *language* remains the master of man'.[42] For Lawrence, as for Heidegger, there are crucial ways in which art *renounces* all claims on the earth, paradoxically through a full acknowledgement of the earth's (or the body's) place within the aesthetic domain. This is something which is brought out very clearly in *Studies in Classic American Literature*.

For Lawrence, the 'lust of control' which seems to him to have beset American culture has led to a kind of imperialism on a vast scale, to 'the development of the orthodox European ideal on American soil' (Heidegger, in parallel fashion, was to speak of 'the complete Europeanization of the earth and of man' through reason).[43] But at the level of his *art*, the French-American writer Crèvecoeur refuses to colonize or be colonized: 'the artist is no longer European. Some little salt of the aboriginal America has entered into his blood.'[44] At the level of art lies 'a rebellion against the old parenthood of Europe'; art cannot suppress the soul of the Red Indian inhabiting the American or the Aztec inhabiting the Mexican.[45] There is an interesting parallel here with Paul de Man's criticism of Husserl in *Blindness and Insight*. Husserl, writing 'as a European', that is to say within a discourse of what he sees to be enlightened, disinterested knowledge, is in fact blinding himself to the rhetorical complications and aporias of his philosophical text: 'The privileged viewpoint of the post-Hellenic, European consciousness is never for a moment put into question . . . As a European, it seems that Husserl escapes from the necessary self-criticism that is prior to all philosophical truth about the self.'[46] For Lawrence, this self-criticism is germane to art, even if the artist is unconscious of it.

Like the American texts, but, in Lawrence's view, more successfully, Cézanne's art attempts to subvert the colonizing gaze, a gaze which (when the paintings were first exhibited) insisted that things ought to be seen and presented in a particular way. Cézanne's struggle against such authoritarianism, against what was in fact a rationalization of sight, leaves its mark on his art as a kind of passive resistance or non-violent protest. In Lawrence's late essay 'Introduction to Pictures', art is singled out from all other human pursuits on precisely these grounds:

[42] 'Building Dwelling Thinking', in *Poetry, Language, Thought*, 146.
[43] 'A Dialogue on Language', in *On the Way to Language*, 15; *The Symbolic Meaning*, 19.
[44] *The Symbolic Meaning*, 61. [45] *Studies in Classic American Literature*, 4.
[46] *Blindness and Insight*, 16.

The queen bee of all human ideas since 2000 B.C. has been the idea that the body, the pristine consciousness, the great sympathetic life-flow, the steady flame of the old Adam is bad, and must be conquered. Every religion taught the conquest: science took up the battle, tooth and nail: culture fights in the same cause: and only art sometimes—or always—*exhibits an internecine conflict* and betrays its own battle-cry.[47]

Lawrence had formulated his ideas on this internal struggle in art as early as the 'Study of Thomas Hardy'. The study was written after reading Lascelles Abercrombie's book on Hardy, which contained a passage presenting an aesthetic theory precisely the inverse of Lawrence's own, and which enabled Lawrence to define his own position more clearly. Abercrombie writes:

The highest art must have a metaphysic; the final satisfaction of man's creative desire is only to be found in aesthetic formulation of some credible correspondence between perceived existence and a conceived absoluteness of reality. Only in such art will the desire be employed to the uttermost; only in such art, therefore, will *conscious mastery* seem complete. And Thomas Hardy, by *deliberately putting the art of his fiction under the control of a metaphysic*, has thereby made the novel capable of the highest service to man's consciousness . . .

For if the metaphysic be there at all, it must be altogether in control . . .[48]

Abercrombie's emphasis on control and mastery in art is at the opposite pole from Lawrence's own aesthetics; it led to Lawrence's celebrated dictum, in 'Study of Thomas Hardy', that 'The degree to which the system of morality, or the metaphysic, of any work of art is submitted to criticism within the work of art makes the lasting value and satisfaction of that work . . . Indeed the overstrong adherence to a metaphysic usually destroys any possibility of artistic form' (pp. 89–90). Lawrence sees the need to imprint a 'metaphysic' or 'text' upon art as symptomatic of a more widespread urge to control and possess the earth. On the very first page of his study of Hardy, Lawrence opposes the greedy urge to possession, 'the greedy wish to be secured within triple walls of brass, along with huge barns of plenty' (p. 7), to the supreme superfluity of art.

In 'Etruscan Places' the Lawrentian antithesis between art and imperialism is made literal. Here, the freshness and vitality of the Etruscan tomb-paintings are played off against the art of the 'law-abiding Romans—who believed in the supreme law of conquest' (p. 19); the Etruscan art escapes what Lawrence terms the 'Latin-Roman mechanism and suppression'

---

[47] 'Introduction to Pictures', in *Phoenix*, 765–71 (p. 769), my emphasis.
[48] Lascelles Abercrombie, *Thomas Hardy: A Critical Study* (London, 1912), 19–20, 22, my emphases.

(p. 29). The Etruscan vases are not governed by the 'elegance and convention' of the Greek ones; they 'open out like strange flowers, black flowers with all the softness and the rebellion of life against convention' (p. 32). In the Romans we encounter 'the power of resistance to life, self-assertion and overbearing . . . a power which must needs be moral, or carry morality with it, as a cloak for its inner ugliness'. This, argues Lawrence, 'would always succeed in destroying the natural flowering of life', as well, it would seem, as destroying the *poiesis* of art (pp. 48–9). Lawrence singles out one of the latest tombs (from the second century BC, when the Romans had long been masters of Tarquinia) and points out that it has been created 'from quite a new consciousness, external, the old inwardness has gone', suggesting that art has been demeaned into 'object' (p. 73). The 'subjective power' of the Etruscans has fallen before the 'objective power' of the Romans (p. 74). Heidegger was to see a parallel appropriation of Greek words by an 'objective' Latin-Roman thought.[49] Lawrence writes:

The old religion of the profound attempt of man to harmonise himself with nature, and hold his own and come to flower in the great seething of life, changed with the Greeks and Romans into a desire to resist nature, to produce a mental cunning and a mechanical force that would outwit Nature and chain her down completely, completely, till at last there should be nothing free in nature at all, all should be controlled, domesticated, put to man's meaner uses. (p. 75)

Etruria corresponds to Spengler's 'metaphysical springtime', when, in Lawrence's words, 'the cosmos was alive, like a vast creature. The whole thing breathed and stirred' (p. 49). Eventually, however, 'inwardness' gives way to 'outwardness', to Spengler's expansionist 'civilization' (of which Lawrence is far more critical than Spengler): 'the dancing Etruscan spirit is dead' (p. 73). Military conquest and a blighted art go hand in hand. And some of the Etruscan places Lawrence visits bear the traces of another wave of militarism: pro-Mussolini graffiti on the walls (p. 100).

Art, then, becomes in Lawrence's work a metaphor for freedom and nonviolence, and this freedom is precluded by a rigid, logocentric model of language, by what Lawrence calls in 'Etruscan Places' the Fascist power to name and unname' (p. 24). The reference to authoritarianism is important. Lawrence's art-criticism can be opposed to the leadership politics of, say, *The Plumed Serpent*; it takes a stand against authoritarianism, against mass feeling and dangerous forms of consensus. Lawrence praises the Etruscan art for its ability to elude such consensus: 'If you want uplift, go to the Greek and the Gothic. If you want mass, go to the Roman. But if you love the odd spontaneous forms that are never to be standardised, go to the Etruscans'.[50]

---

[49] Heidegger, 'The Origin of the Work of Art', 23.   [50] 'Etruscan Places', 32.

Imperialism, on the other hand, entails a dangerous homogenization: 'To get any idea of the Pre-Roman past we must break up the conception of oneness and uniformity, and see an endless confusion of differences'.[51] Once again, we see how precariously close Lawrence comes to the position of *völkisch* ideologues like Spengler. 'Etruscan Places' hinges on exactly the same culture–civilization distinction used by Spengler in *The Decline of the West*. Yet Lawrence manages, in the nick of time, to wrench his argument away from a potentially totalitarian position by splintering the organic into 'an endless confusion of differences'. This release of difference and polygeny is central to what he calls the 'subterfuge' of art.[52] Ultimately, Lawrence's art-criticism is a celebration, not a suppression, of difference.

[51] Ibid. 38.   [52] *Studies in Classic American Literature*, 2.

EPILOGUE: AN AESTHETICS OF THE BODY?

What might it mean to posit 'the body' as a challenge to discursive practices, when 'the body' is itself, for many theorists and philosophers, an effect of those discursive practices? And even *if* we see the body as a discursive or linguistic effect, does that mean that we should not posit it? Similar questions are posed by the category of 'woman' for contemporary feminists. Some critics of essentialism still think that the category of 'woman' should be preserved on a practical level as long as the world continues to behave as if 'women' existed.[1] Moreover, for the feminist sociologist Janet Wolff, 'The critique of essentialism does *not* amount to a proof that there *is* no body', and 'there are pragmatic, political, and philosophical reasons for resisting a total agnosticism of the body'.[2]

The same doubts surrounding the positing of a (human) body outside discourse must surround the positing of that other body upon which the human body depends. Marx calls it 'Nature':

Nature is man's *inorganic body*—nature, that is, in so far as it is not itself the human body. Man *lives* on nature—means that nature is his *body*, with which he must remain in continuous interchange if he is not to die. That man's physical and spiritual life is linked to nature means simply that nature is linked to itself, for man is a part of nature.[3]

One could argue that if 'the earth' is, like 'the body', an effect of discourse, there may none the less be important political or practical reasons for positing it.

Lawrence's stance is, in the final analysis, apolitical, if by politics we implicate large, controlling organizations. His position as an outsider, socially, geographically, and professionally, meant that he was peculiarly well placed to criticize in terms of broad contours and large principles. He took full advantage of his marginality, launching wholesale attacks on movements right across the political spectrum. It is on account of what I see to be this apolitical cast of mind that Lawrence can be, and has been, appropriated at different points in literary critical history by socialism, by right-wing mysticism, and, more recently, by green thinking.[4] It would, I think, be vain to try

---

[1] Denise Riley, '*Am I That Name?': Feminism and the Category of 'Women' in History*, 112.
[2] *Feminine Sentences: Essays on Women and Culture* (Cambridge, 1990), 135, 134.
[3] *Economic and Philosophical Manuscripts of 1844*, 112.
[4] One of the sessions at the *International D. H. Lawrence Conference*, Montpellier, June 1990, was devoted to 'Lawrence and Deep Ecology'.

to make Lawrence toe any party line. He rests as uneasily with communism as with capitalism, as uneasily with liberalism as with totalitarianism.

Yet Lawrence's 'anti-imperialistic' aesthetics does not deny the importance (or the inescapability in practice) of political ideologies. Indeed, for Lawrence, art's 'openness' is only conceivable as openness by virtue of the meaningful and necessary ideologies both surrounding it and vying for attention within it. The keystone of Lawrence's aesthetics is not really the Schopenhauerian notion of 'disinterestness', whereby art momentarily ruptures the teleological chain, rescuing objects from the greed of the will. What he posits instead is rather the opposite of this, a plurality of conflicting wills or ideologies which in their struggle (Lawrence's 'internecine conflict') prevent the final *implementation* of any single one of these ideologies. Art is seen by Lawrence to be *both* a site of conflict *and* the one refuge from instrumentality, the one place in which ideologies can be expressed and tested without the risk of disastrous consequences in the practical world.

In recent years, critics have been on their guard against those philosophers who commit the fatal error of aestheticizing reality.[5] The argument stems from Walter Benjamin, who warns that 'All efforts to render politics aesthetic culminate in one thing: war':

> '*Fiat ars—pereat mundus*', says Fascism, and, as Marinetti admits, expects war to supply the artistic gratification of a sense perception that has been changed by technology. This is evidently the consummation of 'l'art pour l'art'. Mankind, which in Homer's time was an object of contemplation for the Olympian gods, now is one for itself. Its self-alienation has reached such a degree that it can experience its own destruction as an aesthetic pleasure of the first order. This is the situation of politics which Fascism is rendering aesthetic. Communism responds by politicising art.[6]

It is important here to attend to Benjamin's particularized use of the term 'aesthetic'. Benjamin's vocabulary ('the artistic gratification of a sense perception'; mankind as 'an object of contemplation . . . for itself'; 'aesthetic pleasure') makes plain the fact that he is using the term 'aesthetic' in the pejorative sense in which Lawrence uses it; for Lawrence, as for Benjamin, 'aestheticism' implies acute self-consciousness and self-obsession. And Lawrence, like Benjamin, immediately recognized this kind of aestheticism in Marinetti, whose Futurist manifesto he read. He would certainly have agreed with Benjamin that *this* kind of aestheticism, based on 'objectifying' (Benjamin argues that humanity has become an *object* of contemplation for itself), *is* dangerous. It is because he acknowledges this danger that Lawrence

---

[5] See e.g. Eagleton, *Literary Theory*, 64, 66.
[6] 'The Work of Art in the Age of Mechanical Reproduction', in *Illuminations*, 244.

takes a stand against Futurism, associating it, as we saw in Chapter 9, with Nietzsche's will to power. For in Nietzsche we find precisely that '*Fiat ars— pereat mundus*' stance against which Benjamin warns. Nietzsche's aesthetics is one which makes the earth curiously dispensable, and this is something of which Nietzsche himself was fully conscious: 'One is an artist at the cost of regarding what all non-artists call "form" as *content*, as "the thing itself"*. To be sure, then one belongs in a topsy-turvy world: for henceforth content becomes something merely formal—our life included.'[7] By turning 'nature' and 'the natural' into aesthetic constructs, by supplanting the world itself with an artistically woven web of illusion, Nietzsche becomes for Lawrence the most metaphysical of metaphysicians, rendering the physical redundant.

I have tried to show throughout the book that Lawrence's aesthetics remains firmly bound up with the material world in a way in which Nietzsche's does not; symptomatic of Lawrence's position is the fact that the natural world itself remains, throughout his work, an aesthetic touchstone. It is as a result of this that, from Lawrence's point of view, aestheticizing reality (i.e. seeing the natural world as a work of art) seems a far less destructive prospect than the inverse process of *realizing* aesthetics, of *implementing* ideas of the True, the Good, and the Beautiful, and wrenching the world into conformity with those ideas. Here Lawrence's version of the aesthetic is at the opposite pole from Marinetti's, where the world becomes raw material fuelling an overwrought aesthetic sensibility; it corresponds more closely to the 'aesthetic' relationship between humanity and the natural world envisaged by Adorno in his 1942 'Theses on Need'. I am concerned here with the *second* part of the following prediction (Adorno uses the term 'art' in two very different senses): 'When classless society promises the end of art, because it overcomes the tension between reality and the possible, it promises at the same time also the beginning of art, the useless, whose intuition tends towards the reconciliation with nature, because it no longer stands in the service of the exploiter's use.'[8] Lawrence's reverence for the natural landscape is not reducible to the desire for an aesthetically pleasing backdrop to human activity; he does not wish to aestheticize the world in this way. Instead, he wishes to counter a situation in which everything which is not a tool or a raw material is treated as refuse.

It is easy to see how, for some readers, what I defined in the last chapter as an 'anti-imperialist' aesthetics might be seen to correspond too closely to an anti-humanist reverence of Being which can be linked with fascism. Terry Eagleton is justifiably wary of those ontologies which, like Heidegger's, dethrone the autonomous subject, turning him/her into a mere shepherd

---

[7] *The Will to Power*, 433.
[8] 'These über Bedürfnis', *Gesammelte Schriften*, viii. 396, cited in Jay, *Adorno*, 100.

or preserver of Being.[9] But, to invoke Adorno one last time as an illustration of the way in which similar starting-points can lead to very different
ideological ends, we find in Adorno's aesthetic theory an emphasis on the
need for a 'fearless passivity' if the subject is to succeed in rending the veil
it has woven around the object, and approach the object itself.[10] This does
not, however, involve the Schopenhauerian merging of subject and object,
whereby the viewer is utterly decentred into the object of her/his contemplation. For both Lawrence and Adorno, aesthetics is a question of non-
hierarchical relationships between subjective and objective forces; both writers
use the image of the constellation to express such relationships.[11] Adorno
defines peace in terms which sound very like Lawrence's description of the
perfect relationship, as the state of 'distinctness without domination', and
both writers see art as a locus in which this kind of relationship can be
enacted.[12]

In 'Introduction to These Paintings', Lawrence attempts to shock his
readers into an awareness of the 'living, substantial world' (p. 556), in the
hope that this awareness will supplant the traditional 'aesthetic response'. He
rewrites art-history in these terms, seeing Cézanne's arrival to coincide with
a point at which 'paint had found the spirit out' (p. 564): with Cézanne, 'art
made its first tiny step back to real substance, to objective substance' (p. 567).
If, for Lawrence, the impulse of aestheticism is simply 'to state this self, and
the reactions upon this self',[13] and thus, by implication, to appropriate and
dematerialize the world, his own model of the aesthetic rests on a kind of
de-aestheticized art which is not guilty of coercing nature, or of sacrificing
matter to spirit.

In conclusion, I want to return to Barbara Johnson's recent essay on Paul de
Man and the holocaust, cited in the Introduction. We find reference there to
de Man's notorious article 'Jews in Contemporary Literature', where
he speaks of the need to preserve Western literature from Jewish influences,
and advocates 'the creation of a Jewish colony far from Europe'. Johnson
comments:

In his eagerness to preserve differences *between* European national traditions (including Flemish) and to allow for productive cross-fertilization and exchange among
them, de Man judges as extraneous and distracting any 'foreign' influences *within*,

---

[9] Eagleton made this point in his lecture series 'Aesthetics and Ideology from Kant to
Derrida', University of Oxford, 1988 (now incorporated into *The Ideology of the Aesthetic*).
[10] 'Subject-Object', in Arato and Gebhardt (eds.), *The Essential Frankfurt School Reader*,
506.   [11] See *Women in Love*, 319; *Negative Dialectics*, 162–3.
[12] 'Subject-Object', 500.
[13] 'The Crown', in *Reflections on the Death of a Porcupine*, 251–306 (p. 280). This essay was
first published in *Signature*, 1–3 (4 Oct., 18 Oct., 4 Nov. 1915).

which might blur the picture of the organic development of forms. Never has the repression of 'differences within' had such horrible consequences.[14]

I have tried to argue throughout the book that this kind of organicism was quite the reverse of that governing Lawrence's writings on art; far from wishing to eliminate differences within the art-work, Lawrence positively emphasized them as an indispensable feature of art. He was only too aware of the dangers inherent in the repression of difference. Totalities are seen by Lawrence to be inherently dangerous in that, by their very nature, they dematerialize: they allow everything to be read off as a sign or cipher of the whole. They are not to be confused with the version of the organic implicit in Lawrence's art-criticism, where the emphasis is on *materiality*, on semantic conflict and on the impossibility of reading off the parts as signs of the whole. The difference between totality and organicity, is, for Lawrence, that between a denial and an affirmation of the body. Ironically, it is in itself an organicist proposition (in the pejorative sense of the term) to suggest that, because Lawrence's aesthetics and fascism share certain philosophical and cultural 'roots', they must inevitably evolve or grow into the same thing. Adorno's dictum is worth remembering here: 'Psychological dispositions do not actually cause fascism; rather, fascism defines a psychological area which can be successfully exploited by the forces which promote it for entirely nonpsychological reasons of self-interest.'[15]

Lawrence's art-criticism emerges, then, as an antidote to his own worst excesses in novels like *The Plumed Serpent* (1926), where the 'metaphysic' (to use Lawrence's expression in 'Study of Thomas Hardy') threatens to destroy the work. Here the theme of *authoritarian* leadership *within* the novel runs parallel to Lawrence's attempt *as author* to occupy a transcendent, enlightened site in relation to his material. But such 'enlightenment' could only be, according to Lawrence's writings on art, synonymous with a barbaric instrumentalism, an imposition of identity (the author's 'metaphysic') onto heterogeneity and polysemy. We should not forget Lawrence's attack, in his study of Hardy, on the author who can assert a particular point and 'exclude or suppress all the rest'.[16]

---

[14] Barbara Johnson, 'The Surprise of Otherness', in Collier and Geyer-Ryan (eds.), *Literary Theory Today*, 17.

[15] 'Freudian Theory and the Pattern of Fascist Propaganda', in *The Essential Frankfurt School Reader*, 135.   [16] 'Study of Thomas Hardy', 89.

BIBLIOGRAPHY

I. LAWRENCE BIBLIOGRAPHY

Only works cited in the text or footnotes have been included in this bibliography. Wherever possible, the Cambridge edition of Lawrence's works has been listed.

The Letters of D. H. Lawrence, ed. James T. Boulton, 7 vols. (Cambridge, 1979–), i, ed. James T. Boulton (1979); ii, ed. George J. Zytaruk and James T. Boulton (1981).

The Collected Letters of D. H. Lawrence, ed. Harry T. Moore, 2 vols. (London, 1962).

Apocalypse and the Writings on Revelation, ed. Mara Kalnins (Cambridge, 1980). (For first publication details of individual essays, see footnotes.)

Fantasia of the Unconscious and Psychoanalysis and the Unconscious (London, 1961). (First published separately, 1922, 1921.)

The First Lady Chatterley (1944; London, 1972).

'Introduction to These Paintings', in *Phoenix: The Posthumous Papers of D. H. Lawrence* (q.v.), 551–84.

John Thomas and Lady Jane (London, 1972).

Kangaroo (1923; London, 1955).

Lady Chatterley's Lover (1928; London, 1972).

The Lost Girl, ed. John Worthen (1920; Cambridge, 1981).

Love Among the Haystacks and Other Stories, ed. John Worthen (Cambridge, 1987). (For first publication details of individual stories, see footnotes.)

Mornings in Mexico and Etruscan Places (London, 1956). (First published separately, 1927, 1932.)

The Paintings of D. H. Lawrence, ed. Mervyn Levy (London, 1964).

Phoenix: The Posthumous Papers of D. H. Lawrence, ed. Edward McDonald (London, 1936). (For first publication details of individual pieces, see footnotes.)

Phoenix II: Uncollected, Unpublished and Other Prose Works by D. H. Lawrence, ed. Warren Roberts and Harry T. Moore (London, 1968). (For first publication details of individual pieces, see footnotes.)

The Plumed Serpent, ed. L. D. Clark (1926; Cambridge, 1987).

The Complete Poems of D. H. Lawrence, ed. Vivian de Sola Pinto and Warren Roberts (1964; New York, 1971).

The Prussian Officer and Other Stories, ed. John Worthen (Cambridge, 1983). (For first publication details of individual stories, see footnotes.)

The Rainbow, ed. Mark Kinkead-Weekes (1915; Cambridge, 1989).

Reflections on the Death of a Porcupine and Other Essays, ed. Michael Herbert (Cambridge, 1988). (For first publication details of individual essays, see footnotes.)

Sons and Lovers, ed. Helen Baron and Carl Baron (1913; Cambridge, 1992).

Studies in Classic American Literature (1923; London, 1964).

Study of Thomas Hardy and Other Essays, ed. Bruce Steele (Cambridge, 1985). (For first publication details of individual essays, see footnotes.)

The Symbolic Meaning: The Uncollected Versions of Studies in Classic American Literature, ed. Armin Arnold (Fontwell, Arundel, 1962).

The White Peacock, ed. Andrew Robertson (1911; Cambridge, 1983).

Women in Love, ed. David Farmer, Lindeth Vasey, and John Worthen (1920; Cambridge, 1987).

2. GENERAL BIBLIOGRAPHY

(i) Works Cited

ABERCROMBIE, LASCELLES, *Thomas Hardy: A Critical Study* (London, 1912).

ADORNO, THEODOR W., *Aesthetic Theory*, trans. C. Lenhardt, ed. Gretel Adorno and Rolf Tiedemann (London and New York, 1984). (First published as *Aesthetische Theorie*, Frankfurt, 1970.)

—— *Minima Moralia: Reflections from a Damaged Life*, trans. E. F. N. Jephcott (London, 1974). (First published as *Minima Moralia: Reflexionen aus dem beschädigten Leben*, Berlin, 1951.)

—— *Negative Dialectics*, trans. E. B. Ashton (London, 1973). (First published as *Negative Dialektik*, Frankfurt, 1966.)

—— *Prisms*, trans. Samuel and Shierry Weber (London, 1967). (First published as *Prismen: Kulturkritik und Gesellschaft*, Frankfurt, 1955.)

ALLDRITT, KEITH, *The Visual Imagination of D. H. Lawrence* (London, 1971).

ANGELLOZ, J. F., *Rainer Maria Rilke* (Paris, 1936).

ARATO, ANDREW, and GEBHARDT, EIKE (eds.), *The Essential Frankfurt School Reader* (New York, 1978).

BAKHTIN, MIKHAIL, *Problems of Dostoevsky's Poetics*, ed. and trans. Caryl Emerson (Minneapolis, 1984).

BALBERT, PETER, and MARCUS, PHILLIP, *D. H. Lawrence: A Centenary Consideration* (Ithaca, NY, 1985).

BARTHES, ROLAND, *Critical Essays*, trans. Richard Howard (Evanston, Ill., 1972). (First published as *Essais critiques*, Paris, 1966.)

—— *S/Z*, trans. Richard Miller (London, 1975). (First published as *S/Z*, Seuil, 1970.)

BAUMGARTEN, ALEXANDER GOTTLIEB, *Reflections on Poetry*, trans. K. Aschenbrenner and W. B. Holther (Berkeley, Calif., 1954). (First published as *Meditationes philosophicae de nonnullis ad poema pertinentibus*, Halle, 1735.)

BEER, GILLIAN, *Darwin's Plots: Evolutionary Narrative in Darwin, George Eliot and Nineteenth-Century Fiction* (London, 1983).

BEER, JOHN, 'D. H. Lawrence and English Romanticism', *Aligarh Journal of English Studies*, x/2 (1985), 109–21.

BELL, CLIVE, *Art* (London, 1914).

BELL, CLIVE, 'The Allied Artists', *The Nation* (2 Aug. 1913), 676–7.
—— *Landmarks in Nineteenth Century Painting* (London, 1927).
—— 'Mr Roger Fry's Criticism', *The Nation* (22 Feb. 1913), 853–4.
BELL, MICHAEL, *F. R. Leavis* (London, 1988).
BELL, QUENTIN, *Bloomsbury* (London, 1968).
BELSEY, CATHERINE, *Critical Practice* (London, 1980).
BENJAMIN, WALTER, *Charles Baudelaire: A Lyric Poet in the Era of High Capitalism*,
    trans. Harry Zohn (London, 1973). (First published as *Charles Baudelaire: Ein
    Lyriker im Zweitalter des Hochkapitalismus*, Frankfurt, 1969.)
—— *Illuminations*, ed. Hannah Arendt, trans. Harry Zohn (London, 1973).
—— *One Way Street and Other Writings*, trans. Edmund Jephcott and Kingsley
    Shorter (London, 1978).
BERGSON, HENRI, *Time and Free-Will: An Essay in the Immediate Data of Conscious-
    ness*, trans. F. L. Pogson (London, 1910). (First published as *Essai sur les données
    immédiates de la conscience*, Paris, 1889.)
BERSANI, LEO, *The Freudian Body: Psychoanalysis and Art* (New York, 1986).
—— *A Future for Astyanax: Character and Desire in the Novel* (Boston, 1976).
BLAMIRES, DAVID, *David Jones* (Manchester, 1978).
BLOOM, HAROLD, 'Freud and the Poetic Sublime', *Antaeus* (Spring 1978), 355–77.
BONDS, DIANE S., *Language and the Self in D. H. Lawrence* (Ann Arbor, Mich. 1987,
    1978).
BOURDIEU, PIERRE, *L'Ontologie politique de Martin Heidegger* (Paris, 1988).
BOWIE, MALCOLM, *Freud, Proust and Lacan: Theory as Fiction* (Cambridge, 1987).
BRAMWELL, ANNA, *Blood and Soil: Richard Walther Darré and Hitler's Green Party*
    (Bourne End, 1985).
BRET HARTE, FRANCIS, 'The Rise of the "Short Story" ', in *The International Library
    of Famous Literature*, ed. Richard Garnett, 20 vols. (London, 1899), xv, pp. xi–xix.
BREWSTER, BEN, 'From Shklovsky to Brecht: A Reply', *Screen*, 15/2 (1974).
BROOKS, PETER, FELMAN, SHOSHANA, and MILLER, J. HILLIS (eds.), 'The Lesson of
    Paul de Man', *Yale French Studies*, 69 (New Haven, Conn., 1985).
BRYSON, NORMAN, *Word and Image: French Painting of the Ancien Régime* (Cambridge,
    1981).
BULLEN, J. B., introduction to *Art* by Clive Bell (Oxford, 1987), pp. xxi–l.
BURGIN, VICTOR, *The End of Art Theory* (Basingstoke and London, 1986).
BURKE, KENNETH, 'Freud—and the Analysis of Poetry', in *The Philosophy of
    Literary Form: Studies in Symbolic Action*, 3rd edn. (Berkeley, Calif., and Los
    Angeles, 1973), 258–92.
BURNET, JOHN, *Early Greek Philosophy* (London, 1892).
BYWATER, WILLIAM G., Jr., *Clive Bell's Eye* (Detroit, 1975).
CARDINAL, ROGER, *Expressionism* (London, 1984).
CARLYLE, THOMAS, *The Works of Thomas Carlyle*, 30 vols. (London, 1896–9).
CARSWELL, CATHERINE, *The Savage Pilgrimage* (London, 1932).
CASSIRER, H. W., *A Commentary on Kant's Critique of Judgement* (New York and
    London, 1938).
CHAMBERS, JESSIE, *D. H. Lawrence: A Personal Record* (1935; Cambridge, 1980).

CHATWIN, BRUCE, *The Songlines* (London, 1987).

COLERIDGE, SAMUEL TAYLOR, *Collected Letters*, ed. E. L. Griggs, 6 vols. (Oxford, 1956–71).

—— *The Collected Works of Samuel Taylor Coleridge*, vi (*Lay Sermons*), ed. R. J. White (Princeton, NJ, and London, 1972).

COLLARD, ANDRÉE, with CONTRUCCI, JOYCE, *Rape of the Wild* (London, 1988).

COLLIER, PETER, and GEYER-RYAN, HELGA (eds.), *Literary Theory Today* (Oxford, 1990).

COWARD, ROSALIND, ' "This Novel Changes Lives": Are Women's Novels Feminist Novels? A Response to Rebecca O'Rourke's Article "Summer Reading" ', *Feminist Review*, v (1980), 53–64.

DAVIDSON, ARNOLD I. (ed.), 'Symposium on Heidegger and Nazism', *Critical Inquiry*, xv/2 (Winter 1989), 407–88.

DELANY, PAUL, *D. H. Lawrence's Nightmare* (New York, 1978).

DE MAN, PAUL, *Blindness and Insight: Essays in the Rhetoric of Contemporary Criticism* (1971; 2nd edn. London, 1983).

—— 'The Resistance to Theory', in Barbara Johnson (ed.), *The Pedagogical Imperative*, Yale French Studies, 63 (1982).

DENIS, MAURICE, 'Cézanne, II', trans. Roger Fry, *Burlington Magazine*, xiv (1909–10), 27.

DERRIDA, JACQUES, *Margins of Philosophy*, trans. Alan Bass (Chicago, 1982). (First published as *Marges de la philosophie*, Paris, 1972.)

—— *Writing and Difference*, trans. Alan Bass (Chicago, 1978). (First published as *L'Écriture et la différence*, Paris, 1967.)

DIJKSTRA, BRAM, *Idols of Perversity* (Oxford, 1986).

DOWLING, DAVID, *Bloomsbury Aesthetics and the Novels of Forster and Woolf* (London and Basingstoke, 1985).

DRAIN, RICHARD LESLIE, 'Formative Influences on the Work of D. H. Lawrence' (unpublished Ph.D. dissertation, University of Cambridge, 1962).

DUBE, WOLF-DIETER, *The Expressionists* (London, 1972).

EAGLETON, TERRY, *The Ideology of the Aesthetic* (Oxford, 1990).

—— *Literary Theory: An Introduction* (Oxford, 1983).

—— *Walter Benjamin, or Towards a Revolutionary Criticism* (London and New York, 1981).

ERMARTH, ELIZABETH DEEDS, *Realism and Consensus in the English Novel* (Princeton, NJ, 1983).

FELSKI, RITA, *Beyond Feminist Aesthetics: Feminist Literature and Social Change* (London, 1989).

FLETCHER, JOHN GOULD, review of E. H. Goddard and P. A. Gibbons, *Civilisation or Civilisations: An Essay in The Spenglerian Philosophy of History*, Monthly Criterion, vi/3 (Sept. 1927).

FLINDERS PETRIE, W. M. *The Revolutions of Civilisation* (London and New York, 1911).

FREUD, SIGMUND, *Letters of Sigmund Freud, 1873–1939*, ed. Ernst L. Freud (London, 1961).

FREUD, SIGMUND, *The Standard Edition of the Complete Psychological Works of Sigmund Freud*, trans. from the German under the General Editorship of James Strachey, in collaboration with Anna Freud, 24 vols. (London, 1953–74).

FROBENIUS, LEO, *The Voice of Africa*, trans. Rudolf Blind, 2 vols. (London, 1913).

FRY, ROGER, 'The Allied Artists', *The Nation* (2 Aug. 1913), 676–7.

—— *The Artist and Psycho-Analysis* (London, 1924).

—— *The Arts of Painting and Sculpture* (London, 1932).

—— 'The Case of the Late Sir Lawrence Alma-Tadema, O.M.', *The Nation* (18 Jan. 1913), 666–7.

—— *Cézanne: A Study of His Development* (London, 1927).

—— 'Mr MacColl and Drawing', *Burlington Magazine*, xxxv (1919), 84–5.

—— 'A New Theory of Art', *The Nation* (7 Mar. 1914), 937–9.

—— 'Post-Impressionism Again', *The Nation* (29 Mar. 1913), 1060–1.

—— *Transformations* (London, 1926).

—— *Vision and Design* (London, 1920).

FULLER, PETER, *Art and Psychoanalysis* (1980; 2nd edn. London, 1988).

GILBERT, SANDRA M., and GUBAR, SUSAN, *No Man's Land: The Place of the Woman Writer in the Twentieth Century*, 3 vols. (New Haven, Conn., and London, 1988–), i: *The War of the Words* (1988).

GREEN, MARTIN, *The Von Richthofen Sisters: The Triumphant and the Tragic Modes of Love* (London, 1974).

HAMACHER, WERNER, HERTZ, NEIL, and KEENAN, THOMAS, (eds.), *Responses on Paul de Man's Wartime Journalism* (Lincoln, Nebr. 1989).

HAYWOOD, BRUCE, *Novalis: The Veil of Imagery: A Study of the Poetic Works of Friedrich von Hardenberg (1772-1801)* (The Hague, 1959).

HEIDEGGER, MARTIN, *Basic Writings*, ed. David Farrell Krell (New York, 1977).

—— *Distanz und Nähe: Reflexionen und Analysen zur Kunst der Gegenwart*, ed. P. Jaeger and R. Lüthe (Würzburg, 1983).

—— *Nietzsche, I (The Will to Power as Art)*, trans. David Farrell Krell (New York, 1979). (First published as *Nietzsche, I [der Wille zur Macht als Kunst]*, Pfullingen, 1961.)

—— *On the Way to Language*, trans. Peter D. Hertz (New York 1971). (First published as *Unterwegs zur Sprache*, Pfullingen, 1959.)

—— *Poetry, Language, Thought*, trans. Albert Hofstadter (New York, 1971).

—— *The Question Concerning Technology and Other Essays*, trans. William Lovitt (New York, 1977).

HELLER, ERICH, *The Disinherited Mind: Essays in Modern German Literature and Thought* (Cambridge, 1952).

HERZINGER, KIM A., *D. H. Lawrence in His Time* (Lewisburg, Pa., and London, 1982).

HORKHEIMER, MAX, and ADORNO, THEODOR W., *Dialectic of Enlightenment*, trans. John Cumming (New York, 1978). (First published as *Dialektik der Aufklärung: Philosophische Fragmente*, Amsterdam, 1944.)

HUGHES, RICHARD, 'A Day in London Life', *Saturday Review of Literature* (16 May 1925), 755.

IRIGARAY, LUCE, *This Sex Which Is Not One*, trans. Catherine Porter with Carolyn Burke (Ithaca, 1985). (First published as *Ce Sexe qui n'en est pas un* (Paris, 1977.)

JAMES, WILLIAM, *Some Varieties of Religious Experience* (London, 1903).

JAMESON, FREDRIC (ed.), *Aesthetics and Politics: Debates Between Bloch, Lukács, Brecht, Benjamin, Adorno* (London, 1977).

JAY, MARTIN, *Adorno* (London, 1984).

JONES, ERNEST, *Sigmund Freud: Life and Work*, 3 vols. (London, 1953–7).

KANDINSKY, WASSILY, *Concerning the Spiritual in Art*, trans. M. T. H. Sadler (London, 1977). (First published in English as *The Art of Spiritual Harmony*, London, 1914; first published as *Über das Geistige in der Kunst*, Munich, 1912.)

—— and MARC, FRANZ (eds.), *The Blaue Reiter Almanac*, trans. H. Falkenstein, with the assistance of M. Terzian and G. Hinderlie (London, 1974). (First published as *Der Blaue Reiter Almanach*, Munich, 1912).

KANT, IMMANUEL, *The Critique of Judgement*, trans. James Creed Meredith (Oxford, 1952). (First published as *Kritik der Urteilskraft*, Berlin and Liebau, 1790.)

—— *Prolegomena to Any Future Metaphysics*, trans. P. G. Lucas (Manchester, 1953). (First published as *Prolegomena zu einer jeden Künftigen Metaphysik die als Wissenschaft wird auftreten können*, Riga, 1783.)

KEYNES, JOHN MAYNARD, *Two Memoirs, Dr Melchior: A Defeated Enemy and My Early Beliefs* (London, 1949).

KIERKEGAARD, SØREN AABYE, *Concluding Unscientific Postscript*, trans. D. F. Swenson, with an introduction and notes by Walter Lowrie (Princeton, NJ, 1941).

KLEE, PAUL, *On Modern Art* (London, 1954).

KOCKELMANS, JOSEPH J., *Heidegger on Art and Art Works* (Dordrecht, 1985).

KRIS, ERNST, *Psychoanalytic Explorations in Art* (New York, 1952).

KRISTEVA, JULIA, *Desire in Language: A Semiotic Approach to Literature and Art*, trans. Thomas Gora, Alice Jardine, and Leon S. Roudiez (Columbia, Mo., 1980).

—— *A Kristeva Reader*, ed. Toril Moi (Oxford, 1986).

LANGER, SUSANNE, *Philosophy in a New Key* (Cambridge, Mass., 1942).

LAWRENCE, FRIEDA, *Not I but the Wind* (New York, 1934).

LEAVIS, F. R., *Thought, Words and Creativity: Art and Thought in Lawrence* (London, 1976).

LÖWY, MICHAEL, *Georg Lukács: From Romanticism to Bolshevism*, trans. Patrick Camiller (London, 1979).

MACHEN, ARTHUR, *Hieroglyphics: A Note upon Ecstasy in Literature* (1902; London, 1960).

MCLAURIN, ALLEN, *Virginia Woolf: The Echoes Enslaved* (Cambridge, 1973).

MARINETTI, F. T., *Marinetti: Selected Writings*, trans. R. W. Flint and Arthur A. Coppotelli, ed. R. W. Flint (New York, 1972).

MARKS, ELAINE, and COURTIVRON, ISABELLE DE, *New French Feminisms* (Amherst, Mass., 1980).

MARX, KARL, *Economic and Philosophical Manuscripts of 1844*, ed. Dirk J. Struik, trans. Martin Milligan (London, 1970).

MASON, EUDO C., *Rilke, Europe, and the English Speaking World* (Cambridge, 1961).

MATISSE, HENRI, *Matisse on Art*, ed. J. D. Flam (London, 1978).

MERCHANT, CAROLYN, *The Death of Nature: Women, Ecology, and The Scientific Revolution* (London, 1982).

MERLEAU-PONTY, MAURICE, *The Primacy of Perception* (Chicago, 1968).

MEYERS, JEFFREY, *Painting and the Novel* (Manchester, 1975).

MIESEL, V. H. (ed.), *Voices of German Expressionism* (London, 1973).

MILLER, J. HILLIS, 'Stevens' Rock and Criticism as Cure, II', *Georgia Review*, xxx/2 (Summer 1976), 335–8.

MILNER, MARION, *On Not Being Able to Paint*, 2nd edn. (London 1957). (First published in 1950 under the pseudonym of Joanna Field.)

MILTON, COLIN, *Lawrence and Nietzsche: A Study in Influence* (Aberdeen, 1987).

MOORE, G. E. *Principia Ethica* (1903; Cambridge, 1971).

MORRIS, WILLIAM, *The Collected Works of William Morris*, 24 vols. (London, 1910–15).

MORRISON, CLAUDIA C., *Freud and the Critic* (Chapel Hill, NC, 1968).

MÜLLER, KARL ALEXANDER VON, *Deutsche Geschichte und Deutscher Charakter* (Stuttgart, 1926).

NEHLS, EDWARD (ed.), *D. H. Lawrence: A Composite Biography*, 3 vols. (Wisconsin, 1959).

NIETZSCHE, FRIEDRICH, *The Birth of Tragedy and The Genealogy of Morals*, trans. Francis Golffing (New York, 1956). (First published separately as *Die Geburt der Tragödie aus dem Geiste der Musik*, Leipzig, 1872, and *Zur Genealogie der Moral*, Leipzig, 1887.)

—— *Ecce Homo: How one becomes what one is*, trans. R. J. Hollingdale (Harmondsworth, 1979). (First published as *Ecce Homo: Wie man wird, was man ist*, Leipzig, 1908.)

—— *Twilight of the Idols and The Anti-Christ*, trans. R. J. Hollingdale (Harmondsworth, 1968). (First published separately as *Götzen-Dämmerung*, Leipzig, 1889, and *Der Antichrist*, Leipzig, 1895.)

—— *The Will to Power*, trans. Walter Kaufmann and R. J. Hollingdale, ed. Walter Kaufmann (New York, 1968). (First published as *Der Wille zur Macht*, Leipzig, 1911.)

NORRIS, CHRISTOPHER, *The Contest of Faculties: Philosophy and Theory After Deconstruction* (London and New York, 1985).

—— *Paul de Man: Deconstruction and the Critique of Aesthetic Ideology* (New York and London, 1988).

PHILLIPSON, MICHAEL, *Painting, Language and Modernity* (London, 1985).

PICASSO, PABLO, *Picasso sculpteur: Cahiers d'art*, ed. Julio Gonzalez (Paris, 1954).

PINKNEY, TONY, *D. H. Lawrence* (Hemel Hempstead, 1990).

RAGUSSIS, MICHAEL, *The Subterfuge of Art: Language and the Romantic Tradition* (Baltimore and London, 1978).

READ, HERBERT, *Education Through Art* (London, 1943).

—— *Icon and Idea* (London, 1955).

—— *The Meaning of Art* (London, 1931).

REMSBURY, JOHN, ' "Real Thinking": Lawrence and Cézanne', *Cambridge Quarterly*, ii (1966–7), 117–47.

RICHARDSON, DOROTHY, *Pilgrimage*, 4 vols. (1967; London, 1979). (For first publication details of individual volumes, see footnotes.)

RICOEUR, PAUL, *Freud and Philosophy: An Essay on Interpretation*, trans. Denis Savage (New Haven, Conn., and London, 1970). (First published as *De l'interprétation: Essai sur Freud*, Paris, 1965.)

RILEY, DENISE, *'Am I That Name?': Feminism and the Category of 'Women' in History* (Minneapolis, 1988).

RILKE, RAINER MARIA, *Ausgewählte Werke* (Leipzig, 1938).

—— *The Book of Pilgrimage*, in *The Book of Hours*, trans. A. L. Pack (London, 1961), 87–114. (First published as *Das Stunden-Buch*, Leipzig, 1905.)

—— *Letters on Cézanne*, ed. Clara Rilke, trans. Joel Agee (London, 1988). (First published as *Briefe über Cézanne*, Wiesbaden, 1952.)

—— *Tagebücher aus der Frühzeit* (Leipzig, 1942).

RINGER, FRITZ, *The Decline of the German Mandarins: The German Academic Community 1890–1933* (Cambridge, Mass., 1969).

ROSE, MARGARET A., *Marx's Lost Aesthetic: Karl Marx and The Visual Arts* (Cambridge, 1984).

RUSKIN, JOHN, *The Works of John Ruskin*, ed. E. T. Cook and Alexander Wedderburn, 36 vols. (London, 1903–12).

RUSSELL, BERTRAND, 'Portraits from Memory, III: D. H. Lawrence', *Harper's Magazine*, ccvi/1233 (Feb. 1953), 93–5.

RYCROFT, CHARLES, *Psychoanalysis and Beyond* (London, 1985).

SAGAR, KEITH (ed.), *A D. H. Lawrence Handbook* (Manchester, 1982).

SCHOPENHAUER, ARTHUR, *The World as Will and Representation*, trans. E. F. J. Payne, 2 vols. (New York, 1969). (First published as *Die Welt als Wille und Vorstellung*, Leipzig, 1819.)

SHELSTON, ALAN, introduction to *Thomas Carlyle: Selected Writings* (Harmondsworth, 1971), 7–31.

SHRIMPTON, NICK, ' "Rust and Dust": Ruskin's Pivotal Work', in Robert Hewison (ed.), *New Approaches to Ruskin* (London, 1981), 51–67.

SOMBART, WERNER, *The Jews and Modern Capitalism*, trans. M. Epstein (London and Leipzig, 1913).

—— 'Technik und Kultur', *Archiv*, 33 (1911), 305–47.

SPENGLER, OSWALD, *The Decline of the West*, trans. Charles Francis Atkinson, 2 vols. (London, 1926). (First published as *Der Untergang des Abendlandes*, Vienna, 1918–22.)

STEINER, GEORGE, *Heidegger* (London, 1978).

STOKES, ADRIAN, 'Form in Art: A Psychoanalytic Interpretation', *Journal of Aesthetics and Art Criticism*, 2 (1959), 193–203.

SYCHRAVA, JULIET, *Schiller to Derrida: Idealism in Aesthetics* (Cambridge, 1989).

SZASZ, THOMAS, *Karl Kraus and the Soul-Doctors* (London, and Henley, 1977).

THATCHER, DAVID S., *Nietzsche in England 1890–1914* (Toronto, 1970).

TRACY, BILLY T., Jr., *D. H. Lawrence and the Literature of Travel* (Epping, 1981).

WEISS, DANIEL A., *Oedipus in Nottingham: D. H. Lawrence* (Seattle, 1962).

WHEELER, KATHLEEN M. (ed.), *German Aesthetics and Literary Criticism: The Romantic Ironists and Goethe* (Cambridge, 1984).

WINNICOTT, D. W., *Playing and Reality* (London, 1971).

—— *Through Paediatrics to Psycho-Analysis* (London, 1975).

WOLFF, JANET, *Feminine Sentences: Essays on Women and Culture* (Oxford, 1990).

WOOLF, VIRGINIA, *Collected Essays*, 4 vols. (London, 1966–7).

—— *Between the Acts* (London, 1941).

—— *The Diary of Virginia Woolf*, ed. Anne Olivier Bell, 5 vols. (London, 1977–84).

—— *Flush: A Biography* (London, 1933).

—— *The Letters of Virginia Woolf*, ed. Nigel Nicolson, 6 vols. (London, 1975–80).

—— *Roger Fry: A Biography* (London, 1940).

—— *To the Lighthouse* (London, 1927).

—— *The Waves* (London, 1931).

WORRINGER, WILHELM ROBERT, *Abstraction and Empathy: A Contribution to the Psychology of Style*, trans. M. Bullock (London, 1953). (First published as *Abstraktion und Einfühlung*, Munich, 1908.)

(ii) Works Consulted

ALBRIGHT, DANIEL, *Personality and Impersonality: Lawrence, Woolf and Mann* (Chicago and London, 1978).

ALDRICH, VIRGIL C., *Philosophy of Art* (Englewood Cliffs, NJ, 1963).

ANTOR, HEINZ, *The Bloomsbury Group: Its Philosophy, Aesthetics, and Literary Achievement* (Heidelberg, 1986).

BALBERT, PETER, *D. H. Lawrence and the Psychology of Rhythm: The Meaning of Form in The Rainbow* (The Hague, 1974).

BARON, CARL E., 'D. H. Lawrence's Early Paintings', in *Young Bert: An Exhibition of the Early Years of D. H. Lawrence*, compiled by Lucy I. Edwards and David Phillips (Nottingham, 1972).

—— 'The Nottingham Festival D. H. Lawrence Exhibition, 1972', *The D. H. Lawrence Review*, 7 (1974), 19–57.

BELL, CLIVE, 'Dr Freud on Art', *The Dial* (Apr. 1925), 280–4.

—— 'Post-Impressionism Again', *The Nation* (29 Mar. 1913), 1060–1.

—— 'Post-Impressionism and Aesthetics', *Burlington Magazine* (22 Jan. 1913), 226–30.

BELL, MICHAEL, *Primitivism* (London, 1972).

BETTELHEIM, BRUNO, *Freud and Man's Soul* (London, 1983).

BONAPARTE, MARIE, *Edgar Poe, étude psychoanalytique* (Paris, 1933).

BOWIE, ANDREW, *Aesthetics and Subjectivity: From Kant to Nietzsche* (Manchester, 1990).

BROOKS, CLEANTH, *The Well-Wrought Urn* (London, 1949).

BRUNSDALE, MITZI M., *The German Effect on D. H. Lawrence and His Works, 1885–1912* (Berne, 1978).

BUDD, MALCOLM, *Music and the Emotions: The Philosophical Theories* (London, 1985).

BURNS, AIDAN, *Nature and Culture in D. H. Lawrence* (New York and London, 1980).

BUTLER, CHRISTOPHER, *Interpretation, Deconstruction, and Ideology* (Oxford, 1984).

CALINESCU, MATEI, *Five Faces of Modernity: Modernism, Avant-Garde, Decadence, Kitsch, Postmodernism* (Durham, NC, 1987).

CARRINGTON, DORA, *Carrington: Letters and Extracts from Her Diaries*, ed. David Garnett (London, 1970).

CASSIRER, ERNST, *The Philosophy of Symbolic Forms*, trans. R. Mannheim, 3 vols. (New Haven, Conn., 1953–7). (First published as *Philosophie der Symbolischen Formen*, Berlin, 1923–9.)

CHAMBERLAIN, ROBERT L., 'Pussum, Minette, and the Afro-Nordic Symbol in Lawrence's *Women in Love*', *PMLA* 78 (1963), 407–16.

CLARKE, COLIN, *The River of Dissolution: D. H. Lawrence and English Romanticism* (London, 1969).

COWARD, ROSALIND, and ELLIS, DAVID, *Language and Materialism* (London, 1977).

CULLER, JONATHAN, *On Deconstruction: Theory and Criticism after Structuralism* (London and Henley, 1983).

DERRIDA, JACQUES, *The Truth in Painting*, trans. Geoff Bennington and Ian McLeod (London, 1987). (First published as *La Vérité en peinture*, Paris, 1978.)

DERVIN, D. A., 'D. H. Lawrence and Freud', *American Imago*, 36/2 (1979), 95–117.

EAGLETON, TERRY, 'Capitalism, Modernism and Post-Modernism', in *Against the Grain* (London, 1986), 131–47.

—— 'The Emptying of a Former Self', *Times Literary Supplement* (26 May–1 June 1989), 573–4.

EBBATSON, ROGER, *Lawrence and the Nature Tradition: A Theme in English Fiction 1859–1914* (Brighton, 1980).

EHRENFELD, DAVID, *The Arrogance of Humanism* (Oxford, 1981).

EHRENZWEIG, ANTON, *The Hidden Order of Art* (London, 1967).

ELLIS, DAVID, and MILLS, HOWARD, *D. H. Lawrence's Non-Fiction: Art, Thought and Genre* (Cambridge, 1988).

FIRCHOW, PETER EDGERLY, *The End of Utopia: A Study of Aldous Huxley's Brave New World* (Lewisburg, Pa., 1984).

FISHMAN, SOLOMON, *The Interpretation of Art* (Berkeley, Calif., and Los Angeles, 1963).

FRAZER, JAMES GEORGE, *The Golden Bough: A Study in Magic and Religion* (London, 1900).

FRIEDMAN, ALAN, *The Turn of the Novel* (New York, 1966).

FRY, ROGER, 'The Grafton Gallery: An Apologia', *The Nation* (9 Nov. 1912), 250–1.

FYRSTE, CHRISTOPHER, *Heidegger, Thought and Historicity* (Ithaca, NY, 1986).

GERTLER, MARK, *Selected Letters*, ed. Noel Carrington (London, 1965).

GILLESPIE, DIANE FILBY, *The Sisters' Arts: The Writing and Painting of Virginia Woolf and Vanessa Bell* (Syracuse, NY, 1988).

GLASER, GERHARD, *Das Tun ohne Bild: Zur Technikdeutung Heideggers und Rilkes* (Munich, 1983).

GOLDWATER, R., *Primitivism in Modern Art* (New York, 1967).

GOMBRICH, E. H., 'Freud's Aesthetics', *Encounter*, 26 (Jan. 1966), 30–40.

GOMBRICH, E. H., 'Psycho-Analysis and the History of Art', *International Journal of Psycho-Analysis*, 35 (1954), 401–11.

GOODHEART, EUGENE, *The Cult of the Ego: The Self in Modern Literature* (Chicago and London, 1968).

—— 'Freud and Lawrence', *Psychoanalysis and the Psychoanalytic Review*, 47/4 (1960), 56–64.

—— *The Utopian Vision of D. H. Lawrence* (Chicago, 1963).

GORDON, JAN, *Modern French Painters* (London, 1923).

GOTTFRIED, PAUL, 'Heidegger and the Nazis', *Salisbury Review* (Sept. 1988), 34–8.

HAECKEL, ERNST, *The Riddle of the Universe at the Close of the Nineteenth Century*, trans. Joseph McCabe (London, 1900).

HAFLEY, JAMES, *The Glass Roof* (New York, 1963).

HARRISON, JANE ELLEN, *Ancient Art and Ritual* (London, 1913).

HERBART, JOHANN, *The Science of Education and the Aesthetic Revelation of the World* (London, 1897).

HEYWOOD, CHRISTOPHER, 'African Art and the Work of Roger Fry and D. H. Lawrence', *Sheffield Papers on Literature and Society*, i (1976), 102–13.

—— (ed.), *D. H. Lawrence: New Studies* (Basingstoke, 1987), esp. Michael Bentley, 'Lawrence's Political Thought: Some English Contexts, 1906–19', pp. 59–83.

HOFFMAN, FREDERICK J., 'Lawrence's Quarrel with Freud', in Frederick J. Hoffman and Harry T. Moore (eds.), *The Achievement of D. H. Lawrence* (Norman, Okla., 1953).

HOLDERNESS, GRAHAM, *D. H. Lawrence: History, Ideology and Fiction* (Dublin, 1982).

HOLROYD, MICHAEL, *Lytton Strachey: A Critical Biography*, 2 vols. (London, 1967–8).

HORDEN, PEREGRINE, *Freud and the Humanities* (London, 1985).

HUTCHEON, LINDA, *Formalism and the Freudian Aesthetic: The Example of Charles Mauron* (Cambridge, 1984).

JANIK, DEL IVAN, *The Curve of Return: D. H. Lawrence's Travel Books* (Victoria, BC, 1981).

—— 'Toward "Thingness": Cézanne's Painting and Lawrence's Poetry', *Twentieth Century Literature*, 19 (1973). 119–28.

JENNER, KATHERINE L., *Christian Symbolism* (London, 1910).

JUNG, CARL GUSTAV, *Psychology of the Unconscious*, trans. Beatrice M. Hinkle (London, 1916). (First published as *Handlungen und Symbole der Libido*, Leipzig and Vienna, 1912.)

KERMODE, FRANK, *Lawrence* (London, 1973).

KIELY, ROBERT, *Beyond Egotism: The Fiction of James Joyce, Virginia Woolf and D. H. Lawrence* (Cambridge, Mass., and London, 1980).

KUTTNER, ALFRED BOOTH, ' "Sons and Lovers": A Freudian Appreciation', *Psychoanalytic Review*, 3 (1916), 295–317.

LACOUE-LABARTHE, PHILIPPE, *Heidegger, Art and Politics*, trans. Chris Turner (Oxford, 1990).

LANGBAUM, ROBERT, *The Poetry of Experience* (London, 1957).

LAWRENCE, FRIEDA, *The Memoirs and Correspondence*, ed. R. W. Tedlock (London, 1961).

LODGE, DAVID, 'Lawrence, Dostoyevsky, Bakhtin: D. H. Lawrence and Dialogic Fiction', *Renaissance and Modern Studies*, 29 (1985), 16–32.

LOW, BARBARA, *Psycho-Analysis: A Brief Account of the Freudian Theory* (London, 1920).

LUHAN, MABEL DODGE, *Lorenzo in Taos* (New York, 1932).

LYON, JOHN MCARTHUR, 'Thought and the Novel: James, Conrad and Lawrence' (unpublished Ph.D. dissertation, University of Cambridge, 1985).

MCGANN, JEROME J., *The Romantic Ideology: A Critical Investigation* (Chicago and London, 1983).

MCLAUGHLIN, THOMAS M., 'Clive Bell's Aesthetic: Tradition and Significant Form', *Journal of Aesthetics and Art Criticism*, 35 (Summer 1977), 433–43.

MALRAUX, ANDRÉ, *The Psychology of Art*, 2 vols., trans. Stuart Gilbert (London, 1949). (First published as *Psychologie de l'art*, Geneva, 1947.)

MARCUSE, HERBERT, *The Aesthetic Dimension: Toward a Critique of Marxist Aesthetics*, trans. Herbert Marcuse and Erica Sherova (Basingstoke and London, 1979). (First published as *Die Permanenz der Kunst: Wider eine bestimmte Marxistische Aesthetik*, Munich, 1977.)

MARCUSE, LUDWIG, 'Freud's Aesthetics', *Journal of Aesthetics and Art-Criticism*, 17 (Sept. 1958), 1–21.

MARNAT, MARCEL, *David-Herbert Lawrence* (Paris, 1966).

MEGILL, ALAN, *Prophets of Extremity: Nietzsche, Heidegger, Foucault, Derrida* (Berkeley, Calif., and Los Angeles, 1985).

MEISEL, PERRY, *Freud* (Englewood Cliffs, NJ, 1981).

MERRILD, KNUD, *A Poet and Two Painters: A Memoir of D. H. Lawrence* (London, 1938).

MEYERS, JEFFREY, *D. H. Lawrence and the Experience of Italy* (Philadelphia, 1982).

MICHAELS-TONKS, JENNIFER, *D. H. Lawrence: The Polarity of North and South, Germany and Italy in His Prose Works* (Bonn, 1976).

MIKO, STEPHEN J., *Toward Women in Love: The Emergence of a Lawrentian Aesthetic* (New Haven, Conn., and London, 1971).

MOHLER, ARMIN, *Die Konservative Revolution in Deutschland 1918–1932* (Stuttgart, 1950).

MOORE, HARRY, T., *The Intelligent Heart* (New York, 1954).

MOSSE, GEORGE L., *The Crisis of German Ideology: Intellectual Origins of the Third Reich* (New York, 1964).

MURRAY, MICHAEL (ed.), *Heidegger and Modern Philosophy* (New Haven, Conn., 1978).

MURRY, JOHN MIDDLETON, *Reminiscences of D.H. Lawrence* (New York, 1933).

—— *Son of Woman: The Story of D. H. Lawrence* (New York, 1931).

—— and MANSFIELD, KATHERINE (eds.), *The Blue Review* (London, 1913).

OGDEN, CHARLES K., and WOOD, JAMES, *The Foundations of Aesthetics* (New York, 1925).

RANTAVAARA, IRMA, *Virginia Woolf and Bloomsbury* (Helsinki, 1953).

REMSBURY, JOHN and ANN, 'Lawrence and Art', in *D. H. Lawrence: A Critical Study*, ed. Andor Gomme (New York, 1978), 190–218.

Rhythm (periodical), i.–2ix (London, 1911–12).

RICHARDSON, JOHN ADKINS, and ADES, JOHN I., 'D. H. Lawrence on Cézanne: A Study in the Psychology of Critical Intuition', *Journal of Aesthetics and Art Criticism*, 28 (1970), 442.

RIEFF, PHILIP, 'Two Honest Men', *Listener*, 63 (1960), 794–6.

ROSENTHAL, T. G., 'The Writer as Painter', *Listener*, 68 (1962), 349–50.

RUSSELL, JOHN, 'D. H. Lawrence and Painting', in *D. H. Lawrence*, ed. Stephen Spender (London, 1973), 234–43.

SAUSSURE, FERDINAND DE, *Course in General Linguistics*, ed. Charles Bally and Albert Sechehaye, in collaboration with Albert Riedlinger; trans. Wade Baskin (New York, 1966). First published as *Cours de linguistique générale* (Paris, 1916).

SCHAPIRO, MEYER, 'Leonardo and Freud: An Art-Historical Study', *Journal of the History of Ideas*, 17 (1956), 147–78.

SCHNEIDER, DANIEL, *The Psychoanalyst and the Artist* (New York, 1950).

SEGAL, HANNA, 'A Psychoanalytical Approach to Aesthetics', *International Journal of Psychoanalysis*, 33 (1952), 196–207.

SPALDING, FRANCES, *Roger Fry: Art and Life* (London, 1980).

SPECTOR, JACK J., *The Aesthetics of Freud* (London, 1972).

STANGOS, NIKOS (ed.), *Concepts of Modern Art* (London, 1981).

STERBA, RICHARD, 'The Problem of Art in Freud's Writings', *Psychoanalytic Quarterly*, 9 (1940), 256–68.

STEWART, JACK F., 'Expressionism in The Rainbow', *Novel*, 13 (1980), 296–315.

—— 'Lawrence and Gauguin', *Twentieth Century Literature*, 26 (1980), 385–401.

—— 'Primitivism in Women in Love', *The D. H. Lawrence Review*, 13 (1980), 45–62.

STEWART, JAMES ECCLESTONE, 'The Evolution and Source of Themes of Spontaneity in Lawrence's Writing Until 1914' (Unpublished Ph.D. dissertation, University of Cambridge, 1968).

STOLL, JOHN E., *The Novels of D. H. Lawrence: A Search for Integration* (Columbia, Mo., 1971).

STORR, ANTHONY, 'Psychoanalysis and Creativity', in *Freud and the Humanities*, ed. Peregrine Horden (London, 1985), 38–57.

SUSSMAN, HERBERT L., *Victorians and the Machine: The Literary Response to Technology* (Cambridge, Mass., 1968).

SUTTIE, IAN, *The Origins of Love and Hate* (London, 1935).

THISTLEWOOD, DAVID, *Herbert Read, Formlessness and Form: An Introduction to His Aesthetics* (London, 1984).

TATARKIEWICZ, WLADYSLAW, *A History of Six Ideas: An Essay in Aesthetics* (Warsaw, 1980).

THORNHAM, SUSAN, 'Lawrence and Freud', *Durham University Journal*, 71 (Dec. 1977), 73–82.

THORSLEY, PETER L., Jr., *Romantic Contraries: Freedom versus Destiny* (New Haven, Conn., and London, 1984).

TODOROV, TZVETAN, *Theories of the Symbol*, trans. Catherine Porter (Oxford, 1982). First published as *Théories du symbole* (Paris, 1977).

TORGOVNICK, MARIANNA, *The Visual Arts, Pictorialism and the Novel: James, Lawrence and Woolf* (Princeton, NJ, 1985).

TRILLING, LIONEL, *Freud and the Crisis of Our Culture* (London, 1966).

—— *The Liberal Imagination* (London, 1951), esp. 'Art and Neurosis' (pp. 160–80) and 'Freud and Literature' (pp. 34–57).

ULMER, GREGORY L., 'D. H. Lawrence, Wilhelm Worringer, and the Aesthetics of Modernism', *The D. H. Lawrence Review*, 10 (1977), 165–82.

VAN GOGH, ELIZABETH DU QUESNE, *Personal Recollections of Vincent van Gogh* (London, 1913).

VON KLEMPERER, KLEMENS, *Germany's New Conservatism: Its History and Dilemma in the Twentieth Century* (Princeton, NJ, 1957).

WARNER, ERIC, and HOUGH, GRAHAM (eds.), *Strangeness and Beauty: An Anthology of Aesthetic Criticism 1840–1910*, 2 vols. (Cambridge, 1983).

WHYTE, LANCELOT LAW, *The Unconscious Before Freud* (New York, 1960).

WILLET, JOHN, *The New Sobriety 1917–1933: Art and Politics in the Weimar Period* (London, 1978).

WILLIAMS, RAYMOND, *The Country and the City* (London, 1973).

WIMSATT, W. K., and BEARDSLEY, MONROE, *The Verbal Icon* (Lexington, Ky., 1954).

WOLLHEIM, RICHARD, *Freud* (London, 1973).

—— 'Freud and the Understanding of Art', in *On Art and the Mind* (London, 1973), 202–19.

WOODESON, JOHN, *Mark Gertler: Biography of a Painter, 1891–1939* (London, 1972).

INDEX